THE END OF SATISFACTION

THE END OF SATISFACTION

*Drama and Repentance in the
Age of Shakespeare*

HEATHER HIRSCHFELD

CORNELL UNIVERSITY PRESS
ITHACA AND LONDON

First published 2014 by Cornell University Press

Printed in the United States of America

Library of Congress Cataloging-in-Publication Data

Hirschfeld, Heather Anne, 1968–, author.
   The end of satisfaction : drama and repentance in the age of Shakespeare / Heather Hirschfeld.
      pages cm
   Includes bibliographical references and index.
   ISBN 978-0-8014-5274-1 (cloth : alk. paper)
1. Shakespeare, William, 1564–1616—Criticism and interpretation.
2. English drama—Early modern and Elizabethan, 1500–1600—History and criticism. 3. Repentance in literature. 4. Desire in literature.
I. Title.

   PR658.R44H57 2014
   822'.309353—dc23

                                                                    2013038570

Cornell University Press strives to use environmentally responsible suppliers and materials to the fullest extent possible in the publishing of its books. Such materials include vegetable-based, low-VOC inks and acid-free papers that are recycled, totally chlorine-free, or partly composed of nonwood fibers. For further information, visit our website at www.cornellpress.cornell.edu.

Cloth printing   10 9 8 7 6 5 4 3 2 1

For Anthony

Dayenu!

Contents

ACKNOWLEDGMENTS

A book on satisfaction opens itself up to many puns and allusions, often starting with the Rolling Stones. I try to avoid them here. Instead, I enjoy the opportunity to turn from a vocabulary of repentance, compensation, and atonement to the related, but distinct, language of gratitude and thanks.

This project would not have been possible without the financial and administrative support of scholarly institutions. I am grateful to have held a short-term fellowship at the Folger Shakespeare Library and to have received from the National Endowment for the Humanities a summer stipend as well as a year-long fellowship. All three were essential to the completion of this book. I have also been the beneficiary of various sources of support at the University of Tennessee: the Department of English, the Office of Research, the College of Arts and Sciences, the Humanities Center, and the Marco Institute for Medieval and Renaissance Studies.

Friends and colleagues have listened to me opine about satisfaction more than I had a right to expect. At UT, this includes Donna Bodenheimer, Katy Chiles, Dawn Coleman, Margaret Lazarus Dean, Mary Dzon, Rachel Golden,

Laura Howes, Rob Stillman, Judith Welch, and especially Urmila Seshagiri, a model of intellectual as well as material kindness and care. A number of colleagues and members of the Renaissance Humanisms reading group also screened parts of the manuscript at various stages, including Bob Bast, Jane Bellamy, Palmira Brummett, Stan Garner, Katherine Kong, Jeri McIntosh, Samantha Murphy, Brad Pardue, and Anthony Welch. John Zomchick read the introduction more times than he should have. Amy Elias embraced the idea behind this project from its inception and discussed all aspects of it on our weekly walks with compassion as well as theoretical acumen. Graduate students Ashley Combest and Lewis Moyse offered important contributions along the way. Vera Pantanizopoulos-Broux has offered much support and guidance.

I am grateful for the interest and encouragement of friends and colleagues beyond UT, including Barbara Baines, Sarah Beckwith, Lara Bovilsky, Al Braunmuller, Kent Cartwright, Carrie Euler, Raphael Falco, Natalie Houston, Nora Johnson, Erika Lin, Kate Narveson, Gail Paste, Garrett Sullivan, Susan Zimmerman, and members of the monthly reading group of the Appalachian Psychoanalytic Society. Graham Hammill was especially generous in sharing his time and insights with me. I hope he enjoys the epigraph. Leigh DeNeef was a demanding as well as kind reader of this material in all of its many incarnations. Frances and Emery Lee continue to be a source of great insight and understanding. Ken Jackson and Kevin Curran invited me to participate in seminars and panels at the Shakespeare Association of America (SAA) and the Renaissance Society of America, respectively, and I profited from these opportunities. I thank the members of my own 2008 SAA seminar, "Would I were satisfied," who challenged and broadened my own notions of "enough." I was honored to have been asked to present parts of this work in various venues and grateful for the feedback I received. Thanks go to Thomas Fulton and Ann Baynes Coiro, for having me speak at the "Rethinking Historicism" symposium; to Molly Murray, for asking me to the Columbia University Early Modern Colloquium; to Erika Lin and Matthew Biberman, for asking me to the University of Louisville; and to Garrett Sullivan, for inviting me to speak at Pennsylvania State University.

I owe particular debts to the readers for the press. The anonymous reader captured and recast the argument for me in ways which are reflected in the final product and for which I am deeply grateful. And John Parker's engagement with the project was extraordinary. He read the manuscript sympathetically and rigorously, and I have learned much from his intellectual generosity. This is a different and better book because of his responses. I thank Peter Potter at the press for having faith in the project and for his scrupulous attention to details of the manuscript.

I am singularly lucky to have the continued support of my parents, Pam and Henry Hirschfeld.

Anthony Welch was not a part of my life at the start of this project. But he was the first to ask what it meant that I was working on satisfaction, a question that expresses in little his characteristic curiosity, charm, intuition, patience, and sensitivity to things that matter. All of these qualities, as well as the more general erudition and delight he brings to our home with Henslowe, make me spectacularly thankful that he is the central part of my life now. It is to him that this book is dedicated.

An earlier version of chapter 2, titled "'The verie paines of Hell': *Doctor Faustus* and the Controversy over Christ's Descent," appeared in *Shakespeare Studies* 36 (2008), published by Associated University Presses. An earlier version of the second half of chapter 4, titled "'And he hath enough': The Penitential Economies of *The Merchant of Venice*," appeared in *Journal of Medieval and Early Modern Studies* 40.1 (2010), published by Duke University Press. I am grateful to the publishers for permission to make use of this material. For permission to reprint photographs from its collection, I am grateful to the Folger Shakespeare Library.

When quoting from primary texts in original or facsimile editions I have retained original orthography except for silently modernizing i, j, u, and v. For early modern English texts I have included standard reference numbers (abbreviated RSTC) from the revised *Short-Title Catalogue of Books . . . 1475–1640*, edited by A. W. Pollard and G. R. Redgrave, 2nd ed. (London: Bibliographic Society, 1986).

THE END OF SATISFACTION

INTRODUCTION

Where's Satisfaction?

"Would I were satisfied!" laments Shakespeare's Othello in the tortured crescendo of act 3, scene 3. "You would be satisfied," confirms Iago, whose poisonous suggestions about Desdemona's infidelity have prompted Othello's plaint. "And may, but, how, how satisfied, my lord? Would you, the supervisor, grossly gape on, Behold her topp'd? . . . What shall I say? Where's satisfaction?"[1]

Where's satisfaction? Iago's question is directed at Othello's specific struggle, often understood as the effect of a corrosive skepticism, with the nature of evidence and the problem of other minds.[2] But the deep force of the query derives from the explicit, categorical challenge it poses to "satisfaction" as a horizon of human experience. Iago's prompt makes harrowingly plain that if Othello were to obtain what he seeks—the ocular proof of his wife's unfaithfulness—he would have to forfeit the circle of marital content he traced so publicly in the play's first act: "She lov'd me for the dangers I had pass'd, / And I lov'd her that she did pity them" (1.3.168–69). For Othello, in other words, finding or locating one kind of satisfaction means losing another, dearer one more surely.

Othello's predicament, which I study in greater depth in chapter 5, represents the extreme instance of a conceptual and affective dilemma—a problem of satisfaction—central to the language, plots, and characters of the early modern theater. The sources of this dilemma in Reformation doctrine, its place in early modern structures of thought and feeling, and its imaginative representation on the English Renaissance stage are my subjects here. I begin by recovering both the historical specificity and the significance for the sixteenth and early seventeenth centuries of the term "satisfaction," neglected today by literary scholars who tend to treat it as the interpretively transparent—if always elusive—terminus of the seemingly more compelling category of desire. As I will show, however, satisfaction's conceptual vigor gave it discursive purchase across multiple sociocultural vocabularies, including those associated with revenge, finance, and marriage.[3] In each of these realms satisfaction (from the Latin *satisfacere*, to do or to make enough) functioned as an organizing principle underwriting complex compensatory exchanges or "economies": of violation and vendetta, of debt and repayment, of erotic desire and fulfillment. I explore these economies, and the contested place of satisfaction within them, as they feature in a sequence of sixteenth- and early seventeenth-century plays.

I do so by orienting these other economies to the term's religious import in Christian doctrines of repentance. In this realm, satisfaction named a special calculus between transgression and atonement; it signified the "doing enough" or the "enough done" that compensated God for human sin. As I show, this theological meaning, and particularly the technical understanding of satisfaction as the third stage of the sacrament of penance, was a focal point of early modern religious controversy. Indeed, in the process of confessional upheaval we call the Protestant Reformation, the meanings and values of satisfaction were fundamentally shifted, redefined. This redefinition, in turn, put tremendous pressure on the term's conceptual and experiential viability in the other, seemingly more "secular" realms in which it was active.

The effects of this pressure can be heard and seen on the early modern stage. The plays I study document thematically and linguistically the problem of satisfaction as it emerges from the Protestant de-sacramentalization of penance and the challenges to traditional notions of repentance that accompanied it. All the plays share a basic internal logic: their protagonists, driven to balance individual transgression with appropriate payback, acknowledge both the desirability and the impossibility of "making enough" in matters of atonement, whether to God or to intimate others. But each play offers a particular, idiosyncratic approach to this logic and its intersection with the worldly concerns of revenge, commerce, sex. I discuss these different approaches across multiple social, psychological, and generic realms: first in the study of the Wittenberg scholar Dr. Faustus; then in the vengeful courts of Hieronimo's Spain, Hamlet's Denmark, and Vindice's Italy; again in the marketplace of Antonio and Shylock's Venice; and finally in the Mediterranean and Iberian bedrooms of *Othello* and Francis Beaumont and John Fletcher's *Love's Pilgrimage* (c. 1613–1614). In each case I call fresh attention to the plays' penitential underpinnings, to the inflection of their secular engagements by concerns of sin, punishment, and reparation; I also show the way in which each play hinges on a unique penitential economy, the specific equations that their characters assume between offence and reparation. In so doing I reveal each play as a unique venue in the processing of religious change. For each testifies to—and invites their audiences to recognize—the residual allures of penitential satisfaction at the moment of its doctrinal displacement.

What's Satisfaction?

The idea of satisfaction as an early modern cultural concern has either gone uninterrogated by literary scholars or has been treated largely as a threat or obstacle to the voracious desire and ambition that have become synonymous with the era.[4] As I suggest below, this critical disregard can be seen as a consequence of the Protestant rescripting of the term, so that it is understood today almost solely in its "appetitive" or "receptive" dimension: as something that humans get and consume, and thus as a synonym for the simple (and what has become the suspect) fulfilment of needs and wants.[5] But it signified more dynamically during the early modern period, referring to a principle of commensuration which underwrote a range of theological and secular transactions or exchanges.[6] The clergyman Thomas Wilson's *Christian Dictionarie* (1612) provides what we will come to recognize as the early Protestant definition: satisfaction is "a worke doone by vertue, and merit, whereof Gods wrath against the sinnes of the elect is fullie and sufficiently appeased. This worke is Christes Oblation of himselfe upon the Crosse."[7] This reading of Jesus's Passion, to which chapter 1 is devoted, was heralded in Scripture; it was elaborated in early Christian exegesis, which drew on classical Roman civil law and the latter's deployment of satisfaction as a standard of fitness, repayment, discharge, and fulfilment.[8]

Bishop Thomas Cooper's late sixteenth-century *Thesaurus* maps the term's Latinate scope with several examples of classical usage. It stresses the juridical, compensatory and even sacrificial meanings of *satisfacere*—"to content: to make satisfaction: to paye a debte: to purge"—and then goes on to offer definitions that stress the word's social, affective, and erotic implications: "*Cupiditatem satiare,*" translated as "To satisfie luste or desire"; "*Amicitiae satisfacere,*" "To doe as much as friendshippe can require"; "*Suspicioni alicuius satisfacere,*" "To satisfie or content ones suspicion."[9] Thomas Elyot's *Biblio-theca Eliotae* (1545) offers a similar range, defining *satio* as "to saciate or fylle, whiche hath relation not onely to the bodye and sences, but also to the mynde."[10] Or in Robert Cawdrey's efficient definition from 1604, "making amends for wrongs, or displeasures."[11]

This wide range of meaning and usage is reflected in the early modern drama. Thomas Kyd, in his *Spanish Tragedy* (c. 1588), plays on the evidentiary and penitential meanings when he has the protagonist Hieronimo demand that a convicted murderer "Stand forth . . . / And here, for satisfaction of the world, / Confess thy folly and repent thy fault."[12] Ben Jonson, working off of the term's sexual and economic dimensions in *Volpone* (1606), has the endangered wife Celia plead against her impending ravishment: "Would my life would serve / To satisfy—" she starts, before being attacked by her husband-turned-bawd.[13] And no play better exploits and parodies the term's signifying potential than Francis Beaumont's jovial mockery of stage conventions, *The Knight of the Burning Pestle* (1607), in which the thwarted apprentice-lover Jasper, having escaped from blocking parents with his beloved Luce, pretends to slay her because of her father's resistance to their match:

> Canst thou
> Imagine I could love his daughter
> That flung me from my fortune into nothing,
>
> .   .   .   .

Come, by this hand you die,
I must have life and blood to satisfy
Your father's wrongs.[14]

These varied registers and uses of the term resonate with Raymond Williams's understanding of "keywords" as terms whose narrow meanings in
technical discourses become over time available for broad use in "wider ar-
eas of thought and experience."[15] But in the case of satisfaction it is not clear
that its semantic trajectory followed Williams's movement from the esoteric
to the colloquial, the specialized to the common. Indeed, in the case of satisfaction it would seem that a general, affect-tinged understanding of the
term informed even its most rigorous denotations in law. So although it has
been suggested that the definition of satisfaction migrated from an objective
to a subjective one—from a sense "related to debt discharge and repayment"
to one that "indicated a feeling . . . of having desires fulfilled"[16]—the term's
emotional, qualitative associations seem always already to have inhabited
the more literal or quantitative ones. That is, econo-juridical satisfaction—a
technical principle of adequate though never perfect compensation—
depended upon the perceptions and feelings of the compensated person or
institution: "when or whether . . . 'satisfaction' had taken place was decided
solely from the creditor's own point of view."[17] In the plays I go on to study,
it is the position of the debtor/sinner, rather than the creditor, that is under
the most scrutiny. But for now the important point is that the term
describes—assumes, even—a special exchange or *circuit* between self and
other in which activity and emotional state are deeply integrated. This circuit governs satisfaction's signifying capacity across discourses concerned
with fault, debt, and recompense, and it takes special shape in theologies of
repentance, where the circuit includes the divine.

This capacity originates in the Latin root *satis*, enough. The principle of
"enough" upon which the term relies is deliberately equivocal, straddling an
endlessly generative border between ideals of moderation, equivalence, and
abundance. For the early modern period, then, satisfaction's most significant
dialectical relationships were not only to physical or psychological desire per se
(though this binary between desire and fulfillment will certainly concern us),
but also to standards of sufficiency, efficacy, necessity, equity, and excess—to
definable but highly variable or negotiable criteria of what counts as "too
little" or "too much" in matters of punishment, payment, and reward.

In her moving account of the use of the term satisfaction in medieval English literature, Jill Mann explores the ways in which *satis*, "enough," became "a poetic word, a word that vibrates with emotional and intellectual connotations." Its poetic power, she explains, derives from its "semantic ambivalence," the fact that "in one sense it represents a point of balance between extremes. But in another sense, 'ynough' is itself a superlative; it indicates fullness, abundance, satisfaction to the utmost limits."[18] This remarkably labile signifying capacity, as Mann points out, is an inheritance of an Aristotelian confidence in the mean as the key to the *summum bonum*.[19] Thus her examples, governed by the classical ideal of moderation as sign of perfection, use "enough" to describe God's grace and eternal rewards: "In the heavenly kingdom renunciation is paradoxically rewarded with satisfaction. In its fullness the desire for 'more' always falls away, not because one prudently settles for 'less' but because that endless desire is endlessly satisfied, and it is the completeness of that satisfaction that constitutes 'enough.' "[20]

The literature I study here is similarly driven by the promise of enough, but in these texts the promise becomes a problem, inviting concern and anxiety rather than confidence.[21] The authors and characters of these works resist or rue the oscillation between sufficiency and plenitude: they differentiate between exactitude and increase, interrogate the precise lineaments of enough, and identify where it shades into more or too much. They are, in other words, preoccupied, even threatened, by the definitional mobility of satisfaction: the way in which it embraces contraries as synonyms so that adequation becomes a conceptual as well as computational asymptote. The idea of enough, ironically, takes on the characteristics of the excessive or infinite, and with it a "despair, not only of ever subjugating [the idea], but of making any kind of sense of it."[22] The compulsive emphasis on the word of the "silver-tongued" sixteenth-century minister Henry Smith presents the dilemma with particular urgency: "Every word may be defined, & every thing may be measured, but *enough* cannot be mesured [*sic*] nor defined it changeth every yeare: when we had nothing wee thought it *enough* if wee might obtaine less then we have: when we came to more we thought of an other *enough*: nowe we have more wee dreame of another *enough*, so *enough* is alwayes to come though to [*sic*] much be there already."[23]

Smith's comment on the always-receding quality of enough is especially resonant, because he struggles with the problem in the context of a sermon that calls for repentance for worldly desires and acquisitions. His preoccupation with enough, in other words, is joined to a pastoral concern with penitence, the realm in which *satis* does not stand for the mean between extremes but rather for appropriate, proportionate, or efficacious restitution and penalty—a measure of what humans do or make to atone to God, rather than as a measure (in Mann's reading) of what God gives to humans. These categories are not exclusive, of course; they intersect in Christian theology in the figure of Jesus, who, in an act of incalculable grace, satisfied for human sin precisely in order that humans could themselves "make enough" on account of his blessings. But in so far as this intersection is premised on compensating God for wrongdoing, it requires extraordinary attention to determining what constitutes "enough" to merit—for Christ and for human beings—divine forgiveness. In this realm the proximity of enough and more (precisely what Mann's texts celebrate) can become or be felt as an excruciating demand. We might call this the penitential dilemma or problem of enough.

The penitential concept of satisfaction has a juridical and Roman, rather than a metaphysical and Aristotelian, pedigree. In Roman law, a sustained influence in the development of Christian theology, satisfaction was governed by a simultaneously vague and exacting notion of "enough" as the amount that would mollify a creditor or an injured party: it meant "generally to fulfill another's wish, to gratify the desire of a person; when used of a debtor = to carry out an obligation whatever is its origin (a contract, a testament, a statute)."[24] The *Dictionnaire de Théologie Catholique* cites Justinian's *Digest*: "Satisfaction is doing as much as is enough for the angered person intent on vengeance (*Satisfacere est tantum facere quantum satis est irato ad vindictam*)."[25] The mid-seventeenth-century jurist Hugo Grotius explains the Roman principle as the repayment of an obligation by "another thing . . . than what was in the Obligation," thus requiring "that some Act of the Creditor or Governour should be added thereto."[26] This was a substitutionary, equitable, and "lowest common denominator" principle: "To offer satisfaction was not to acquit oneself completely of debt or to avoid submitting to deserved punishment; it was, however, to recognize the law, confess one's wrongdoing, accept the principle of reparation, that is, to conform to justice, and in appealing to good will and applying oneself to obtain it, by the confession of debt or guilt, no longer to be treated according to the absolute rigor of the law."[27] The equitable sense is retained today in contemporary legal parlance, which takes satisfaction as "the giving of something with the intent, express or implied, that it is to extinguish some existing legal or moral obligation . . . it is always something given as a substitute for or equivalent of something else."[28] But in the instances we will consider, minimalism and equity can quickly give way to maximalism or scrupulosity, so that enough is only satisfactory (only enough) when it becomes excessive or exacting. The most astonishing instance of this movement between minimal and maximal, as we shall see in the next chapter, is the theory of Christ's satisfaction; but the movement, and all its potential complications, extends more broadly into general concerns of crime, punishment, and payback.

The penitential as well as legal usage returns us to the other powerful aspect of satisfaction: its transactional sensibility. The term is built upon the premise of a circuit between the performer and receiver of gratification. One makes or does *satis* for—or receives or takes it from—another. The term thus prescribes a direct, although flexible, interaction between the maker and the recipient of repayment or reparative action, so that both sides are understood as participants in its accomplishment. Scholars frequently neglect or disable this basic circuitry, separating satisfaction as an objective deed from satisfaction as a subjective experience (this distinction, as we will see in the next chapter, structures many interpretations of the dynamics of penance). Bossy distinguishes between these two poles in terms of strong and weak meanings. The strong sense of satisfaction, he explains, refers to "making up for, paying for, making amends, making reparation"; it "is always other-directed." The weak sense connotes "contentment, gratified desire . . . what you can't get none of"; it "is principally self-directed."[29] But the commonplace distinction here neglects the fundamental reciprocity of these meanings, since the premise of satisfaction is that it traverses activity and sensation *intersubjectively*, connecting what one party does to what another party has or feels. We might usefully compare this kind of circuitry to the work of the early modern humors and passions. Although satisfaction is not a synonym for or a category of the early modern passions—it is properly understood as a condition that a passion seeks—it resembles these complex physiological and psychological systems in that it "comprise[s] an ecology or a transaction."[30] In its idealized form, then, the satisfactory transaction is not a unidirectional exchange between the one who makes, and the one who gets, enough.[31] Rather, satisfaction describes an arc or circuit according to which satisfying the other rebounds to the self. (To rephrase Jacques Lacan, "satisfaction is always satisfaction of the Other.") The late fifteenth-century morality play *Everyman* offers a particularly rich dramatization of this arc: Everyman, frightened by the approach of death, is invited by Knowledge to go "together lovingly / To Confession, that cleansing river." When, after doing penance and receiving the last sacraments, Five Wits sees the protagonist approaching, he announces: "I see Everyman come, / Which hath made *true satisfaction*," as though the internal accomplishment of penance, of making enough, is visible on the protagonist's body.[32] Five Wits thus presents penitential satisfaction as a simultaneously objective and subjective accomplishment, so that *making* or *doing enough* remains intimately connected to *having* or *feeling enough*.

The prevailing, and pejorative, tendency of scholars to overlook the circuitries of satisfaction is, I suggest, a semantic and affective inheritance of the Reformation. The inheritance begins with the efforts of Continental and English Protestant theologians to distinguish their understanding of repentance from traditional ones. This understanding, grounded in their fundamental conviction in the incapacity of a human will disabled by original sin, involved the rejection of the notion that men and women could satisfy God for their wrongdoing.[33] The long-term consequence of this rejection, part of the paradoxically secularizing effects of early modern religious change,[34] has been the "banalization" of the idea of satisfaction, so that it no longer designates a standard of active, extroverted exchange but rather has become a synonym for "totally privatized happiness," the demonized stepsister of authentic philosophical happiness or an unexamined category on business or psychology surveys.[35]

But the more immediate effect of the Reformation approach to satisfaction was to raise the dilemmas inherent in its "semantic ambivalence" to a new conceptual level. Protestant theology, in keeping with its fundamental belief in the inadequacy of the human will, insisted that humans could not make enough, regardless of how enough was determined or defined. Protestant theologians resolved this shock to human agency by preaching the utter sufficiency of Christ's sacrifice to make amends for the faithful.[36] But the plays I study expose the complications and fault lines in this supposed resolution, activating their protagonists' struggles not only with the residual problem of *defining* enough but also with the emerging problem of the *impossibility* of enough. As we shall see, this fresh problem only exacerbated the definitional demand it was trying to eliminate, triggering new sensitivities to or longings for a *satis* now announced off limits or unavailable. In contemporary theoretical terms, we might say that the plays work through a pursuit of satisfaction that arises precisely when and because it is declared "impossible."[37]

How To Do Satisfaction?

Of course, challenges to the meaning of the word "enough" in the early modern period were not confined to the realm of penitential theology. Developments in early modern systems of calculation, changes in prevailing cultures of honor, modifications in legal practice and evidentiary theory, increases in the availability of consumer and intellectual goods, expanding international trade and travel, technologies of print culture and the rapid dissemination of texts: all were part of the period's re-defining and re-experiencing of making as well as having enough.[38]

It is my contention, however, that Reformed theology was the period's most significant and fundamental source of pressure on the idea of satisfaction, a pressure that subsequently complicated the term's meaning in the various other discourses in which it functioned. Such an approach follows scholars such as Debora Shuger, who has eloquently written that religion in this period was "the cultural matrix for explorations of virtually every topic."[39] But in the case of satisfaction, we can be even more specific in identifying the conceptual reach of theology into multiple discursive fields. First, satisfaction per se, as the organizing principle of the Incarnation and Passion as well as a specific stage in the Catholic sacrament of penance, was explicitly, self-consciously re-evaluated in the process of Reformation doctrinal change.[40] Chapter 1 examines this re-evaluation, sketching a broad history of early approaches to satisfactory atonement and then dwelling on the sixteenth- and seventeenth-century dismantling of the sacrament and related shifts in penitential practices and affects. Second, human thought and behavior in worldly contexts supplied *occasions* for both sin and repentance, so participation in secular economies was never separable from participation in penitential ones.[41] If penitential exchange, that is, shared a conceptual vocabulary with legal, economic, and sexual exchanges, it also intersected with them in more concrete, practical ways. Thus the study of repentance is not fully comprehended by an interpretive paradigm, supplied so convincingly for money and language or bookkeeping and confession, which would feature it as one among other structurally homologous discourses or "systems of substitution or its correlative, value."[42] Rather repentance, given its orchestrating sway in early modern individual and communal life, needs to be seen as organizing or intervening directly in other forms of exchange. Chapters 3, 4, and 5 make clear the ways in which repentance was implicated in—and not simply structurally or analogically related to—enterprises such as revenge, trade, and marriage. The language of satisfaction across the period's "lateral workings of verbal networks," I suggest, was extravagantly *overdetermined* by its penitential character even as it signified richly in other contexts.[43]

Such an approach to the language of penitential satisfaction draws on the theoretical and historiographical re-orientation over the past several decades of scholars who no longer assume a progressive or singular model of the English Reformation.[44] Their studies have been especially sensitive to the tumultuous, complicated process of religious change, to the ideological and political fissures even within established doctrinal positions, and to the persistence of earlier forms of worship and belief even amidst the most concerted attacks on "old" religion. Following these models I have refused the temptations of either naïve nostalgia for a pre-Reformation "world we have lost" or triumphalist celebrations of a purified, post-Reformation Anglican polity. My study is predicated neither on a view of the Roman sacrament of penance as a perfectly or endlessly fulfilling rite destroyed by the forces of reform nor on a view of Protestant repentance as a purified recuperation of the earliest, most principled forms of Christian atonement. Rather, I offer an analysis of the unique emphases of Protestant doctrines of repentance as they were deliberately fashioned against—though necessarily descended from and in conversation with—the sacramental tradition they were dismantling.

I also acknowledge continuities of penitential thought across a medieval divide while stressing, to a greater degree, the distinctive features of English Protestant doctrine and practice against its predecessors and Roman Catholic counterparts.[45] This emphasis on the ways that Reformers accentuated their differences from the Roman Church of the past is especially appropriate to a study of penitence, which was at the center of both Catholic and Protestant theologies: "the issue at hand is a great one, the chief doctrine of the Gospel, the forgiveness of sins."[46] In such a case the establishment of confessional distinctions was particularly pressing. As the Catholic author of *The Christians Manna* insists, "in points doctrinall . . . who erreth litle [*sic*], erreth much."[47] Protestant efforts to divide and distinguish may now look like "anxious attempts to suppress the early modern period's medieval heritage," which only call attention both to the longing for a disavowed tradition and to the remnants of that tradition present in the new.[48] But it would be a mistake to underestimate the ways in which Reformation thinkers overtly constructed their theological positions through "sustained attack[s] upon the doctrines, rites, and ceremonies of the Roman Church" in order to accentuate their difference from late medieval ones.[49] So if, as Alexandra Walsham suggests, "the relation between [the culture of] evangelical Calvinism and the eclectic culture it sought to efface and replace was far more intimate and intricate than is still widely assumed," then it is important to recognize that this very intimacy was often characterized by stark, explicit confrontations between these cultures and their conceptual vocabularies.[50]

These confrontations were not limited to those between emerging English Protestantism and the theology and institutions of late medieval Catholicism. As the following chapter demonstrates, Reformed writings on repentance and satisfaction took shape against the mandates of the post-Tridentine Roman Church and the pressures of English Catholicism as well as in conversation with competing brands of Protestantism, themselves being shaped and reshaped during the late sixteenth and early seventeenth centuries.[51] Indeed, within what historians have labeled a "Calvinist consensus," Tudor and Stuart religious thought fostered varieties of Protestant conviction which asserted their ecclesiastical and doctrinal differences through "the polemical manipulation of what remained a set of essentially shared assumptions."[52] Reformed teachings on repentance, whether aimed at the Church of Rome or at representatives of alternative Protestant views, lie at the heart of the specifically early modern dilemma of satisfaction. If its practitioners did not expect or intend to initiate such a dilemma—as the following chapter explains, they were trying to *solve* the problem of sinful mankind's endless indebtedness, not reinforce it—the demands of early modern religious controversy and polemic, what Jesse Lander calls its "unbecoming certitude, passionate conviction, and remorseless logic," was nevertheless the source of a conceptual and experiential pressure on the possibilities of fulfillment.[53]

Our most dynamic archive of the contemporary pressures on repentance and the meaning of satisfaction is the early modern theater. The drama inherited this cultural role from its medieval predecessors, which were "eschatalogical and apocalyptic but primarily penitential" in orientation, both teaching and interrogating contemporary understandings of sin and salvation.[54] But in so far as it trafficked in secular subjects and stories that were also, as I have proposed, inseparable from penitential impulses and demands, the early modern drama absorbed and represented in new forms and terms a distinctly contemporary problem of repentance and satisfaction. In chapter 2 I show how *Doctor Faustus*'s fascination with hell—Western culture's most aggressively imagined site of eternal dissatisfaction—was a symptom not only of its protagonist's "over-reaching" aspirations but also of his inability to qualify or quantify what counts as "enough." I link this inability to his suspicion, occasioned by a specific late sixteenth-century debate about Christ's descent to hell, that no savior is sufficient—can do enough—for his redemption. The third chapter examines the genre of revenge tragedy and its protagonists' demands for commensurate, eye-for-an-eye justice as well as amplified, excessive punishment and pain. Glancing at Thomas Kyd's *The Spanish Tragedy* and Shakespeare's *Hamlet* but focusing on Thomas Middleton's *Revenger's Tragedy*, I explain the impulse to revenge in terms of Reformed debates about both original sin and the efficacy of confession, and thus in terms of the impossibility of "setting things right." Chapter 4 looks at the penitential bonds between Antonio and Shylock in *The Merchant of Venice* and their background in economic morality plays, particularly William Wager's aptly titled *Enough Is as Good as a Feast*. Chapter 5 suggests that the full scope of the Reformation challenge to satisfaction is comprehended in the marital anguish of Shakespeare's *Othello*, whose racially different protagonist suffers most exquisitely from a comprehensive loss of satisfaction, as "enough" is removed for him as spiritual and erotic possibilities within marriage. The chapter concludes by looking at a mid-Jacobean romance, Beaumont and Fletcher's *Love's Pilgrimage*, which both parodies and nostalgically longs for the sacraments of penance and matrimony and their promises of penitential and marital satisfaction. A brief coda discusses the intersection of the aesthetic satisfactions of the commercial drama with the theatricality or staginess of early modern repentance.

In focusing on the penitential dispositions of these plays, I extend to Shakespearean and non-Shakespearean tragedy some of Sarah Beckwith's recent concerns in *Shakespeare and the Grammar of Forgiveness*, which traces the "complex afterlives" of penance in the romances, as Shakespeare grappled with the epistemological effects of the "vast transformation in whole categories of speech acts consequent on a reformed liturgy and a transformed theology of the sacraments."[55] Although I treat the plays as less recuperative in their sensibilities than Beckwith does, our approaches to the particularities of repentance take as their starting points the current "turn to religion" in English studies, which includes a broad range of work on the entanglements between spirituality and the Renaissance stage. The theater's institutional role in religious change, as either an arena for appropriating ritual and devotional practices or an agent of Erasmian tolerance born of its practitioners' commitment to "evangelical inclusiveness," has been central to this work.[56] More recently, scholars have focused on the specifically performative dimensions of the theater, emphasizing both the ways that "the theater's own practices of meaning-making were conditioned by an extraordinary diversity of religious practice" and the ways that the material conditions of the stage could "destabilize polemical debates and ideological affiliations."[57]

But although I share these investments in the theater's institutional place in negotiating religious change, I stress, like critics such as Beckwith, Huston Diehl, Bryan Crockett, Elizabeth Mazzola, Michael O'Connell, John Stachniewski, and Adrian Streete, the drama's more particular engagements with signature elements of Reformation doctrine and controversy, which made it an "arena in which the disruptions, conflicts and radical changes wrought by the Protestant Reformation [were] publicly explored."[58] Indeed, the chapters that follow witness the imaginative resources of doctrine in reciprocal relation to the drama—that is, doctrine as an impetus for drama and narrative as well as doctrine as incorporating or determined by drama and narrative. This connection is intimated by John Bossy when he notes that "theological or ecclesiastical distinctions [are] important and historically creative," and it is perhaps the most pressing lesson of John Parker's *The Aesthetics of Antichrist*, which reminds us of the "centrality to Christianity . . . of playacting."[59] I am thus uncomfortable with the kinds of oppositions drawn by scholars who, in efforts to embrace or express the capaciousness of religious culture, argue that "religion was not just about doctrine, liturgy or ecclesiastical government; it was a language, an aesthetic, a structuring of meaning, an identity, a politics."[60] In fact, doctrine is itself a language, an aesthetic, and a structuring of meaning; and it remained in our period in crucial, mutual dialogue with the lived practices we associate with dramatic performance and content.[61] In this book I explore in detail what happens—first offstage and then onstage—when Christian understandings of repentance changed in ways that literally displaced the language and meaning of satisfaction.

Chapter 1

"ADEW, TO AL POPISH SATISFACTIONS"

Reforming Repentance in Early Modern England

"Adew, to al Popish satisfactions," proclaimed the Protestant clergyman Thomas Wilson in his monumental *Christian Dictionarie* (1612).[1] The exclamation is representative of the robust efforts by early modern Protestants to "bend the language of satisfaction . . . to a new purpose."[2] The "language of satisfaction" to which theologian Timothy Gorringe refers here is a vocabulary of divine and human atonement intimated in the Scriptures and established in early and medieval Christian doctrine. The "bending" of this language was a discrete element of the doctrinal program of the European and English Reformations, consistent with their epochal redescription of the relation between humans and God in the process of salvation. Its purpose was to articulate a "new Protestant theology of repentance"—for many the essence of devotional life—which was both distinct from the sacrament of penance of medieval and post-Tridentine Catholicism and congruent with doctrinal commitments to a Reformed soteriology.[3]

In their written and spoken pronouncements, Reformers invoked and then rejected the sacrament and its definition of satisfaction ("penal works performed as restitution for offenses against God, neighbor, or church");[4] they explained penitential emotions as the effects, rather than the cause, of God's grace and forgiveness; and they defended penitential practices as divine chastisement and correction rather than revenge or punishment. The result was a theology that both denied the possibility of "making enough" to compensate for sin and replaced the possibility of "feeling enough" with an affective condition called assurance, the consolation or comfort that accompanied the sense that one's "salvation was built upon a rock that could not fail."[5] It offered, that is, a model of Protestant repentance whose disciplinary procedures and emotional scope *did not include satisfaction*, enough, as something one made, had, or felt.

Repentance, as recent scholars suggest, was a key "Reformation battleground on which vital issues of theology, authority, and social mores were fought out," and theologians on both sides of the confessional divide presented their models with great rhetorical and polemical urgency.[6] Such energy informs their treatments of sacramental satisfaction as both a technical stage in, as well as a synecdoche for, the sacrament of penance; it also informs their treatment of the Crucifixion as the moment of Christ's satisfaction to God on behalf of humanity. In this chapter I study these approaches, paying special attention to the verbal styles and conceptual logics with which Reformers "bend" the language of satisfaction. I begin by rehearsing briefly the early and late medieval cure of souls, the history of which has been the object of increased scrutiny in the past two decades.[7] Although I move chronologically and at times schematically in this discussion, my organizing focus on satisfaction as both a calculable accomplishment and an affective experience acknowledges that "the variety and complexity of penance ... cannot be neatly contained in a single narrative."[8] In so doing I prepare the background for a detailed, nuanced examination of English Reformers' recalibration of the term and the complex assumptions about accounting and atoning for sin the recalibration involved.

Satisfaction Theory

What did Thomas Wilson mean by "Popish satisfactions"? His phrasing is deliberately controversial and pejorative, but in more neutral terms he is referring to the Catholic sacrament of penance, which had developed from the early church's penitential procedures into an elaborate, institutionalized theory and program for cleansing human sin after baptism through the specific stages of contrition, confession, and satisfaction, the latter having come to include indulgences and masses for the dead in purgatory. Implicit in Wilson's formula is a contrast between Christ's satisfaction, *singular*—the once-and-for-all work of the Cross—and Catholic satisfactions, *plural*—the human works which threatened the dignity of the former. The latter, for Protestants, was seen as a blasphemous assertion of the sufficiency of the self in relation to the gravity of sin, the omnipotence and alterity of God, and the untrammeled grace of Christ's sacrifice on the cross. As Alexander Nowell states in his *Catechism*: "There is no mercie due to our merites, but God doth yeld and remitte to Christ his correction and punishment that he would have done upon us. For Christ alone, with sufferance of hys paines, and with hys death, wherwith he hath payed and performed the penaltie of our sinnes, hath *satisfied* God."[9]

Nowell's assertion looks back to a central strand of atonement theory that stressed the sacrificial and satisfactory nature of the redemptive work of the Crucifixion.[10] Formulated in the Gospels and Pauline epistles and explicated by Latin fathers such as Tertullian and Cyprian, both of whom were deeply influenced by Roman civil and criminal law as well as the expiatory strategies of the Hebrew Bible, satisfaction theory stresses the juridical, sacrificial, and substitutionary nature of Christ's Passion.[11] According to the account, Adam and Eve's sin in the garden, an act of disobedience so devastating that no human effort could repair it, required the vicarious, punitive suffering of God's own self, in the figure of Jesus, to reconcile the divine with the humans who had inherited Adam's sin and continue to enact it.[12] Thus Mark 10:45: "For even the Son of man came not to be served, but to serve, and to give his life a ransom for many." The basic framework of this account was articulated in distinct and complicated ways by theorists of both the early Greek and Roman churches, including Irenaeus, Athanasius, and Augustine, but they all assume that God, as wrathful judge, must be placated or compensated for sins committed against him. The account, as scholars have noted, relies upon the deep linguistic, structural and conceptual homologies between economic, legal, and religious spheres insofar as they are organized by principles of exchange.[13] I stress here the way in which their literal and metaphorical correspondences are poised upon a notion of *satis*, enough, as a form of appropriate compensation or punishment that makes it aesthetically as well as juridically appealing. As Augustine says in his *De Libero Arbitraro*: "In order that the *beauty of the universe* not remain soiled, the disgrace of the crime [against God] must not remain without the beauty of vengeance."[14]

The doctrine reached its fullest, most compelling elaboration in the late eleventh-century theologian St. Anselm's *Cur Deus Homo*.[15] Part of the period's revaluation of the humanity of the incarnate Christ and its "new concern for [his] corporeality," Anselm explained Christ's incarnation and eventual death on the cross according to principles of order and hierarchy meant "to vindicate the whole scheme from the point of view of justice instead of falling back at every turn upon the arbitrary will of God."[16] Anselm's account of the Crucifixion as the restoration of divine justice— rather than the fulfillment of divine wrath—relies on Christ's willing, un-compelled embrace of suffering on behalf of men and women who lack the power to redeem themselves: "Christ of his own accord gave to his Father what he was never going to lose as a matter of necessity, and he paid, on behalf of sinners, a debt which he did not owe."[17]

According to Gorringe, this approach "refers us back to the beauty of divine nature,"[18] and indeed Anselm himself celebrates the "indescribable beauty" of the relation of opposites he discerns in the atonement: "If man sinned through pleasure, is it not fitting that he should give recompense through pain? And if it was in the easiest possible way that man was de-feated by the devil, so as to dishonour God . . . is it not justice that man, in giving recompense for sin, should, for the honour of God, defeat the devil with the greatest possible difficulty? Is it not fitting that man, who, by sin-ning, removed himself as far as he possibly could away from God, should make a gift of himself in an act of the greatest possible self-giving?"[19] But Anselm's balance and reason (made rhetorically available in the passage's moving anadiplosis) nevertheless insist upon the rigorous nature of the satis-faction that reconciles God and man through Christ. Anselm's God is not arbitrary, but he is punitive and exacting.[20] As Gorringe explains of the *Cur Deus*, "Compassion without satisfaction is not possible, for God's justice al-lows nothing but punishment as the recompense for sin."[21] That satisfac-tion, as Anselm makes explicit, is based upon a paradoxical understanding of *satis* deeply engrained in earlier theologies of the Passion: enough is the exact but also infinite amount that will compensate for human sin in the face of God. And when that compensatory "enough" is furnished by Christ, it is exactly equivalent to, *yet always in excess of*, the human debt incurred for sin.[22] As Anselm writes, "the life of this man [Christ] is so sublime and so precious that it can suffice to repay the debt owed for the sins of the whole world, and infinitely more besides."[23] This astonishing vacillation between the minimal and maximal values of *satis*, between precision and excess, is a key feature of Christ's atonement. It is also one with which theologians have grappled in their discussions of *human* atonement.

Human atonement lies at the intersection of Christology and anthropology in satisfaction theory.[24] Even as the theory registers the enormous gap between the individual and the divine, the irreconcilable distance between sinful creature and perfect Creator, it also grounds programs of human penitence and expiation—programs that blend punishment and repayment—in Christ's perfect atonement.[25] The connection is made explicit in the Gospels, with the resurrected Jesus's message to the Apostles that "So it is written that the Christ would suffer and on the third day rise from the dead, and that, in his name, repentance for the forgiveness of sins would be preached to all nations" (Luke 24:46–7). It is reframed in the Epistles, with Paul's praise for that "distress that . . . led to repentance" (2 Cor. 7:10) along with his identification in Galatians of offenses—"works of the flesh"—that require repentance: "sexual vice, impurity, and sensuality, the worship of false gods and sorcery, antagonisms and rivalry, jealousy, bad temper and quarrels, disagreements, factions and malice, drunkenness, orgies and all such things" (Galatians 5:19–21). It is fully calculated and institutionalized in the early church, with a penitential discipline that involved rigorous forms of public confession and shaming as well as physical punishment. Designed both to restore the individual soul to health and to insure communal purity, this was a discipline "meant for man's prostration and humiliation requiring a behavior conducive of mercy,"[26] and it depended upon a calculus of punishment according to which the "penalty [was] proportionate to the crime."[27] Undergirding it was the implicit understanding that humans, though dependent on Christ's Passion, were agents in their own repentance, participants in a complex transaction between the individual and God and the individual and the holy community. "We confess our sin to the Lord, not as though he were ignorant of it, but because *satisfaction* receives its proper determinant through confession, confession gives birth to penitence and by penitence God is appeased."[28] Tertullian here is interested specifically in confession, but his language assumes more generally the agency of the individual in appealing to the divine. In the course of their own proportionate suffering, that is, humans do enough to compensate for sin, to merit forgiveness, and to return to the solidarity of the church.

Calculating this "enough," according to John T. McNeill, began as early as the fourth century, as various councils as well as individual writers attempted to clarify the precise duration and depth of penitential activity.[29] Calculating it to a meticulous, exacting degree became the work of the early medieval penitentials. Beginning roughly in the sixth century, these guidebooks, growing out of monastic tradition, supplied priests with instructions for prompting contrition and hearing confession as well as with "a catalogue of sins and proportionate penances" which matched wrong with right according to careful ratios, assuming sin, crime, and restitution to be measurable entities.[30] (We thus have, for instance, the macabre formula in the *Canones Hibernensis* (675 CE) that allows as a valid substitution for a year of penance on bread and water "three days with a dead saint in a tomb without food or drink and without sleep.")[31] The penances provided in the penitentials may have been punitive and rigorous—John Bossy refers to their demands for fasting, vigils, and flagellation as "drastic penitential machinery"—but they were also meant to be sensitive to the conditions of the individual sinner, to accommodate the contingencies of the world outside the monastery, and to support devotion as well as discipline.[32] The linked provisions for proportionality and individuality represent an important difference between the early medieval church and its late antique ancestor.[33] But their structures and concepts of satisfaction remained fundamentally similar. As Thomas Tentler explains, in both systems sinners confessed their sins to a priest and followed the confession with deeds since "forgiveness rested most surely on *works* of expiation."[34] Or in Isidore of Seville's seventh-century definition of penance in his *Etymologies*: "Penitence is so called as if it were *poenitentia*, because by means of his own repenting (*poenitere*, i.e. *paenitere*) a person punishes (*punire*) the wrong he has done. Indeed, they who truly do penance do nothing other than not permit what they have done wrong to go unpunished."[35]

The individual's contribution to his or her forgiveness remained part of the penitential curriculum of the High Middle Ages, during which time the specific sacramental status of penance was affirmed and a careful distinction between the mortal guilt or debt of sin (*culpa*) and the temporal penalty or punishment of sin (*poena*) was drawn.[36] This distinction, historians concur was part of a new "stress on contritionism" which was heralded by figures as ideologically distinct in other ways as Abelard, St. Anselm, St. Bernard, and Hugh of St. Victor and which located the active scene of penance in the sinner's conscience, in his or her cultivation of sorrow, rather than in his or her deeds.[37] Jacques LeGoff places the change between the late eleventh and early thirteenth centuries, a period which included both the institutionalization of penance as a sacrament as well as the canon *Omnis Utriusque Sexus* by the Fourth Lateran Council of 1215, which mandated annual confession for both men and women.[38] During this period, LeGoff summarizes, the concept of sin and penance became "spiritualized and internalized. The gravity of a sin was henceforth measured in terms of the sinner's intention. It was therefore necessary to determine whether this intention was good or bad. This morality of intention was taught in every major twelfth-century theological school."[39] The focus on intention was matched by an equivalent emphasis on auricular, private confession, so that "the penitent was expected to comment on the sin as it related to his familial, social and professional situation, and explain the circumstances and motives involved. The confessor had to keep these individual parameters in mind and show as much concern, if not more, for soliciting the sinner's *confession* and for obtaining his *contrition*, as he did for 'satisfaction,' that is, for penance."[40] The result, in addition to the "cultivation of interiority concentrated on the confessional" and the "aggrandize[ment of] the powers of the clergy" who could absolve *before* deeds of atonement were performed, was that "contrition became the essential element for the penitent and pushed penitential exercises into a subservient position."[41] According to this scheme, satisfaction as a penitential stage "lost the preeminence it had enjoyed in the early church."[42] For the immensely influential Peter Lombard, for instance, "true repentance which abolishes sin" could hinge on the sinner's internal disposition, his "hatred of the offence committed and of committing it, together with the desire to make satisfaction."[43] Desire could, in certain instances, trump doing—or, more precisely, desire *was equivalent to* doing.

Such growing emphasis on intention indicates the subtlety and flexibility of medieval theologies of penance. It also indicates the extent to which medieval doctrine assumed the sinner's psychic interiority and individuality. My goal here is neither to argue on behalf of a developed sense of medieval subjectivity (this has already been done with great persuasiveness)[44] nor to adjudicate which part of penance gains or loses "preeminence" in the period as a result. (Recent work by Joseph Goering, for instance, suggests that theologians and canonists through the Middle Ages continued to "underscore the fruitful balance between the internal freedom of contrition and the external order of confession and satisfaction.")[45] Instead, I wish to emphasize that if satisfaction as a stage of penance "loses its preeminence," it is not itself lost.[46] Rather, in a movement that Mary Mansfield characterizes as a measure of scholastic theologians' "deep ambivalence about secrecy" and "longing for [the] public humiliation" of sinners, subjective experience takes on the role of objective satisfactory expiation.[47] Or, in other terms, the "shame of exposure [becomes] part of the satisfaction for the sin."[48] As Lombard offers, looking back to Chrysostom: "Perfect penance compels the sinner to bear all things cheerfully; in his heart contrition, in his mouth, confession, in deed all humility. This is fruitful penance; that just as we offend God in three ways, that is, with the heart, the mouth, and the deed, *so in three ways we make satisfaction.*"[49] Lombard thus sees satisfaction as a penitential stage, following contrition and confession; but he also sees it as the entire work of penance, the accomplishment of all "three ways" taken together. That work, including feelings of guilt and shame, is understood as pleasurable ("cheerful") as well as painful and punitive.

Such a combination of accomplishment and affect was the design of penitential practice in medieval England, including the various Latin and vernacular writings which provided "a substantial amount of educational literature on the subject of penance—confessional manuals, synodalia, sermons, and the like."[50] The fourteenth-century handbook *Fasciculus Morum*, for instance, insists that "even if we offend God when we sin but afterwards have been reconciled to him through contrition and confession, yet *this is not enough without our making satisfaction* and bettering our ways."[51] *Of Schrifte and Penance*, a Middle English prose translation of *Le Manuel des Péchés*, for instance, explains that "by the schame that ye haue in schryfte the peyne is made lasse for thy synne. *For the moste satisfaction is schame and contrition.*"[52] Contrition and confession, in this commonplace view, *become* satisfaction: they make enough in the theater of God's judgments. "Contrition came to serve *in the place* of satisfaction," Anne Thayer explains, as preachers taught "that deep contrition can be powerful enough to completely satisfy for sin."[53] So what the idea of satisfaction "loses" as a specific stage in the sacrament of penance it gains in its role as naming the total accomplishment of penance as a *conversion du coeur* shared by the sinner and the priest who grants absolution.[54]

The status of contrition and confession as vehicles of satisfaction opened up new realms for the investigation and measurement of "enough" in the process of placating God and assuaging the self. If the early medieval penitentials were preoccupied with assigning exact numbers to fast days, to prayers, and to sleepless vigils, the later medieval guides and manuals exhibited a "scholastic mania for subdividing and categorizing" in order to determine the sinner's levels of motivation and self-awareness and thus his or her sin's precise and proportionate penalty. The *Speculum Sacerdotale*, a guidebook for priests, suggests that "the quantitie of [penance] is noȝt to be considred but with what mynde *and* what affeccion he doþ it with."[55] Mirk's fifteenth-century *Instructions for Parish Priests* offers similar advice, diminishing the heaviness of the penance in inverse proportion to the sinner's sorrow: "But fyrst take hede, by gode a-vys, / Of what contrycyone þat he ys, / Ȝef he be sory for hys synne, / And fulle contryte as þou myȝt kenne; / Wepeþ faste, and ys sory, / And asketh yerne of mercy, / A-bregge hys penaunce þen by myche, / For god hym self for-ȝeueth syche."[56]

Delumeau suggests that manuals like the *Speculum* and *Instructions*, as they became "increasingly exhaustive and overloaded lists," risked "turning confession into a formalized and almost mechanical recitation of a certain number of excessively catalogued offenses." But he also notes the authentic, urgent motive behind those lists: "fear of incorrect and sacrilegious confession . . . and the conviction that God the Creditor kept an exact account of every sin and debt."[57]

These twin pressures—of automization and exactitude—are deeply related to the problem of enough: the difficulty of determining what counts as *satis* in the enumeration of sins or the prescription and performance of penalties. "It is difficult to assign for men what is necessary and what is superfluous (*Sed difficile est assignare que sint necessaria homini et que sint superflua*)," wrote Thomas of Chobham in his influential thirteenth-century *Summa*.[58] This same difficulty was echoed in other medieval contestations about penance: between the efficacy of attrition (regret for sin based on fear) versus contrition (regret for sin based on genuine sorrow in the face of God), or between the concepts of *opus operato* (which emphasized the objective status of the sacrament and the power of the clergy to absolve) and *opus operantis* (which stressed the subjective status of the sacrament and the internal disposition of the sinner).[59]

But these difficulties, however urgent, never eliminated the basic human ability to *satisfacere*, to make enough. This ability, of course, was understood to be dependent upon the grace of God and enabled by the sacramental in-frastructure and penitential tradition of the church, which was "devoted to assisting the penitent to do his best to prepare for this divine gift [of grace]."[60] But late medieval theologians continued to teach that "sinners co-operated with God to make progress toward their justification."[61] And what they did was "enough": enough defined as some sort of compensatory activity, whether it was pursuing a virtue to correct a vice, giving alms, extracting mental or physical self-punishment, or, most controversially, purchasing indulgences or sponsoring masses for the dead.

The quintessential articulation of this premise in the late Middle Ages, based on a belief in a divinely instituted, unilateral pact between God and man, was the dictum of Gabriel Biel and the late medieval *via moderna*: "*Facere quod in se est,*" to do what is in oneself. The sinner needed the "the exterior rite of the sacrament of penance [to] serve as the means to strengthen man's natural powers," but the thrust of this thinking was to make clear the role of human activity, alongside God's covenantal disposition, in atonement.[62] Such thinking would be echoed in Counter-Reformation defenses of the sac-rament; the Italian cardinal Thomas Cajetan, for instance, explained in an early response to Luther that although "in so far as our works proceed from ourselves they are not meritorious and consequently not of satisfactory value," nevertheless "in so far as they proceed from the divine grace that precedes, accompanies, and completes them, our works are meritorious and conse-quently of satisfactory value."[63]

"*Facere quod in se est*": this efficient phrase crystallizes the prevailing logic of penitential satisfaction against which the Reformers, although sensitive to Biel's emphasis on contritionism against Scotist sacerdotalism, would take their stand.[64] According to its logic, and the logic of its ancillary, "*facienti quod in se est, Deus non denegat gratiam,*" Christ satisfied God's justice in a way that makes it possible for humans, according to their own distinct, mundane abilities, to satisfy God for their shortcomings and sins.[65] Graced by God and directed by priestly authorities, individuals could make enough to answer the demands of divine justice, so that God became the satisfied object of the satisfying work his subjects did. The transaction was complete when it bent back on the subject, who was transformed—the popular devotional word was "cleansed"—in the process. Fundamental to late medieval and Tridentine penitential practice, this circuit of satisfaction presumes that an outer-directed but self-generated action oriented towards a sacred other accomplishes something in and for the actor, so that the individual has participated in his or her own justification. The allegory of the well and "scoop" underlying the late medieval manual *Jacob's Well* rests on the fundamental activity and participation of the sinner in satisfactory cleansing: "But þou take þis handyl of satysfaccyoun wyth þin handys, vp-on þi power to makyn amendys for þi false wrongys & harmys, wyth-outyn dowte, þi scope of penaunce is nouþt ellys spedy to casteyn out spedyly þe watyr of þis curs, to save þi soule fro drenchyng."[66] The same approach to the integrity and necessity of satisfaction as part of the three-stage process is emphasized in the early sixteenth century by Bishop John Fisher: "All though by contricyon & confessyon the payne eternall that we sholde have suffred be done away, nevertheles there abydeth in the soule a certayne taxacion or duty whiche without doubte must nedes be content & satysfyed eyther here in this lyf by temporal payne or elles after this lyfe in purgatory."[67]

It is precisely this transaction which the Reformers of the sixteenth century confronted. Grounded in Luther's recoil from the potential endlessness of confessional "enough,"[68] the challenge organized a broader attack on Catholic penance: on its sacramental status; its ascription of merit and agency to humans; its prescription of a mediating role for the priest, particularly in confession and in the granting of absolution; its emphasis on legalistic, ritualistic, and comprehensive accounting of sins, prayers, and pains; its deep, necessary connection to the reviled purgatory; and its vulnerability to abuse by the church in the shape of indulgences. At the same time, since "the doctrine of penitence and the doctrine of justification are very closely related," the challenge bred a new theology of repentance, one consonant with Reformed convictions about the depravity of the human soul and the omnipotence of divine will.[69] The result was a definition of repentance as a total change of personality and life, enabled by the Holy Spirit, which issued in, rather than derived from, good works: "Repentance is the free gift of the grace of God, who giveth it to every man, when he will, to whom he will, and in what measure hee will according to the riches of his mercie which is free, and not tyed to the will and pleasure of man."[70] This definition, as scholars routinely note, was encouraged and enabled by a humanist philology that had replaced the Vulgate's *poenitentiam agite*, "do penance"— Jerome's translation of *metanoeite* in Matthew 3:2—with Erasmus's *resipiscite*, "come to one's senses."[71] It led to the sustained, often polemical, reorientation of satisfaction as a technical stage in, as well as the total accomplishment of, repentance as something that human beings do, make, and, ultimately, feel.

Re-valuing Satisfaction: The English Reformation of Repentance

What did Thomas Wilson mean when he bid "adew to all Popish satisfactions"? His farewell condenses in prankish tones the rejection of human satisfaction for sin initiated by Luther and other European Reformers and then inherited and worked through in England as a central feature in the process of English confessional and national self-definition.[72] Luther set the terms of the rejection in 1517 in his Ninety-Five Theses, but it took more concentrated form in a 1519 discussion of the sacrament of penance, in which he insisted that "the forgiveness of guilt, the heavenly indulgence, is granted to no one on account of the worthiness of his contrition over his sins, nor on account of his works of satisfaction, but only on account of his faith in the promise of God," and in the *Babylonian Captivity*, in which he argued that the Catholic Church has "grossly abused it [penitential satisfaction], to the ruin of Christians in body and soul" and accused the church of instructing people so that they "never learned what satisfaction really is, namely, the renewal of a man's life." Not knowing or teaching the correct definition, leaders of the church then make their gravest error: "They so harp on it and emphasize its necessity, that they leave no room for faith in Christ."[73] Luther thus traced out a concatenation of mistakes at the heart of the sacrament of penance, deriding its reliance on human agency and its diminishment of Christ's satisfaction on the cross.[74]

For Luther, Christ's sacrificial suffering was a *"satisfactio sufficientissima,"* a wonderfully paradoxical use of the superlative that recalls Anselm.[75] But, as John Bossy makes clear, Luther, and the Reformers who followed him, differed fundamentally from Anselm in their understanding of the Passion. Although it might appear that Luther concurred with the Anselmian explanation of the Incarnation and Crucifixion, he in fact differed significantly:

> He continued to speak of the satisfaction of the wrath of the Father by Christ's passion and death . . . . But he did not mean what Anselm meant by satisfaction . . . . What in Anselm had been an offer of compensation adequate to turn away due vengeance and restore amicable relation between offended

God and offending man was taken by Luther as a submission to the punishment required of a criminal offence of public character. In Luther's penal or
criminal theory of the Atonement, there was no transaction; the parties were
not reconciled in the sense entailed by the English word, that two should
become one, since the act was purely one-sided. There was no natural or
social axiom to explain God's accepting Christ as a substitute for man in
general . . . it remained an impenetrable decision.[76]

Bossy sees this difference as a measure of "something happening to language."[77] But that "happening" is not unmotivated: Luther himself is behind it, inaugurating a semantic shift in—a transvaluation of—the word
satisfaction. It was meant to emphasize both mankind's profound inability
and its superfluity in attempting to compensate for sin; it was also meant to
reinforce the sheer generosity and grace of God in dealing with His crea-
tures. And, as Debora Shuger has recently suggested, it was also meant to
reject a model of divine justice as retributive, organized in terms of "the
language of debt and payback."[78]

Continental and English Reformers maintain this shift. Philip Melanchthon attacks the idea of satisfaction particularly for literalizing the economic metaphors of salvation—and thus for doing too much in a way that
belittles Christ:

There remains the third step, satisfaction. Here their discussions really become confused. They imagine that eternal punishments are changed into
punishments of purgatory, that of these one part is forgiven by the power of
the keys and another part is redeemed by satisfactions. They add further that
satisfactions ought to be works of supererogation, and these consist of stupid
observances like pilgrimages, rosaries, or similar observances that do not have
divine command. As they buy off their purgatory with satisfactions, so later
on a most profitable way of buying off satisfactions was invented. They sell
indulgences, which they interpret as the remission of satisfactions, and collect
this revenue not only from the living but even more from the dead . . . . In
short, the whole business of satisfactions is endless, and we cannot list all the
abuses. Beneath these scandalous and demonic doctrines the doctrine of the
righteousness of faith in Christ and of the blessing of Christ lies buried.[79]

Swiss Reformed positions on satisfaction are similar to the German ones, as
sixteenth-century English translations make clear. Calvin, who was more

concerned about the leniency than the severity of the sacrament, complains that Catholics "say that it is *not enough* for him that repenteth, to absteyne from his former evels, and chaunge his behavior into better, unlesse he make satisfaction to God for those things that he hath donne." This need for satisfactory activity suggests that God's mercy has no sway except "by meanes of ye deserving of our workes," a premise which takes away both the work and the sheer gift of the cross.[80] Calvin protests against the idea that "the crosse of Christe and our penaunce maye worke together," since Christ "alone . . . is the oblation for sinnes, he alone the propitiatory sacrifice, he alone the satisfaction."[81] The Zurich theologian Heinrich Bullinger hit the same notes, emphasizing the absolute sufficiency of Christ's Passion: "The priests and Monks do teache that repentaunce of the sinne committed, and faith in Christ, are not sufficient for the purgeing of sinnes, without the satisfaction of our owne workes and merites." But true believers understand that "if we are not justified by workes, then doe wee not with our woorkes make satisfaction for our sinnes." Rather, "by the justification of Christ we are absolved. By the satisfaction of Christ, or rather, for his satisfactions sake wee are also absolved. Christ is our righteousnesse, & therefore also our satisfaction."[82]

English theologians and other writers interrogate the term—"bend the language"—with similar energy and commitment. But their treatment of satisfaction in organizing penitential practices and affects has been either subsumed by contemporary scholars into the issue of predestination or disregarded in favor of more spectacular points of religious conflict, such as purgatory, iconoclasm, or the Eucharist.[83] Satisfaction is intimately bound, of course, to these issues. But it also stands independently as an essential aspect of Reformation theology and the changes in thinking about human agency and affect which this theology both assumed and fostered. For satisfaction, understood as the overall outcome as well as a specific stage of the sacrament of penance, gives what we might consider a local habitation and a name to the more abstract, umbrella category of atoning works, as it designates *a concrete principle of both exchange and contact* between the individual and the divine in a circuit of sorrow, expiation, and forgiveness. The term is invoked with an almost compulsive regularity by English Reformers to define their "new theology of repentance" and to manage new forms of penitential thinking and feeling.

Penance as a sacrament was officially preserved in Henrician and Edwardian articles of religion as late as 1553, testimony to both official acknowledgment of its strong theological attraction and official reluctance to dispense with it.[84] But attacks on it began far earlier. William Tyndale's *Obedience of a Christian Man* (1528) follows Lutheran models in opposing Christ's satisfaction to that of humans: "God anointed his son Jesus with the Holy Ghost, and therefore called him Christ, which is as much to say as anointed . . . . and sent him into the world to bless us and to offer himself for us a sacrifice of a sweet savour, to kill the stench of our sins . . . and to make full and sufficient satisfaction or amends for all them that repent." According to this model, the human claim to be able to satisfy was blasphemous: "Whosoever goeth about to make satisfaction for his sins to Godward, saying in his heart this much have I sinned, this much will I do again, or this wise will I live to make amends withal, or this will I do to get heaven withal, the same is an infidel, faithless and damned in his deed doing."[85] Thomas Cranmer, as Ashley Null has recounted in scrupulous detail, rejected the sacrament by 1540, when he "fundamentally repudiated the notion that Christians in this life could ever be fully pleasing to God in their own person. Rather, justification consisted solely in appropriating the 'righteousness of Christ' so as to be 'reputed righteous' for Christ's sake."[86] Null cites Cranmer's direct attack on the sacrament and its three stages: "Of penaunce also I finde in the scripture, Whereby synners after baptisme returnyng holly vnto god be accepted againe vnto god*des* favour and mercye, But the scripture speaketh not of penaunce as we call yt a sacrament, consistyng in iii partes | Contrition | Confession | and Satisfaction, but the scripture taketh penaunce for a pure Conversion of a synner in harte and mynde frome his synnes vnto god, makyng no me*ntion* of private Confession of all deadly synnes to a preiste, *nor of ecclesiasticall satisfaction to be enjoyned by hym*."[87] And in 1553, John Bradford, in an oft-reprinted sermon on repentance, called the idea of human satisfaction a "monstruous abhomination, blasphemie, and even open fyghtyng agaynste God. For yf Satisfaction can be done by man, then Christ died in vaine."[88]

Bradford's position, at the time still representative of what Christopher Haigh considers the country's "minority faith," achieved general acceptance in the early Elizabethan period as part of the national absorption of Calvinist theology, if not ecclesiology, into the Church of England.[89] Repentance, as idea and practice, was thus an integral part of that "interplay of many forces" that defined the complicated, controversial process of Reformation religious change.[90] The sacramental status of penance was eliminated by the time of the Thirty-Nine Articles (1563, revised 1571) and the authorized "Homilie of Repentance" explained that Christ "alone did with the sacrifice of his Body and Blood, make satisfaction unto the Justice of God for our sins," so that "they that think that they have done much of themselves towards Repentance are so much more the farther from God, because they do seek those things in their own works and merits, which ought to be found in our Saviour Jesus Christ."[91]

Variations on these positions, often corresponding to the competing strains of "hotter" and more moderate Protestant thinking, were reiterated by English clergy throughout the later sixteenth and early seventeenth centuries in a wide range of devotional, sermonic, and instructional materials. They were answering to pastoral as well as polemical pressures, from the catechetical need to disseminate basic principles among the young or unlearned to the need to answer doctrinal and practical challenges from the Council of Trent (1545–64) and post-Tridentine Catholicism, including the concerted pressures from the presence of recusant and Jesuit communities.[92] Indeed, the forces of Catholic renewal "developed the internal and spiritual work of confession" in direct response to Protestant critique,[93] emphasizing the importance of satisfaction and critiquing its dismissal by Reformers. In its fourteenth session the Council of Trent, for instance, declared it anathema to believe "that satisfaction of penitents is no other than the faith whereby they apprehend that Christ has satisfied for them."[94] In England the Catholic community, with its network of priests and publications, portrayed the refusal of penitential works as a misinterpretation of Christ's Passion and as a matter of Protestant weakness and indolence.[95] A striking example is the Jesuit Robert Parsons's *Christian Directory*, which was revised for a Protestant readership by Edmund Bunny after its initial publication in 1582 as *The First Book of the Christia Excercise.* In his edition, Parsons offered a long defense, buttressed with references to Jerome, Cyprian, and Augustine, of the necessity of satisfaction: "Thou [must] make satisfaction to Gods justice, either in this life, or in the life to come, for that which now thou passest over so pleasantly. And this satisfaction must be so sharpe and rigorous . . . as it must be answerable to the weight & continuance of thy sinnes . . . so that, by how much the more thou prolongest, and encreasest thy sinne; so much greater must be thy paine and sorrow in satisfaction."[96] This directive, Parsons notes sardonically in a second edition meant to address Bunny's version, was excised from the Protestant book. "Bun. leaveth out and mangleth most impudently," Parsons glosses, reading the absence as a symbol of the incorrigible Protestant, hardened to piety and instruction.[97]

Tudor and Stuart divines, then, actively defined their penitential theology against the church of their forbears *and* against post-Tridentine Catholicism.[98] This engagement could look like the definition of repentance in John Merbecke's commonplace collection, which complains that the Church of Rome had seduced its followers into thinking "that they have repented sufficiently for their sins, in case they observe the same which was appointed them for their penaunce . . . although they never feele one jot of true repentaunce in their hearts."[99] Or it could look like Daniel Dyke's gratuitous swipe in the dedicatory epistle to his *Two Treatises* (1616), which complains that some lackadaisical Protestants do not repent until the last minute, when they "conceit as great an efficacie in these five words, *Lord have mercy upon me*, spoken with their last breath, for the translation of their soules into heaven, *as the papists do* of their five words of consecration."[100] Or it could involve a direct allusion, as in *Davids Faith and Repentance* (1589), which refers directly to Trent (the Sixth Session, which also discussed penitential works) when the Calvinist Henry Holland derides the "best known and most unsaverie dregges of Poperie" and worries that his brethren do not understand "that salvation depends on Christ, not works—and that this is the work of Satan."[101] Archbishop Edwin Sandys defines the difference between confessions precisely in terms of satisfaction: while Protestants "wil have the scriptures to be read of all men, prayer to be made with understanding, Christ to be a full satisfaction for sinne," papists "upon their foundations have builded a doctrine that forbiddeth Gods people to read his word, that teacheth them to powre out their prayer in a tongue which they cannot understand, that hath found *a way to satisfie the wrath of almightie God* in this life by penaunce, and after this life by indurance in purgatorie."[102] And William Perkins, one of the period's leading Calvinist divines, condemns the "opinion of the papists, who besides the alone passion of Christ, maintaine workes of satisfaction, partly of their owne, and partly of the Saints departed."[103] Usually such attacks aimed at Catholic satisfaction for being *not* enough, for being *not satis*: but for Perkins penitential satisfaction marks a Catholic mistake in thinking that humans can do *more* than they are able and thus feel *more* than they should.

As Anne Thayer and Katherine Lualdi have suggested, this kind of polemical jousting was a matter of "Protestant self-definition and communal identity."[104] The engagement was particularly urgent because, as Reformers were highly aware, their penitential theology could look, at least from the outside, very similar to the Roman one: "Protestants vocally dissociated their own penitential rites from those engaged by their Roman Catholic neighbours and forebears . . . but there was far less difference in practice than Protestants so energetically alleged."[105] The similarity is due partly to the maintenance of an almost sacramental structure of confession and satisfactory penance in the proceedings of the ecclesiastical courts, to which I turn in the coda. But it was also the result of the way in which Protestants preserved the importance of penitential works by explaining them as the fruit, rather than the root, of divine forgiveness—an inversion of traditional cause and effect schemes consistent with the broad shape of Reformed positions on justification and salvation.[106] As evidence of the sought-after "renewal of life," Reformers extolled a contrite disposition as a gift from God, though not a matter of human will. Personal confession to peers and clergy, as long as it was understood as a matter of counsel or education and not as purgative or efficacious, was similarly permitted. "Confession, not in the priest's ear, for that is but man's invention, but to God in the heart and before all the congregation of God," Tyndale offered, in a formula that was to be repeated by other Protestant divines.[107] And good works, with the rise of an experimental approach to salvation, were encouraged as proof of election: "Faith without Charitie is dead: So Repentance without Restitution is a vapour," Arthur Dent warned.[108] Dyke is especially poignant in his calculations: "If the weaknesse of thy repentance trouble thee, remember it is an evangelicall grace: and how little a mite will the gospell accept? Even a penny for a pound. A desire to repent is repentance heere."[109] Such formulations could sound extraordinarily like the calculations of earlier penitential manuals. "The more festred and dangerous the wound is, the sharper must be the cure," Dyke offers, rearticulating an enduring commitment to penitential logics of proportionality and contrariety.[110]

So although Debora Shuger has argued strenuously for the continuities between Catholic and Protestant penitential practices, particularly their demand for restitution to human beings as a condition of divine pardon, Protestants of various stripes themselves had to emphasize the radical difference of their model of repentance and its connection to solifidianism.[111] As Alec Ryrie notes, Reformers "were careful not to claim that ascetic practices could atone or satisfy for sin. Instead, their function was to deter and reform the sinner."[112] And they did this precisely in terms of "*satisfacere*." Perkins is especially explicit in his *Reformed Catholike* (1598), in which he derides the Church of Rome for teaching that "*they themselves must satisfie* the justice of God . . . either on earth or in purgatorie." Protestants, on the contrary, teach and believe "that Christ by his death and passion hath made a perfect and all-sufficient satisfaction to the justice of God for all the sinnes of men, and for the whole punishment of them." The distinction is fundamental, Perkins adds, because it implies that "we for our parts must for ever stand at difference with them: so as if there were no more points of variance but this one, it should be sufficient to keepe us alwaies from uniting our religions."[113] In sum, precisely because of the proximity of this kind of experimentalist thinking and a theology of works,[114] these allowances depended upon the reiterated, reflexive denial of their satisfactory status. As Perkins insists, works are "*not a satisfaction for sinne*, but onely testification of repentance by the fruits thereof."[115] "Satisfaction," by nominating what true penitents could not make and what Christ had done, became a shibboleth—the premier shibboleth—for differentiating Protestant from Catholic repentance as well as the elect from the reprobate.

A pattern of repeatedly invoking and then clarifying penitential satisfaction thus became part of the fabric of English spiritual writing, an engrained impulse as well as deliberate polemical maneuver. The *Path-way to Penitence* (1591) explains that restitution "which some do cal [*sic*] satisfaction," is not to be understood "as though we are able by any workes or merits to deserve the forgivenesse of our sinnes, or to yeelde any meete recompence to God."[116] The prolific Andrew Willet asserted that "by true and faithfull repentance, and other good works proceeding of faith, we may avoyde Gods heavie judgement due to our sinnes, *yet not for the merit or satisfaction of any worke*, but through the merites onely of Christ."[117] Francis Marbury decried the "hypocrisie of the Papists, who have turned [penance] into a sacrament," so that they "bring almost all the power of repentance to consist in the externall affliction & penaltie of the bodie."[118] Thomas Scott's *Godlie Sermon of Repentance* (1585) emphasizes the importance of deeds over words ("Good wordes shall bee found in hell, but good workes go all to heaven"), but he is quick to clarify the claim: "I speake not this as holding, that wee are justified by our woorkes."[119] Richard Stock, who defined repentance to be "when one and the same man is changed in the condition both of his soule and bodie, from iniquitie to righteousnes, from all sinne to the living God, both in the inward man and the outward conversation," attacked Catholics who believe that "those works, which have any shew of goodnes, although they bee never so imperfect, corrupt, and hypocriticall, yet they are good, and may be meritorious to deserve earthlie and heavenlie blessings" and who, even more remarkably, think that "they can free themselves by their works of mercie and other satisfactions, and so say there is no feare."[120]

Even more interesting is Arthur Dent's *Plaine Mans Path-way* (1601), organized in dialogic structure to give the feel of a conversation, however stylized. It features a non-believer, Antilogus, who says in the language of Biel's *via moderna* that if he has time before he dies to "aske God forgiveness, and say my prayers, and cry God for mercy, *I hope I shall do well inough.*" His Protestant admonisher, Theologus, warns him that "repentance is the rare gift of God, & it is given but to a fewe."[121] George Gifford's *Countrie Divinitie* (1582), another multi-speaker text, is especially instructive, since it features a dialogue between Zelotes, a hard-line evangelical, and Atheos, an old-school Christian from the country, who, though he claims to despise the Pope, still clings to good works as the key to his salvation. As Gifford rues in his dedicatory epistle, Atheos, like many others, has not been "taught thoroughly and sufficiently in the Gospel," and is thus in mortal danger, having "arme[d] himself] against true repentance, and right understanding."[122] When Zelotes questions him specifically about repentance, Atheos, like Dent's Antilogus, also echoes the late medieval theology of Biel, convinced that he will be saved as long as he does as much as he is able. But Zelotes warns him that "ye deceive your selfe, when ye think that God can be mercifull unto ye, and you live without repentance." True repentance is not, he tells Atheos, doing one's best, but rather "a returning home unto God for all evill vices and corrupte desires which are in the flesh and in the heart." It is distinguished from "false," or Catholic, repentance precisely because it doesn't imagine itself as satisfactory, especially to God: "This counterfet repentance maketh men bolde all their life to despise the holy worde of God . . . it causeth them at their ende not to feare the wrath of God, nor the vengeance to come: because *they thinke God is satisfied* with this repentaunce."[123]

Such examples are easily multiplied. They testify to a persistent, insistent need to reiterate the solifidian credentials of Protestant repentance in order to guard its difference from Catholic penance and to reinforce its connection to principles of justification by faith and the utter depravity of the human will. This protection, to return to Gorringe, depended on a particular "bending of the language of satisfaction" so that *satis*, as something humans *facere*, is canceled out entirely under the banner of the Crucifixion. As the *Path-way to Penitence* insists, satisfaction "is not to be taken as though we are able by any workes or merits to deserve the forgivenesse of our sinnes, or to yeelde any meete recompence to God." For only Christ "hath wrought satisfaction for us."[124] So although Gregory Kneidel has argued eloquently that, for Protestants engaged in a critique of "medieval economics of afflic-tion," "enough was enough, *satis*faction was *satis*," I would suggest that the Reformation marks the historical juncture at which *satis* was *satis* only for Christ, when humans recalibrated—and rejected—their potential for do-ing enough in matters of atonement.[125]

My final point here is to connect the recalibration of *doing enough* with that of *feeling enough*. As discourse and practice, Reformed repentance was intended to have emotional effects on its followers as well as behavioral and ideational ones. It was intended, in other words, to manage "satisfaction": to manage it as a subjective feeling, the contentment or relief associated with having done enough. So having degraded and eliminated satisfaction as some-thing humans do, Reformers replaced it as something humans feel. Their emotional substitute for the feeling of penitential satisfaction was called *assur-ance*. Assurance involved the cultivation of an important set of pained emo-tions: the "sorrowe and griefe" that signifies "a broken and contrite heart."[126] This is the holy mourning which Gary Kuchar describes as a process of "re-orientating the subject from a worldly to a spiritual comportment." And, as Kuchar explains, it was distinguished from Catholic compunction by a Protestant insistence that such spiritual melancholy was an "irreversible sign of grace."[127] But the central commitment of the doctrine of assurance was that its sense of comfort derived from the fact that it was not associated with a human contribution to salvation.[128] Dyke traces this logic in a series of antitheses: "The deeper is the sense of misery, the sweeter is the sense of mercy," he explains, "the deeper our descent in *humiliation*, the higher our ascent in *consolation*."[129] He is additionally explicit that the feelings of mis-ery and humiliation (which he maintains are the *effects* rather than *causes* of forgiveness and grace) are never to be understood or experienced as enough: "We must feede and nourish this sorrow, *never satisfie our selves*, but wish with the prophet, that *our heads were continuall, unemptiable fountaines of teares*."[130] Humans do not satisfy God, but they also do not satisfy—are not satisfied—themselves. At the heart of this affect, we may read a rejection of

Catholic penance for allowing its followers to feel enough in terms of their own salvation and thus to feel *too much*.

Dyke, like his fellow theologians, championed this approach, returning enough to Christ so that, they claimed, the faithful penitent did not have to experience the doubt inherent in the Catholic sacrament.[131] But some sensed other, darker implications; Samuel Hieron, for instance, acknowledged the residual appeal of this lost possibility. In a remarkably subtle aside in a sermon on one of the Penitential Psalms, Hieron notes that "the popish opinion of satisfaction cleaves close to our nature, and there is an aptnes in us, to thinke by some act of ours, to make some kind of amends for the things we have done amisse inn: we can soon perswade our selves to be able to out waigh, as it were, our evill deeds by our better."[132] Especially sensitive to this recalibration and its potential effects was Richard Hooker, who was unwilling to give up the possibility that "our repentance and the workes thereof, [can be] . . . termed *satisfactorie*" to God.[133] While the Reformers around him had, as we have seen, definitively rejected such a premise, Hooker's rationalism, what Peter Lake calls his "insist[ence] upon the law-bound nature of God's doings," often rendered him at odds with the competing strains of Elizabethan Calvinism.[134] His account of repentance in the sixth book of his *Laws of Ecclesiastial Polity* (composed in the early 1590s, but not published until 1648) balances his sympathy for the virtues of public and private confession as well as penitential works with his systematic suspicion of the sacramentalizing claims of the Fourth Lateran Council and its elevation of the priesthood. When Hooker takes up the specific question of satisfaction, he echoes the Protestant chorus in explaining that only Christ's sacrifice was sufficient for God "to bee satisfyed" for the infinite debt of human sin, and that "faith alone maketh Christ's satisfaction ours."[135] But unlike his "hotter" Protestant peers, Hooker wants to preserve the efficacy—not just the post hoc evidentiary status of election—of the works that stem from this faith. For faith, he says, makes us "willing by repentance *to doe* even that which of in itselfe how unavaylable soever, yet being required and accepted with God, wee are in Christ made capable, and fitt vessels to receive the fruit of his satisfaction."[136] This "doing" is admitted by God "for satisfaction which is due by us, because Christ hath by his satisfaction made it acceptable."[137] Hooker's statement echoes Catholic responses to the rescripting of satisfaction, including claims such as Cardinal Cajetan's, who looks forward to the penitential *increase* of Christ's merits, "if indeed I believe I have shared in them, I also want to add my own satisfactions, not ranking them above the satisfactions of Christ, but because it is better to satisfy in two ways than by one alone. Christ's and my satisfaction are together a multiplication of goods over Christ's satisfaction alone."[138] So although Hooker goes on to criticize the excrescences that developed alongside the sacramentality of Roman satisfaction—priestly absolution before works, clerical power "to determine or define aequivalencie, betweene sinnes and satisfactions," and the treasury of merit that allows for indulgences—he is deeply reluctant to give up the acceptability of individual satisfaction in concert with Christ's sacrifice.[139] He is reluctant, that is, to defend or define a Protestant repentance that does not include the human ability to "please and content God . . . because when wee have offended, he looketh but for repentance att our hands: our repentance and the workes thereof, *are therefore termed satisfactorie.*"[140]

Hooker's approach to the "satisfactorie" is certainly an element of his own understanding of grace, works, and faith. But it can also be read, alongside others such as Hieron's, as an intimation of the lingering appeal of penitential satisfaction and a concern with the broad stakes and consequences of its revaluation as a principle of exchange, payment and punishment as well as an experiential and emotional state. The remainder of this book studies the exploration of those stakes and consequences on the Elizabethan and Jacobean stage.[141] It begins with the generic contortions, wrought by pressures on penitence, of Christopher Marlowe's *Doctor Faustus.*

Chapter 2

THE SATISFACTIONS OF HELL

Doctor Faustus *and the Descensus Tradition*

Could Christopher Marlowe's *Doctor Faustus* be a version of the medieval harrowing of hell play, that cycle pageant which displayed Christ's descent to the underworld where he challenged Satan for the souls of the righteous dead?

Of course, Marlowe's drama, which centers obsessively on the status of the protagonist's repentance, has long been associated with the morality play.[1] But in this chapter I argue that, under the pressure of the period's reconfiguration of satisfaction, the play's generic as well as penitential impulses take shape as an underworld journey as much as they do a psychomachia. In other words, the "form of Faustus' fortunes" has much in common with the *cycle* drama, or at least the special pageant of Christ's descent into hell.[2] If the substance of that form has been significantly altered, it is the result not only of the secularization of the commercial stage and of Marlowe's special imaginative powers but also of a particularly vivid contemporary controversy about the meaning of the third article of the Elizabethan church: "As Christ died for us, and was buried: so also it is to be believed that he went down into hel."[3]

According to Peter Marshall, the Descent controversy, in which a range of Elizabethan and Jacobean divines argued over whether or not Christ literally traveled to hell to confront Satan, was part of a comprehensive effort to "dissociate . . . irrevocably from the typologies and language of pre-Reformation 'geographies of the afterlife.' "[4] But, as my discussion of the controversial literature suggests, the most pressing theological concern exposed by the debate was not Protestant "unease with the conception of the afterlife as a series, or even a pair of concatenated localities,"[5] but rather an uncertainty about what counted as *enough* for Christ to do to redeem fallen humanity. The debate, that is—over whether or not it was *necessary* for Christ to go down to hell or to suffer hell in his soul—rehearses the problem of human satisfaction and redemption that we have chronicled in chapter 1 as a problem for Christ. Faustus, in his fixation on and trafficking with hell, absorbs both sides of the dilemma: he probes not only the limits of his own (in)ability to repent for a life of "all voluptuousness" but also the contours of Christ's satisfaction to God for human sin.[6] In the process his play transforms to tragic effect one of the medieval stage's most powerful representations of the movement of Jesus from suffering to triumph, from *tristia* to *gaudium*.[7] In what follows I discuss the economies of satisfaction at work in contemporary understandings of hell. I then turn to the theological as well as literary debates around Christ's descent to hell to demonstrate how they bleed into Faustus's own salvific concerns, making him the center of a contorted harrowing of hell play.

The Symbolics of Hell

Faustus's fascination with the underworld is not original to Marlowe. It is inherited directly from the play's source, *The Damnable Life*, also known as *The English Faust Book*, hereafter referenced as *EFB* (1592).[8] The magician protagonist of this legendary account, popular with a Renaissance readership on the Continent as well as in England, focuses relentlessly on the shape and place of hell. Having made his pact with the devil, for instance, Faustus "dreamed that he had seen a part of hell, but in what manner it was, or what place he knew not: whereupon he was greatly troubled in mind and called unto him Mephistopheles his spirit, saying to him: 'My Mephistopheles, I pray thee resolve me in this doubt: what is hell, what substance is it of, in what

place stands it, and when was it made?'"[9] Mephistopheles supplies answers—
that God ordained hell even before the Fall of Lucifer, that it "is of no substance, but a confused thing," and that it floats like a bubble moved by the
breath of God—but this information only prompts further questions from
Faustus about hell's geography and the nature of its punishments.[10] Finally
Mephistopheles furnishes him with a baroque description energized by a long
tradition of sermonic and catechistical threat:

> Therefore is hell called the everlasting pain, in which is neither hope nor
> mercy; so is it called utter darkness, in which we see neither the light of sun,
> moon, nor star: and were our darkness like the darkness of the night, yet
> were there hope of mercy, but ours is perpetual darkness, clean exempt from
> the face of God . . . . And mark Faustus, hell is the nurse of death, the heat of
> all fire, the shadow of heaven and earth, the oblivion of all goodness, the
> pains unspeakable, the griefs unremovable, the dwelling of devils, dragons,
> serpents, adders, toads, crocodiles and all manner of venomous creatures; the
> puddle of sin, the stinking fog ascending from the Stygian lake, brimstone,
> pitch and all manner of unclean metals, the perpetual and unquenchable
> fire, the end of whose miseries was never purposed by God . . . . There shalt
> thou abide torments, trembling, gnashing of teeth, howling, crying, burning,
> freezing, melting, swimming in a labyrinth of miseries, scalding, burning,
> smoking in thine eyes, stinking in thy nose, hoarseness of thy speech, deaf-
> ness of thine ears, trembling of thy hands, biting thine own tongue with
> pain, thy heart crushed as in a press, thy bones broken, the devils tossing
> firebrands upon thee, yea, thy whole carcass tossed upon mulchforks from
> one devil to another.[11]

Taken together, Faustus's questions and Mephistopheles's answers provide an anatomy of hell as both a place of positive punishment (*poena sensus*)
and a condition of privation from God's presence (*poena damni*). The latter—
the internalized, psychic torment of the latter—becomes of fresh interest to
Protestant theologians, and I discuss it below.[12] But my concern now is the
depiction of hell's punishments as endless and limitless as well as matched
precisely to the nature and duration of the sin. This is Dante's *contrapasso*, a
program of punitive equivalencies or *lex talionis* observable in the earliest
literatures on hell[13] and explained by Georges Minois as the lingering effect
of Roman legalism on early medieval theology.[14] Persistent well into the
seventeenth century, this paradigm cast hell as the apotheosis of both the

exactitude and the impossibility of expiatory "enough": its penalties represented both precise proportionality and infinite, ineffable punishment, exciting while eluding full description. Efforts to portray hell only accelerated in the literature and art of the fourteenth, fifteenth, and sixteenth centuries, as they became a preoccupation not only for preachers intent on inculcating lay fear but also for artists and dramatists who, in their maps and narratives of underworld travel, brought a "profusion of imagination . . . to their embodiments of hell's demonic inhabitants."[15] Hell pains, in other words, were an intellectual and aesthetic/linguistic as well as a theological challenge, the culture's most aggressively imagined experience of the promise and impossibility of punitive satisfaction. They provoked a set of literary and pictorial conventions—always deeply inflected by political, cultural, and technological contexts[16]—which required constant innovation in the attempt to express the inexpressible, to calculate the incalculable, and to render the infinite and eternal in finite and temporal terms.

It was not only the forms and duration of infernal penalty which demanded more. Hell itself, and not just its punishments, was endlessly appetitive. The locale of "everlasting tormentes" where "the fire goeth not out, but continual weping and gnashing of teeth," hell was a ravenous entity, always on patrol for more sinners.[17] The medieval hell-mouth, a staple of both pictorial and theatrical iconography which usually took the form of the jaws of a devouring beast, offers perhaps the most vibrant image of such an appetite, one that persisted into the Renaissance and onto the Renaissance stage.[18] But the Faust book's Mephistopheles has a verbal way of expressing this notion to Faustus: hell, he tells him, "is bloodthirsty and is never satisfied."[19] This model of insatiety, set against the perfect proportionality of "the greater the sin, the greater the torment," transfixes the *EFB*'s Faustus, prompting the cascading ironies of his unappeasable curiosity about an unappeasable place.[20]

The curiosity he exhibits, and the terrifying images it yields, was sometimes understood as a step in the calling to repentance, a means of provoking attrition, or fear of punishment, in order to move the sinner to contrition, or genuine sorrow for sin as a violation of God's law. Thus *A Breefe Treatise Exhorting Sinners to Repentance* (1580) encourages its audience to compare the pains of hell to the promises of heaven as a way of fostering holy regret, while George Meriton, recognizing that Christ's Passion and "*Gods* continued mercy towards us" should prompt sinners' repentance, acknowledges nevertheless that "were there no *Hell* to receive them; or *Tortures* provided for them," people would never grow contrite.[21] But this is not the effect of thinking about hell on the *EFB*'s Faustus, who responds as preachers expected of the wicked, becoming "more hardened then before": more convinced of his damnation and more dedicated to performing outrageous jests and tricks for princes as well as students.[22] As John Henry Jones summarizes, "Faustus' curiosity is turned into an obsession with hell, which only serves to reveal to him his folly and his plight."[23] And as Faustus himself laments, "Had I not had a desire to know so much I had not been in this case:. . . I thought myself not worthy to be called Doctor Faustus if I should not also know the secrets of hell and be associated with the furious fiend thereof; now therefore must I be rewarded accordingly."[24] After this, Faustus despairs of forgiveness: "his repentance was like to that of Cain and Judas, he thought his sins greater than God could forgive. [He] looked up to heaven, but saw nothing therein; for his heart was so possessed with the devil that he could think of nought else but of hell and the pains thereof."[25]

Marlowe's Faustus takes on his predecessor's fascination, including its precarious status as an ambiguous signal of his own damnation.[26] But to it he adds a special fantasy of Christological imitation: of harrowing hell, of descending to the infernal realm and defeating Satan of his rights to the dead. This fantasy may be traced to the broad influence on Marlowe's dramaturgy of late medieval and Reformation representations of Christ, particularly the influential devotional tradition of *imitatio Christi*, which remained a vibrant genre through the period.[27] I suggest here, however, that it is fueled by the particularly noble, heroic model of divine intercession dramatized so effectively, and with ample doses of mockery, in the cycle plays. Only this model of heroic harrowing had become an object of controversy by the second half of the sixteenth century. The latent preoccupation of the debate, which ostensibly focused on whether or not Christ's soul descended to hell, was with what counted as "enough" for Christ to do to redeem mankind.

The Medieval Descent to Hell Tradition

The harrowing of hell play, versions of which feature in all four of the major medieval cycles, was the dramatic manifestation of a compelling, if scripturally problematic, doctrinal tenet which maintained that between the Crucifixion and the resurrection Christ went to the place of dead souls.[28]

The tenet, formulated by various Greek and Latin fathers including Irenaeus, Origen, Athanasius, Ambrose, and Augustine, first appeared in a creed in 359 at Sirmium, and by the eighth century "He descended into hell" was "part of the universally accepted Apostles' Creed."[29] But its most influential formulation—and certainly its most vibrant—was in the apocryphal *Evangelium Nicodemi*, the Gospel of Nicodemus, "one of the most successfully and culturally pregnant" of the early retellings of the Passion.[30] The Gospel, whose existence in manuscript is documented from the end of the fourth century, was widely disseminated after the fifth century in Latin and Greek, and then in European vernaculars; it "manag[ed] to penetrate into a variety of literary, theological, devotional, and liturgical discourses."[31] In England, the apocryphon left its marks in Old English chronicles and poetry dating from the eleventh century and was reproduced in Middle English translations as well as in prose compilations such as the *Cursor Mundi* (c. 1300) and the *South English Legendary* (c. 1270–85). Its influence was felt most widely in the late medieval civic drama which, as John Parker writes, was fueled by the period's fundamentally "theatrical understanding of atonement."[32]

The narrative of the Gospel begins with Jewish accusations against Jesus and includes a full discussion of both the Passion and of Joseph of Arimathea's burial of Jesus before it presents the account of the two sons of Simeon who, having been roused from death after the Crucifixion, tell "the secretes of [Christ's] devyne mageste whych [he] dedyst yn helle."[33] These "secretes" constitute the harrowing narrative: while the infernal princes, frightened by the prospect of Christ's approaching divinity, encourage Satan to "dyffende thyself a-yenst hym," a tremendous voice calls for the gates of hell to be lifted (*attollite portas*); the devils refuse, shutting the gates more tightly with locks of iron, but they are broken open as Christ enters "yn the forme of man," spreading light through hell as the holy dead, including Adam, Isaac, and David, praise him. Meanwhile the devils, horrified, question him in a way that establishes his heavenly identity and the salvific, triumphal purposes of his earthly and infernal sojourns:

> What art thou that thus lyftest up thy request to God for oure confusyoun? What art thou þat haste broken oure ʒatys? What art thou that art so gret and semest so lytel? What art thou hyghe and meeke emperour yn the forme of man, and Kynge of glorye, put on the crosse and dede, and than leyde yn sepulture by the Jewes? And now art thou come to us alyve. And alle crea-

tures dyd tremble at thy dethe, and alle the foure elementes schewed sygnes and tokenes. And now art thou dessended and arysen from dethe to lyfe and troubles oure peple. What art thou that haste unbounde hem that wer bounde by her synnes, and þou callest hem ageyn to theyr fyrst fraunchyse? What art thou that enlumynest by the dyvyne clerenesse hem that wer blynde yn derknes by her synnes? What art thou wyth-oute corupcyoun yn mageste, and destroyest oure power?[34]

Christ does not answer but simply binds Satan and delivers him to the "power of Helle" before reclaiming his "chyldren þat haue myne ymage and my lyknes" and leading them to Paradise, where they meet Enoch, Elijah, and the thief who died with Jesus on the cross.[35]

Karl Tamburr has described the magnetic appeal of the story: "Its place within salvation history is almost unique because it brings together figures from the Old and New Testaments. It demonstrates the fulfillment of Christ's promise of salvation to the righteous of the Old Testament, while at the same time it makes the same promise of salvation to present-day Christians if only they will truly believe in the Messiah."[36] But as the devils' interrogation of Christ suggests, the core of the Gospel of Nicodemus, as in other earlier and later accounts of the harrowing, is its groping toward a redemptive economy that could organize the competing demands of God, the devil, and man for justice, punishment, and forgiveness—for satisfaction. One such organizing economy, known as the "devil's rights theory," was particularly influential in the formulation and dissemination of the Descent story in the first millennium: it offered an extraordinarily legalistic account according to which Satan, mistaking the supremely innocent Christ as a member of sinful humanity, arranges his death and admits him to hell, forfeiting his rights over all other souls.[37] The theory of the devil's rights was challenged in the twelfth and thirteenth centuries by theologians such as Anselm and Aquinas, who insisted that the Devil did not have rights over man but held him by divine permission only, so that Jesus made satisfaction for man's sin to God alone, and not to the devil.[38] But this emphatic shift in the shape of redemptive economy did not mean that "the issue of the defeat of the Devil vanished from formulations of the redemption."[39] Instead, accounts of the Descent, with its embedded assumption that "Christ's trickery of Satan by disguising His divinity in a human body was a legitimate and fitting payback for Satan's trickery of Eve in the Garden of Eden," remained an essential part of both learned and popular theology, taking on new emphases in the devotional literature and drama of medieval England.[40]

One of these new emphases, appropriate to emerging forms of Franciscan affective piety, was a focus on Christ's humility in descending to hell, resulting in a "transform[ation of] the image of the divine warrior-king."[41] But the most striking feature of later medieval descent literature was its development of a theological debate between Christ and Satan—without precedent in the Gospel of Nicodemus—which allowed Jesus to inhabit his "role as divine conqueror" as well as suffering man.[42] It is included in Middle English harrowing of hell manuscripts and in William Langland's *Piers Plowman*, but it takes perhaps its most compelling form in the cycle plays, where the debate is literally staged. The York "Harrowing" (like the Towneley, for which it was likely the source) begins with Christ's plangent address to the spectators, as he recalls his "pereles paynes" on the cross, but it moves quickly to Christ's plans to unbind souls surrendered to Satan.[43] When Jesus calls for the gates to open, the devils begin to argue with Satan, warning him not to allow Christ through for fear he will "schende / Alle helle," a warning which Satan, mistaking the divine for the human, does not heed.[44] At this point Satan and Christ face off in a verbal version of the "combat myth":[45] after Christ establishes himself not as the son of Joseph (a disguise meant to fool the devil) but as the son of God, both figures claim their rights to mankind. Christ insists that Satan has no true claim over the dead souls;[46] he will "saue my seruauntis fro þat pitte / Wher dampned saulis schall sitte for synne."[47] When Satan continues to protest, Christ admits that some souls—those who neither served nor believed in him—will remain, as punishment and example for the future. Delighted with the prospect of having in hell "moo þanne we haue nowe," Satan promises to go abroad to tempt men, and Christ binds him and sends him sinking "into hell pitte" as the patriarchs and others celebrate their release.[48]

Rosemary Woolf suggests that in the cycle play "Christ's verbal defeat of the devil is a far more impressive symbol of the victory of the redemption than his token destruction of the gates of hell."[49] But in the drama it is not only a *symbol*: it is a material element, a step, in that victory. The theology of the harrowing pageants do not contradict Aquinas's careful wording in the *Summa*, which explains the harrowing as the sacramental application of the redemption rather than its cause.[50] But the pageants literally provide, and would have provided for English audiences until their disappearance in the late sixteenth century, a model of Christ's activity after his death as an integral part of the arc of salvation history. Though they might differ in emphasis from contemporary devotional works as well as redactions of the Gospel of Nicodemus, the cycle plays, like those other texts, preserve the necessity and integrity of a real, or local, descent to hell and of actual contact with devils and other figures. In other words, they make clear what Christ had to do to recover lost souls and where he had to do it.

Reformation debate about the Descent challenged the time, the place, the shape—and ultimately the meaning—of this activity. This particular debate was not the cause, of course, of the exit of the cycle harrowing from the landscape of northern England; that loss was tangled in other economic, doctrinal, and ideological forces prevailing against the incarnational aesthetics of the cycle drama.[51] But the debate did involve a thorough re-negotiation of what one contemporary theologian termed "the sufficiency of Christ's sacrifice,"[52] a re-negotiation that would affect any theatrical thinking about the issues so central to *Doctor Faustus*: Christ, repentance, and hell.

The Reformation Descent to Hell Debate

In the dedication to his 1592 treatise on the credal position that Christ descended to hell after the Crucifixion, the Anglican minister Adam Hill warned that "there is like to be . . . great strife about the true understanding of this Article in England."[53] The strife to which he refers represents what the religious historian Dewey Wallace calls "one of the lesser but vigorous controversies of the Reformation era" in England,[54] an exacting, at times scholastic, disagreement about the nature of Christ's suffering on the cross and whether he literally went down to hell after it. The English controversy, which began in the 1550s, reflected competing interpretations of the creed by Continental Reformers, who explained the Descent either as a physical accomplishment in a real, localized hell or as a particularly internal form of Christ's torment. German Reformers tended toward the first version. The third article of the Augsburg Confession (1530) stated simply that Christ "descended into hell," a principle which Luther endorsed as part of a broader theology of the cross "whereby in life and death Christ both suffered and overcame hell . . . [as] part of God's redemptive work."[55] According to

Luther's *Treatise, Touching the Libertie of a Christian Man*, Christ acts on behalf of the human soul "even as if himselfe had sinned, were travelling, dying, and descending into hell, to bring all things in subjection . . . his righteousness is greater than the sinnes of all men: his life surmounted in power all death, his saving health is more victorious than all hell."[56] Luther's influential disciple Philip Melanchthon endorsed "a real local descent and above all made that descent part of the triumph of Christ,"[57] which ultimately found its way into the important Formula of Concord (1580). The Formula acknowledged the questions generated by the creed, including "when and in what manner the Lord Christ, according to our simple Christian faith, descended to hell: whether this was done before or after His death; also, whether it occurred according to the soul alone, or according to the divinity alone, or with body and soul, spiritually or bodily; also, whether this article belongs to the passion or to the glorious victory and triumph of Christ."[58] Its solution: maintain a triumphant literal descent to a manifest hell, but forestall further speculation: "It is enough to know that Christ went to hell, destroyed hell for all believers, and has redeemed them from the power of death, of the devil, and of the eternal damnation of the hellish jaws."[59]

The Formula of Concord reflects not only intra-Lutheran issues raised by "some theologians who have subscribed to the Augsburg Confession" but also new exegeses of the Descent by Calvin and other Swiss Reformers.[60] The latter's approach was to treat the Descent very differently than the Germans – to see it as an extended metaphor, a way of expressing the principle that "the vertue of Christe his death, did flow even to them that were dead and profited them too."[61] Fear that a real descent smacked of a belief in purgatory was one of the motives for this kind of allegoresis, since the principle of the Descent was intimately bound up with the idea that "the fate of certain men is susceptible to amelioration after death."[62] Indeed, later English writing on the harrowing can be traced to the intense rejection of this third otherworldly realm.[63] But the central concern for the Swiss Reformers was not purgatory but the nature and extent of Christ's sacrificial enterprise. Even when it emphasized that it was Christ's soul, and not his body, that went down to the gates of hell, the idea of a real descent tended to reinforce the image of a material savior conquering a physical place.[64] In response Calvin offered an interpretation that turned *inward*, bringing hell *into* Christ on the cross. In the *Institutes* he suggests that full expiation for mankind's sin required that Christ suffer hell in his soul as part of his Passion.

In this way he became the conqueror not so much of Satan and hell but of his psyche:

> If Christ had died only a bodily death, it would have been ineffectual. No—it was expedient at the same time for him to undergo the severity of God's vengeance, to appease his wrath and satisfy his just judgment. For this reason, he must also grapple hand to hand with the armies of hell and the dread of everlasting death . . . . The point is that the Creed sets forth what Christ suffered in the sight of men, and then appositely speaks of that invisible and incomprehensible judgment which he underwent in the sight of God in order that we might know not only that Christ's body was given as the price of our redemption, but that he paid a greater and more excellent price in suffering in his soul the terrible torments of a condemned and forsaken man.[65]

Against those who suggested that spiritual suffering would be impossible for Christ, Calvin endorsed the glory, rather than the despair, of Christ's pain and estrangement from God. To detractors who claimed that it was "incongruous for [Christ] to fear for the salvation of his soul," Calvin responded that "we must with assurance, therefore, confess Christ's sorrow, as Ambrose rightly teaches, unless we are ashamed of the cross. Unless his soul shared in the punishment, he would have been the Redeemer of bodies alone."[66] Calvin, in other words, pivoted away from the metaphorizing tendencies of Bullinger, Jerome Zanchius, and Huldrych Zwingli (who interpreted the Descent as "the spiritual effects of Christ's death which extended into hell") to insist on a descent that was not local but was nevertheless real: a descent into psychic torment.[67]

By the middle of the sixteenth century, then, English theologians had inherited from the Continent competing interpretive approaches which, though joined by a shared disgust for the Descent's affiliation with purgatory, offered fundamentally different concepts of Christ's satisfactory suffering. In the early 1560s Bishop of Exeter William Alley suggested the potential hazard for English congregations of not clarifying this issue. In a paper drawn up for the Canterbury Convocation of 1563, he offers a summary of the sides and the stakes of the Descent debate which is worth quoting at length:

> There have been in my Dioces great Invectives between the Preachers, one against the other, . . . some holding, that the going down of Christ his Soul to Hell, was nothing else but the Vertue and Strength of Christ his Death, to be

made manifest and known to them that were dead before. Others say that *Descendit ad Inferna*, is nothing else but that Christ did sustain upon the Cross the infernal Pains of Hell . . . . Finally, others preach, that this Article is not contained in other Symbols, neither in the Symbol of *Cyprian*, or rather *Rufine*. And all these sayings they ground upon *Erasmus* and the *Germans*, and especially upon the authority of Mr *Calvin* and Mr *Bullinger*. The contrary side bring for them the Universal Consent, and all the Fathers of both Churches, both of the *Greeks* and the *Latines*. . . . Thus, my Right Honourable good Lords, your Wisdoms may perceive, *what Tragedies* [italics mine] and Dissensions may arise for consenting to, or dissenting from this Article. Wherefore your Grave, Wise, and Godly Learning might do well and charitably, to set some Certainty concerning this Doctrine.[68]

For Alley, the "Tragedies" of doctrinal ambiguity on this point include fighting among ostensibly Protestant allies (to the glee of Roman adversaries) and jeopardizing the faith of congregants. But the other, implicit tragedy of the debate is the blow it levels at the definition of Christ's expiatory suffering and the determination of its sufficiency. It took Christopher Marlowe to dramatize this "tragedy" as a *tragedy*, but he was aided by the language of the competing sides themselves, which struggled over rival definitions of hell and rival criteria of Christ's suffering.[69] And this language is tremendously revealing about both the critical importance of, and the critical disagreement on, what counts as *enough* in matters of atonement.[70]

The language was dominated in the early years of the Anglican Church by the Lutheran approach. *The Institution of a Christian Man* (1537) (also known as *The Bishops' Book*), explained the Descent as a matter of both conquest and merit: "By this descending . . . into hell, not only his elect people . . . were delivered from thence, but also that the sentence and judgment of malediction and of eternal damnation . . . was clearly dissolved, satisfied, released, and discharged, and . . . the devil and hell both have utterly lost and been deprived of all the right claim and interest which they might have pretended to have."[71] But this notion was challenged by at least the 1550s, when the clergyman Christopher Carlile, aiming at the particularly Romish implications of the creed, rejected it in a public disputation with Sir John Cheke at a 1552 Cambridge commencement. Carlile saw it as endorsing multiple levels of hell, including a *limbus patrum* and purgatory, while it also promiscuously mixed pagan and Christian concepts of the afterlife.

"Perhaps we should make the pope, *Pluto,* yᵉ Cardinalle his judges *Rodo-manthus, Aecus, Minos,* and *Triptolomus,* and his *Curtesanes, Tisiphone, Meg-ara, Alecto, Erynies,* and *Furies,* his fery man *Charon,* and his porter, *Cerbrus* [*sic*]."[72] Returning to arguments from the third and fourth centuries and relying on humanist scholarship that translated the Hebrew *sheol* as "grave," Carlile sanctioned the article only if "hell" was read as the grave, the place where Christ was buried. But despite his florid display of philologi-cal exactitude—a tendency that reached its peak with the Hebraist Hugh Broughton at the turn of the century—the heart of Carlile's brand of literal-ism was his emphasis on the absolute sufficiency of the Crucifixion alone for redemption, which rendered belief in any other approach to salvation un-scriptural and excessive. As he writes, "If the price was paide on the crosse, was it not superfluous to be paide againe in hell?"[73]

This attack on the superfluity of the literal descent is echoed in John Northbrooke's 1571 treatise *Spiritus Est Vicarius Christi in Terra,* which reit-erates that "Christes soule should not neede to goe downe thither" to rescue the souls of the righteous dead.[74] But Northbrooke, unlike Carlile, adopts a Calvinist hermeneutic, endorsing a purely metaphoric descent, not a literal one into the grave. Christ's extraordinary suffering, Northbrooke makes clear, was essential to redemption and had real effects in and on hell: "the effica-cie, virtue, and power of his death and passion, did pearce through and into the verie hell it self, by his divine power and godheade: that all the damned soules, felt their full paine, and juste damnation for their infidelitie: and Sathan hym self, felt all the power, and strength of his tyrannie, and dark-nesse, was weakened, vanquished, and fallen." Thus it was not necessary for Christ's soul to descend *to hell,* but it was necessary for him to suffer hell *in his soul.* Christ's death and Passion, insofar as they involve an agony compa-rable to the experience of hell, are the "omnisufficiente Sacrifice unto God his father."[75] Alexander Nowell, in his *Catechism* of 1570, seems to have it both ways, describing a hellish Passion as well as a literal descent. On the cross Christ "was touched with the horror of eternall death: he fought & wrastled as it were hand to hand with the whole army of *hell*: before the judgement seat of God he put himself under the heavy judgement and grevous severitie of Gods punishment: he was driven into most hard dis-tresse: he for us suffered and went through horrible fears, and most bitter greefes of minde, to *satisfie* Gods just judgement in all things to appease his wrath."[76] Afterwards, "as Christ in his bodie descended into the bowels of the earth, so in hys soule severed from the bodie he descended into hell: and that therewith also the vertue and efficacie of hys death so pearced through to the dead, and to very hell it selfe, that both the soules of the unbelevyng felt their most painefull and just damnation . . . and Satan himselfe the prince of hell, felt the power of hys tyrannie, and darknesse, was weakened, vanquished, and fallen to ruine."[77]

Thus by the 1580s "Calvin's nonliteral interpretation of this article [had] gained ground in the Elizabethan Church and was widely accepted."[78] Thomas Rogers's commentary on the Thirty-Nine Articles explains briefly hell "signifieth, The terrors, and torments of the bodie and soule, which Christ suffered" and "not the place of everlasting torments."[79] John Baker, in his *Lectures of J.B. Upon the XII Articles* (1581), insisted on the juridical necessity of inward suffering. Such suffering, he is at pains to explain, is equivalent to the experience of a real or local hell as well as necessary for man's redemption:

> The meaning therefore of this his descension, is this: that Christ our saviour, to redeeme us both in body and soule, which had offended God, suffered the tormentes of hell, the wrath infinite of his father for the time, not onely in body, but also in soule, and did abide the most bitter and unspeakeable so-rowes of death in his minde and conscience, pressed downe with the burden of all our sinnes, as if hee had bene forsaken of God his father . . . . Nothing had bene done for us, if Christ had dyed the common death of the body onely, as other dyd. It was necessarie therefore and very expedient, that we might be perfectly redeemed in both partes both body and soule, that hee shoule feele the severe punishment of the vengeance of God.[80]

And Andrew Willet's position in his *Synopsis Papismi* (1592), a huge tome designed to "set downe the bodie and summe of all Popish opinions whatso-ever, wherein we dissent from them, and they from the truth," aims explic-itly at Cardinal Robert Bellarmine's claim that "the death of the bodie of Christ, without any further anguish in soule, was sufficient."[81] Willett states the Reformed position of Christ's soul-suffering, offering a climactic state-ment of what was "necessary for our redemption": "That Christ our Saviour by the vertue of his death, did overcome hel and the devill, we doe verily beleeve, which may be called a discent [*sic*] into hell: that he suffered the tor-ments of hell upon the crosse and so descended into hell for us, to abide that bitter paine which we had deserved to suffer eternally, we doe also holde and teach: for what rather may be called hell, then the anguish of the soule, which he suffered."[82]

A "counter-attack" to this decidedly Calvinist vision developed in the last decades of Elizabeth's reign, as a number of Anglican divines affirmed a triumphant real Descent rather than one of spiritual suffering.[83] Adam Hill, for instance, offers an expiatory calculus directly opposed to Willet's, according to which the real descent is necessary while the internal one is insufficient. According to Hill, "man being seperate [sic] from God by the desert of sinne had fallen [into hell]," so that "it remained for the full effecting of our redemption, that man assumpted to God [i.e., Christ] should descend thither."[84] Most important to him is the nearly compulsory role of the literal descent in satisfying the demands of God's justice: "The Sonne of God by the efficacy and nature of the divinity had tarried in hell *fulfilling all things marveilouslye*."[85] For Hill, Christ's ability to complete the full redemption of man depended upon his harrowing of hell.

The debate continued into the start of the seventeenth century. The Oxford poet and linguist John Higgins, for instance, agreed with Hill, criticizing the Calvinist position that Christ experienced hell in his soul as the result of estrangement from God. Such a stance, according to Higgins, diminished the idea of the divinity of Christ; it was thus precisely sufficient that Jesus suffer hell in his body and too much that he suffer it in his soul: "We must hold that, Jesus Christ the sonne of God, dying upon the crosse, could neither feele nor suffer the pangs of hel, nor the ful wrath of God seazing upon his soule; because it was neither seperated [sic] from the godhead; nor subject unto sin."[86] A similar argument was formulated from the pulpit by the learned Thomas Bilson, Bishop of Winchester, who insisted that "we are sufficientlie redeemed by the death and bloud of Christ Jesus (without adding of hell paines to bee suffered in the soule of Christ)."[87] Certainly Christ's soul suffered, according to Bilson, only the suffering was a "pained sorrow" for human sin rather than the experience of hell, for "hell is a *totall* and *finall exclusion* of the sinfull *from* enjoying the *presence* or *patience* of God," and Christ could not experience such exclusion.[88] In turn, the semiseparatist minister Henry Jacob, who had attended the bishop's Paul's Cross sermon, attacked Bilson directly, insisting on a sacrificial equation that demanded soul-suffering from Christ that would preserve a direct ratio—a "proportion"—between the Messiah and mankind: "We know by Gods worde, and doe affirme, that God in his justice regarded this proportion, that as we have sinned both in our Bodyes & Soules, so he that was made our propitiation did purposlie and aunswerably suffer both in his Body and Soul."[89] That suffering was the suffering of hell, if not "hell torments in the verie place & condition of the damned," nevertheless the wrath, vengeance and distance from God "which we affirme is equal to Hell itselfe."[90] So by the start of James's reign in 1603, Richard Parkes could look back on these exchanges and lament "what disputes & contentions the denial [of this Article] hath bred of late years, & dayly nourisheth even in the bosome of our Church, no man . . . is ignoraunt; being so notorious that they cannot be suppressed, and so vehement, or rather virulent that they will not be pacified."[91] But he could not resist joining the dispute, and his treatise goes on to defend as integral to man's redemption the literal descent: "You have as it were a golden chaine of four linckes very aptly & artificially framed and compact of those four most gracious and glorious works of our Saviour Christ, that is to say: his Passion, Descension, Resurrection, and Ascension. But if you knapp a sunder the seconde linke . . . you counterfaite that which was currante, disorder the Apostles methode, and dissolve the connexion of his whole discourse."[92]

The threat of "knapp[ing] a sunder" the relay of Christ's redemptive performance, I have been suggesting, was the result of the exigencies of Reformed polemic, as English theologians of the sixteenth and seventeenth centuries tried to articulate a coherent Reformed Christology in relation to Roman Catholic models.[93] The Descent debate, in other words, was part of an effort to clarify what was *enough*, as well as what was *too much*, for Christ to do to meet—to *satisfy*—the demands of divine justice on behalf of sinful humanity whose only true desert was devouring by the jaws of hell. Such a demand is the corollary to a Reformation anthropology which, stressing mankind's essential depravity and inefficacy, had eliminated from its penitential program the role of human participation in atoning or satisfying for sin. For the debate about the descent to hell extends the problem of human satisfaction, the problem of human expiatory agency, *to Christ*. As John Bossy observes, Reformers "g[o]t rid of satisfaction altogether . . . . Or perhaps we should say that where the old Church had shifted the responsibility on to Purgatory, the Reformers shifted it on to Christ."[94] The Calvinist side of the Descent debate, we might say, shifted it further *into* Christ. In Faustus's compromised efforts to harrow hell Marlowe dramatizes the effects of this tug-of-war and the questions about satisfaction it poses.

The Descent to Hell of Doctor Faustus

Doctor Faustus has long been recognized for his *dis*satisfaction, a particularly unquenchable intellectual desire, *libido sciendi*, accompanying his aim to "master the world at large."[95] Edward Snow, in an especially eloquent discussion of this libido, turns this narrative on its head and suggests that Faustus's desires operate to avoid such mastery. As an attempt to "rationalize an alien, anxiously prior inward restlessness by creating around it the appearance of a self that wills it and has it as 'its' desire," Faustus's pursuits—whether for knowledge, power, or fame—are part of a defense mechanism that guards against fulfillment or satiety precisely because, despite their seeming appeal, they can be "the most fearful prospect of all for a self that suspects it has created itself out of nothing."[96] Snow, in other words, diagnoses Faustus's resistance to *being* satisfied—intellectually, erotically, emotionally. I want to suggest that this resistance is best understood as a corollary to what he senses as his inability to *make* satisfaction penitentially.

A substantial tradition of scholarship has suggested that Faustus, poised painfully on the edge of a Protestant notion of human volition that eliminated individual activity in the working of salvation, pursues his various studies and activities as a paradoxical response to his own inefficacy: he turns to magic and jests because "they are something he can do."[97] But Faustus is concerned not only with "doing" in the abstract but also with doing *enough*. Wavering in his commitment to his magical studies at the beginning of the second act, Faustus rejects the persuasions of the Good Angel: "Contrition, prayer, repentance—what of them?" he asks (2.1.16). Whether as a loyal subject of either Lutheran Wittenberg or the more "left-wing Protestant" Württemberg,[98] Faustus has translated the stages of Catholic penance—contrition, confession, satisfaction—into a formula acceptable to Protestant theology, one that has replaced the literal possibility of *making enough* to compensate for wrongdoing with a call to constant repentance as the sign of an unmerited forgiveness. His terrible, and terrifying, meditations on repentance over the course of the play are the ultimate consequence of this replacement, but his famous opening monologue registers it from the start. In its dismissive, grandiose sweep through the academic professions, so exemplary of a Faustian "transgression rooted in an impasse of despair," the speech recasts the fundamental inability to do enough as the intent to do more, to enact a "greater miracle" (1.1.9).[99]

Only one such miracle is named directly. While philosophy and law are rejected on general principle—they are "too servile and illiberal for me" (1.1.36)—physic alone is lamented for a specific failure: it does not enable Faustus to "make men to live eternally / Or, being dead, raise them to life again" (1.1.24–25). This ability, though classified here as the domain of medicine, is, of course, the enduring accomplishment of Christ's life and death.[100] Faustus's first explicit wish, then, establishes the play in the *imitatio Christi* tradition, laying the ground for what Adrian Streete has provocatively analyzed as Faustus's "problematic relation with his putative saviour."[101] But Faustus's version of *imitatio Christi*, I have been suggesting, is indebted to a specific theatrical form: the *descensus* tradition, the dramatic concretization of the credal position we have traced above, according to which Christ's salvific power is proved against the backdrop of devils in hell. Thus in his first encounter with Mephistopheles Faustus hints at his connection to the descending Christ when he claims jubilantly that he "confounds Hell in Elysium" (1.3.59–60). He means not only that he confuses or combines the two (or, as Nashe scorned about Kyd, that he "thrusts" one into the other),[102] but also that he "defeats [hell] utterly, brings [it] to ruin, destroys [it]" (*OED* 1.a). Faustus's boast may indeed be a humanist effort to envision the pagan underworld conquering the Christian one in a "bravuristic sally."[103] But the assertion, made to Mephistopheles and hemmed in by references to Beelzebub and Lucifer, is conditioned by another imaginative model of triumph, the one proclaimed in the Towneley cycle when Jesus causes hell's "yates . . . to crak!"[104] Confounding hell in Elysium promises to reproduce Christ's distinct triumph in the underworld, to allow Faustus to "filter Christian glory back through classical fame," in Patrick Cheney's formulation.[105] As we have seen, however, this triumph had been thoroughly interrogated in the Descent controversy. *Doctor Faustus* is the tragedy Bishop Alley predicted when worried that debate would lead to "strife" as well as "Tragedies and Dissensions": the play is an *imitatio Christi* contorted by controversy, an *imitatio Christi* when the imitator is uncertain of exactly what he is imitating.

Faustus's turn to the magical arts early in the play signals the contortion, as the possibility of descending is replaced by conjuring. Rather than going down to the devils, Faustus will bring them up: "This night I'll conjure, though I die therefore" (1.1.166). Having summoned Mephistopheles from the underworld, Faustus quickly exploits his hydraulic access to infernal realms, charging the devil "to return and change thy shape. / Thou art too ugly to attend on me. / Go, and return an old Franciscan friar; / That holy shape becomes a devil best" (1.3.25–8). The anti-Catholic bias here cloaks the more pressing concern that hell comes to Faustus, rather than vice versa, a pattern that will be startlingly reinforced later in the play when Lucifer, unbidden, presents him with the fantastically metatheatrical pageant of the Seven Deadly Sins (2.3).[106] Of course, Faustus insists that conjuring is a sign of his authority: "I see there's virtue in my heavenly words . . . . Such is the force of magic and my spells. / No, Faustus, thou art conjurer laureate. / That canst command great Mephistopheles" (1.3.27–33). And although Mephistopheles, in the remarkable position of a truth-telling devil, tries to disabuse the protagonist of this impression—Faustus's incantation "was the cause, but yet *per accidens*"—Faustus remains unconvinced (1.3.47). Indeed, he dedicates much of his activity over the remainder of the play to a form of conjuring which, in the service of entertainment, comes to look like a pale version of Christ's release of righteous souls from the underworld. He summons Alexander to appear before the holy Roman Emperor (4.1) and Helen to delight his students (5.1). His admission, "it is not in my ability to present before your eyes the true substantial bodies of those two deceased princes, which long since are consumed to dust," underscores not only the poverty of his accomplishment—the usual critique of the Faustian "falling off"—but also of his distance from a generic ideal (4.1.45–8).

This distance is further revealed in the denial of his fondest wish, to "see hell, and return again, how happy were I then!" (2.3.163–4). Lucifer seems to agree to the request, offering to "send for thee at midnight" (2.3.165), but the trip, unlike its model in the *EFB*, never materializes on Marlowe's stage. The protagonist of the biography, who also "desired to see hell," is tricked at first by Beelzebub but is eventually conveyed to hell where, pulled by dragons, he witnesses "the cries of tormented souls, with mighty thunderclaps and flashing lightnings about his ears."[107] And Faustus's failure here is reinforced by the successes of other imaginative characters. In a play often compared to *Faustus*, Robert Greene's Friar Bacon parades his past: "I have dived into hell / And sought the darkest palaces of fiends, / That with my magic spells great Belcephon / Hath left his lodge and kneeled at my cell."[108] And several of Marlowe's contemporaries, combining Menippean satire and medieval vision narrative, sent their protagonists down to the "inner roomes" of hell, on whose conditions and inhabitants they reported after returning to earth in ghostly or living form.[109] But Marlowe neither stages nor narrates such a scene for his Faustus, whose geographic exploits, majestic as they are, remain restricted to circuits between Wittenberg and the empyrean ("Olympus' top" [3.Chorus.3]) as well as the earthly globe: Trier, Paris, Naples, Venice, Padua, Rome (3.1.1–22). Ironically it is not Faustus's will but rather papal ceremony, treated by Marlowe with such caustic disdain, which proves most dedicated to the protagonist's desires. When the Pope damns "his soul forever," Faustus is prepared: "Bell, book, and candle; candle, book, and bell / Forward and backward, to curse Faustus to hell!" (3.2.94–95). The Pope's plan, however, would eliminate a central part not only of Faustus's stated wish but of his dramatic and Christological exemplar: the possibility of a return.

If the theological ground of Christ's return is his divinity, the dramatic ground is the deceptive guise of his humanity, by which he overpowers and outwits Satan and his cohorts. Herein lies the most compelling reversal of Faustus's *imitatio descensus*: the devils best him. They do this by means of theatrical distraction—the parade of devils in 2.1, the more elaborate pageant of the Seven Deadly Sins in 2.3—which one could read effectively as a means of turning Faustus himself into Satan, fooled by dramatic exploits.[110] But their most effective method is what John Cox singles out as their use of "reverse psychology" according to which they "tempt Faustus to persevere in 'manly fortitude,' because that kind of perseverance is really a submission to the devil."[111] The extended antics of the third and fourth acts, including the jokes on the German knight and the poor horse courser, serve as substitutes for what should be Faustus's defeat of more spiritual—if equally humorous—adversaries. But it is the demonic contract of 2.1, with its extensive catalog of conditions for both parties, which epitomizes not only the devils' domination over Faustus but the most complete reversal of his intended *descensus*. Signed quickly once Faustus's blood resumes flowing, the contract is concluded with Faustus's declaration: "*Consummatum est*" (2.1.74). These are, of course, Christ's final words on the cross, and they were given new interpretive life in the Descent controversy. The scriptural crystallization of the complete satisfaction accomplished by Jesus's death, they could serve as evidence against the necessity—the satisfactory status—of the harrowing. As William Perkins explained, *"consummatum est"* indicates that Christ "had finished his satisfaction to the justice of his father for mans sinne" and thus that "the works of Christs priesthoode which follow his death serve not to make any satisfaction to gods justice for sinne, but onely to confirme or applie it."[112] Andrew Willet was even more emphatic in explaining *consummatum est* as the moment of Christ's victory which rendered a descent superfluous: "The divel was then destroyed and perfectly conquered by Christs death: the conquest being once obtained, hee needed not againe to be conquered."[113] But in Faustus's mouth the words offer precisely the opposite of such closure. Opening immediately onto the warning inscribed on his arm, *"Homo, fuge!"* they represent neither Faustus's instantaneous victory—an "end immediately"—nor the promise of a future one. Whether seen as the symbol of a prior damnation or one he has just initiated, Faustus's *consummatum est*, unlike Christ's, satisfies neither God nor the devil.

But even as the credal narrative warps around and against Faustus, he remains true to its investment—and the Descent controversy's—in using hell as the scenic and symbolic backdrop for penitential quantification. Mephistopheles introduces this approach in his opening exchange with Faustus, when he takes up the protagonist's query about hell's location in order to discourse on its pains: "Why, this is hell, nor am I out of it. / Think'st thou that I, that saw the face of God / And tasted the eternal joys of heaven, / Am not tormented with ten thousand hells / In being deprived of everlasting bliss? (1.3.74–80). Mephistopheles's speech is a watershed moment in the canonical literature of hell, emphatically defining it as a place of spiritual torment, a state of mind, rather than a geographic locale.[114] But his plaint is also linked to a distinct mathematical impulse, commonplace in accounts of the punishments of hell, which relies on escalating numbers to represent unrepresentable suffering. His descriptive efforts mark both the emergence in Renaissance England of what Patricia Cahill has aptly termed the period's "new discourses of quantification and abstraction" as well as the intimate connection between mathematics and the supernatural popular at the time.[115] But they also testify to hell's special role in simultaneously provoking and perplexing calculation, supplying a model for Faustus's efforts not only to "contemplate the difficulties associated with notions of infinite time and space," as Todd Pettigrew has written, but also to determine the parameters of punitive *satis*.[116] Mephistopheles's method is to multiply not just individual punishments but the place itself: "Ten thousand hells" is for him the only way to describe the internalized experience of damnation. Eventually Mephistopheles gives up on numbers altogether: "Hell hath no limits, nor is circumscribed / In one self place, for where we are is hell, / And where hell is, there must we ever be" (2.3.117–9). Faustus picks up on this impulse when he tries to assign a precise, if non-numeric, value to hell in relation to his own soul. "Had I as many souls as there be stars, / I'd give them all for Mephistopheles," he announces (1.3.100–1). Later he deploys numerical terms to conceptualize the same exchange: "There's enough for a thousand souls," he says when Mephistopheles promises him magical powers (2.1.87). If Mephistopheles multiplies hell, Faustus multiplies his own soul, and it is easier for him to imagine providing thousands to Lucifer than compensating God with one.

The characters' numerical excess is opposed by the legalistic details of the demonic contract, according to which Faustus trades his soul to Lucifer for twenty-four years of "living in all voluptuousness." The duration of the contract is not original to Marlowe (he gets it from the *EFB*), but its specificity, juxtaposed with surrounding moments of computational plenitude, emphasizes the efforts to which Faustus will go to name a principle of spiritual adequation.[117] He initiates the terms in 1.3, making hell the precise return on the exchange of a single soul for a certain period of years: "Go bear these tidings to great Lucifer: / Seeing Faustus hath incurred eternal death / By desperate thoughts against Jove's deity, / Say, he surrenders up to him his soul, / So he will spare him four-and-twenty years" (1.3.87–91). But they materialize when he writes the bill, the deed of gift, in his own blood, praying it will "be propitious for my wish" (2.1.58). The contract, then, like Faustus's frequent proclamations to be "resolved" or "resolute," represents his desperate attempt to establish a comprehensible equivalence, a *satis*, between what he does and where his soul goes. Thus both the appeal and necessity of the second contract, again written in blood by Faustus, with which he "confirm[s] / My former vow I made to Lucifer" (5.1.72–3). The same appeal drives Faustus's compulsive return, at the close of the play, to bargaining for his release from hell. Only now his terms are not those of the dramatic unities but of exorbitant numeracy: "O, if my soul must suffer for my sin / Impose some end to my incessant pain. / Let Faustus live in hell a thousand years, / A hundred thousand, and at last be saved" (5.3.161–5). Faustus's plea comes near to transforming hell into purgatory (a concept mocked during his stay in Rome [3.1]), where souls were purified by a strictly determined schedule of suffering. But Faustus's plea has less to do with faith in the possibility of purgatorial cleansing and spiritual rebirth and more with the despair that follows the absence of penitential enough. If pre- and Counter-Reformation theology depended, in matters of penitential exercise, on the possibility that assigned quantities of suffering both on earth and in purgatory resulted in efficacious atonement, then Faustus's desperate negotiations serve as reminders that he lacks an infrastructure that would make his repentance satisfactory or sufficient.

This is so because, as we have seen in the Introduction, human satisfaction was thought by Reformers to undermine Christ's. We can recall Nowell's basic catechistical statement:

> There is no mercie due to our merites, but God doth yeld and remitte to Christ his correction and punishment that he would have done upon us. For Christ alone, with sufferance of hys paines, and with hys death, wherwith he hath payed and performed the penaltie of our sinnes, hath satisfied God. Therefore by Christ alone we have accesse to the grace of God. We receaving the benefite of hys free liberalitie & goodnesse, have nothing at all to offer or render agayne to hym by way of reward or recompense.[118]

True repentance, in this scheme, was necessary to salvation not as something one did to justify oneself but as the signifying outgrowth of God-given faith in that Christ "hath payed and performed the penaltie."

This is the kind of repentance Faustus cannot achieve, as his anguished conversations with the Good and Evil angels in acts 1 and 2 show: "My heart's so hardened I cannot repent" (2.3.18). His inability has been linked both to divine decree as well as to a self-willed failure of faith.[119] I am suggesting, however, that we link it to the way in which contemporary doctrinal controversy, by debating whether Christ had to suffer hell in himself or had to conquer it below ground, pushed the problem of satisfaction back onto—and into—Christ, making the very work of the Passion indeterminate. Such indeterminacy lies behind Lucifer's intervention when Faustus cries out for "Christ, my savior, / Seek to save distressed Faustus' soul," and it drives Faustus's even more stunning utterance: "See, see where Christ's blood streams in the firmament! / One drop would save my soul, half a drop. Ah, my Christ!" (2.3.79–80; 5.2.74–5). One drop or half a drop? Charles Clay Doyle connects this passage to medieval theories of Christ's superabundant merit, particularly to Pope Clement's bull of 1343, which rationalized indulgences on the basis of a surplus of Christ's suffering. Doyle suggests that "Lutheran, Anglican, and Catholic would all concur as to the efficacy of Christ's blood; the dispute was over the means of obtaining its benefits."[120] But the debate about the Descent makes clear that in early modern England different confessions did not at all agree on the efficacy of Christ's bloodshed, and that they were willing to argue with one another about its effects in terms of wholes and fractions. Faustus's computational hesitancy at this moment has been seen as yet another indication of his religious failure, of his inability to believe truly in the saving force of Christ's death on his own behalf. But as an attempt to calculate what is sufficient *not for him but for Christ*, the desperate plea actually repeats contemporary debates about Christ's relation to hell, and thus about what precisely was required of—and what was extraneous to—Christ's satisfaction for human sin. The tragedy of this debate, as Bishop Alley predicted and as Marlowe dramatizes, is that even Christ cannot suffice to get Faustus out of hell.

Marlowe, who was accused of calling Jesus a "bastard" born "of a carpenter" who "used [St. John the Evangelist] as the sinners of Sodom," is too theologically and psychologically honest to lay the burden on Christ.[121] But he does not, contrary to some didactic approaches to the play, blame his protagonist. Neither Faustus's limited achievements in magic nor his tormented ending—his failure, in short, to harrow hell—should be read in the conventionally didactic, accusatory terms which the Prologue and the Epilogue of the B-text present, or even in the terms of so much criticism that sees the broad outline of the plays as a reduction of Faustus "to a caricature, diabolically parodying the divinity he can never attain."[122] For if, over the course of the play, hell has harrowed Faustus rather than vice versa, it is because this model of Christian triumph had been so thoroughly disputed in contemporary Christian polemic. The dramatic effects of this dispute—the wrenching of Faustus's descensus—reach their climax in the play's final scenes. Faustus's famous address to Helen, in which he observes with numerical extravagance the "face that launched a thousand ships / And burned the topless towers of Ilium," reflects Faustus's effort to determine how much Helen is worth and to reconcile that worth with his own soul (5.1.90–1). This calculation involves a mixing of heaven and hell that, as Neil Forsyth has pointed out, is suggested in the femme fatale's very name, Hell-en: "Terms as essentially different as *heaven* and *hell* blur together in the figure of the play's 'Heavenly Helen.'"[123] But the mixing is also the result of Faustus's project of harrowing as it intersects with his interest in the classical past. His proposal to "be Paris, and for love of thee, / Instead of Troy shall Württemberg be sacked; / And I will combat with weak Menelaus / And wear thy colors on my plumed crest. / Yea, I will wound Achilles in the heel / And then return to Helen for a kiss" is Marlowe's most distinctive revision of the Descent, provocative precisely for its formal consistency with, but substantive divergence from, the traditional Christian narrative: Faustus would populate Württemberg, home of the German Reformation, with figures from Hades in order to fight with them on earth (rather than with the devil in hell) (5.1.97–102).

But it is Faustus's last dying speech that is most consistent with both the language and the implications of the Descent controversy. It is a speech of compulsive calculation and measurement, of trying to compare "one bare hour" against "perpetual" damnation, of trying to turn "this hour" into "a year, a month, a week, a natural day," of trying to transform the self into "little water drops," so that they might, in keeping with the ineffectual drop of Christ's blood, not be found. It is also a frenzied speech of multiple addressees—first Christ, then Lucifer, then God, then Lucifer and Mephistopheles again—as if Faustus, channeling the entire exegetical history of Christ's relation to the devil, is searching for the appropriate judge of what he himself must do to be saved. Perhaps the most telling moment of salvific confusion comes in Faustus's pleas to earth and to hell: the former he asks to open up and consume him, the latter he asks not to. Insofar as holes or gaps in the landscape were portrayed, in both classical and Christian iconography, as openings into the underworld, Faustus shows that, even in his final paroxysm of fear—"Ugly hell gape not"—he is still puzzled by the question he posed to Mephistopheles in their perverse catechistical interview: "Where is the place that men call hell?" (5.2.115; 2.1.113).

"Where is that place that men call hell?" Mephistopheles has told him that hell is everywhere. Faustus himself at one point proposes that it is lodged in him: "Hell strives with grace for conquest in my breast" (5.1.64). Such a statement could be seen to turn the play into an allegory of the Descent debate itself: Faustus begins with a medieval or Lutheran project of harrowing a local hell and ends up suffering from the Calvinist hell inside of him.

But *Doctor Faustus* resists such schematizing; indeed, the play may work in the opposite direction. As Cecile Williamson Cary shrewdly observes in an essay on the presentation of hell on the Renaissance stage, "Calvinist determinism leads Doctor Faustus to a medieval hell."[124] Or, in the language of the descent debate, Calvinist soul-suffering leads Faustus, in his effort to do and determine enough, to a medieval or Lutheran real hell. That he suffers on both fronts, in both scenarios, is the result of Faustus's lingering attachment to the idea of an *imitatio descensus Christi* when that creed intersected with broader questions about what counted as enough, as *satis*, for humans and for Christ, to do in matters of atonement.

Chapter 3

Setting Things Right

The Satisfactions of Revenge

"Unto God, satisfaction is due for every sinne . . . by taking vengeance of our selves," explains the *Briefe Fourme of Confession* (1576).[1] Echoing a long tradition of confessional *summa* that build from 2 Corinthians 7:11, the dictum names a special reciprocity, even entanglement, between revenge and repentance. This reciprocity, and the linguistic and conceptual pressures to which it was subject over the course of the Reformation, represent an unexplored core of English Renaissance revenge tragedy, that fantastically successful dramatic genre dedicated to problems of retribution and reconciliation, of "setting things right" in the wake of wrong-doing. At the core of this core is the role of *satisfaction* as the shared aim of both the revenger and the penitent.

As we have seen in the previous two chapters, the promise of penitential satisfaction was rejected by Protestant Reformers who, while advocating various kinds of self-humiliation in the face of the "terrours of the law, and streights of conscience,"[2] nevertheless saw making enough as both an infringement on Christ's passion as well as a suspect assertion of human merit. Here I suggest that Elizabethan revenge tragedy, a form whose development is "virtually synonymous"[3] with the rise of Reformed religion, absorbed in unique and deliberately explosive ways Protestantism's reknitting of the connection between vengeance and repentance, its sanctioning of penitential self-punishment alongside its refusal of penitential satisfaction.[4]

Revenge and Repentance

Revenge and repentance, as responses to wrong-doing, are structurally analogous pursuits. Conceptualized in the discourses of shame and honor as well as sin and redemption, joined in both Augustinian and Anselmian views of the Crucifixion, they share the logic and language of commensuration, proportional payback, of "getting even."[5] And "getting even—repaying one's debts and getting repaid when owed—is legally and technically a matter of satisfaction."[6] The analogy is presented with scribal delicacy in a seventeenth-century commonplace book, whose formula evokes the tripartite organization of sacramental penance:

	revenge
Three things that followe an injurie:	censure
	satisfaction.[7]

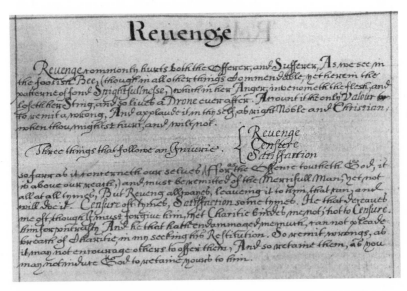

Figure 3.1. Commonplace book, Folger V.A.134. By permission of the Folger Shakespeare Library.

Like those sought in repentance, the satisfactions of revenge depend upon complex, interpersonal orchestrations of particular violations and responses. Like those of repentance, they involve circuitries of self and other, of doing and feeling, orchestrated according to the subtleties of talionic exchange: in revenge a victim "makes enough" for—pays back—an offender by making the offender "make enough" for—pay back—the offense.[8] As a result, the victim-avenger "has enough," has satisfaction, feels satisfied. Of course, because "the talion is understood to state an aesthetic principle of poetic justice, in which the core idea is the exactitude of the fit, the perfection of the matching,"[9] the achievement of that satisfaction varies according to the details of crime, criminal, and revenger. That is, in order to restore honor, balance, and personal integrity—the overarching, *generalizable* goals of revenge[10]—the contours of satisfaction must be highly *individualized*, "respond[ing] to both the crime and the guilty mind of the criminal" as well as the victim.[11] Linda Woodbridge connects such vengeful exactitude in the early modern period to a computational sensibility nurtured in an "age whose great mathematical achievements were algebraic equations and double-entry bookkeeping," and she suggests that both the revenger's and the accountant's satisfaction "rivals atonement for sin."[12] But the affiliation or reciprocity between revenge, repentance, and their satisfactions is not only one of homology. It is also highly *instrumental*. On the one hand, repentance is often integrated into a vengeful scheme, with the revenger anticipating the wrongdoer's acknowledgment of or regret for his misdeeds. On the other hand, the violence of revenge is also considered a *means* of repentance, the engrained result of a popular as well as theological "desire to see bad men humiliated."[13] "Unto God," we recall, "satisfaction is due for every sinne . . . by taking vengeance of our selves." In this case, revenge becomes an intimate part—the supposedly satisfying part—of penitence. When that satisfaction is subject to the kinds of recalibration we have been chronicling, the already complex relationship becomes especially volatile.

Reforming Revenge and Repentance

The *Briefe Fourme*, dedicated in London, translated from Spanish, approved in Louvain, and published in Antwerp, was designed for recusant readers longing for instruction in the stages of penance, which had been eliminated from the sacraments of the English church in the early 1550s. At the heart of the Catholic treatise is the theological premise (rooted in Scripture, repeated in early works on penance such as the pseudo-Augustinian *De Vera et Falsa Poenitentia*, and institutionalized in the twelfth century in Peter Lombard's *Sentences*) that the performance of sacramental penance turns the sinner into an efficacious—satisfactory—avenger of his or her own misdeeds.[14] Assumed in the premise is a conflation of retribution and expiation, of punishment and restitution.[15] As Lombard says, citing the *Vera*, "penance is a sort of vengeance of the one who grieves, always punishing in himself what he grieves to have committed."[16] This formula is repeated and discussed in the medieval confessional manuals and sermon collections which became such a staple feature of late medieval religious culture. Thomas of Chobham's *Summa Confessorum* offers a definition of penitence which includes self-punishment: "*Omnis enim penitentia penalis est: sine enim p[o]ena semper interiori et quandoque exteriori deo pro peccato satisfieri non potest, quia* aut punit deus aut punit homo (Indeed, all penitence is penal: it is not possible for God to be satisfied for sin without punishment on the inside as well as on the outside, *because either God punishes or man punishes*)."[17] The fifteenth-century *Manipulus Curatorum* reflects even more vividly that "*Poenitentia est quaedam dolosis* [sic] *vindicta puniens in se quod se dolet commissise* (Penitence is vengeance, punishing in ourselves that which we regret to have committed)."[18] The same language informs Tridentine and post-Tridentine treatments of penance: the Council of Trent "exhorted confessors to recall that the satisfactions they impose be 'not only for the preservation of a new life *but also for the avenging and punishing of past sins*' "; a seventeenth-century Jesuit catechism defined sacramental satisfaction as "revenge and punishment taken of ones self for his offences, thereby to bring forth fruits worthy of true penance."[19] Such doctrine reinforces the instrumental relation between revenge and repentance according to which vengeance on the self is an element in the process of penance. And as we discussed, such vengeance included both punitive acts associated with the third stage of penance as well as the painful experience of confession, the second stage: "Confession of secret and haynous sinnes, to a mortall man, is one of the most odious things, and most contrarie to humane nature, that may be."[20]

Revenge and repentance were also interwoven in various ways in Protestant discourse. They were connected, for instance, in a rich body of providential literature that explained that *God's* vengeance was the result of a *human* failure to repent. The logic, which presented God as "more like a feudal warlord jealously engaged in a personal vendetta than a stern but benevolent father and redeemer," bred a genre of the "alarum" or "summons" based on the conviction that repentance could avert the avenging force of the Lord.[21] Alexander Nowell's occasional homily during the plague in 1563 is exemplary: "Seeing we have so long despised his justice, requiring our innocency, he can not but visit us with his justice, punishing our iniquity, and that he doth more justly execute upon us, than he did upon his people of any time before us."[22] Nowell offers hope, however, since the godly can still respond with prayer, fasting, and alms to the "particular punishments, afflictions, and perils, which God of his most just judgment hath sometimes sent among his people, to shew his wrath against sin, and to call his people to repentance and to the redress of their lives."[23] The connection between punishment and repentance also informed the public treatment of felons, whose repentance on the gallows, coupled with their ensuing execution, served retributive as well as social functions, meeting a need to "restore the rent in the social fabric caused by a capital crime."[24]

But Reformers also maintained the scriptural alliance between *self-revenge* and repentance, a distinct logical progression according to which Protestant "*self-examination* would lead to *self-revenging*, 'self-chastisement.'"[25] Calvin states that "for the more rigorous that we be to our selves, and the streightlier that we examine our owne sinnes, so much yᵉ more we ought to trust that God is favourable and merciful unto us. And truly it is not possible, but that the soule being stricken with horrour of the judgement of God, muste needes some execution in the punishing of it self."[26] In a popular sermon on the subject, Arthur Dent reminds his audience that a proper penitent should be "so equal offended with the sin he hath committed, that he will be *revenged of himselfe* for it."[27] Stephen Egerton, referring directly to the Pauline verses, extols the "*holy revenge* which the apostle maketh a fruit of godly sorrow bringing forth repentance no[t] to be repented of, when men being pricked in the heart . . . shall even offer violence to themselves." He offers the popular example of the famous martyr Archbishop Thomas Cranmer, who "executed a most memorable *revenge* upon himselfe . . . thrusting his right hand, wherewith he had subscribed against the truth and against his conscience, into the fierie flame."[28] Francis Marbury's *Notes of the Doctrine of Repentance* (1602) suggests "true repentance worketh revenge, & it

pricketh the conscience therby."[29] And George Meriton, glossing the Corinthians passage with reference to Augustine, Gregory the Great, Bede, and
Lombard, explains that "true convertes . . . are so farre from savoring of
their faults: as that they severely punish them upon them-selves." The unrepentant, he goes on to say, are those "who use not the meanes to *cleare* the
score: who be not *angry* with them-selves for their sinnes: who *feare* not
Gods judgements, who *desire* not his mercie . . . who *revenge* not their sinnes
uppon them-selves: *Irridentes sunt, non paenitentes* (saith *Gregory*) they are
proud mockers: not true repenters."[30]

Reformers, we thus see, were deeply committed to reinforcing a relation
between penitence and self-revenge or self-punishment. But there were
theological risks to this commitment, since it seemed to ascribe to sinners an
agency and efficacy in their own salvation which was anathema to Protestant thought generally and the source of its rejection of the sacrament of
penance specifically. Sensitivity to this interpretive predicament is visible
in early- and mid-sixteenth-century vernacular treatments of 2 Corinthians
7:11, including Tyndale's New Testament (1526), the Great Bible (1539), the
Geneva Bible (1560), and the Bishops' Bible (1568), which all translate the
"*vindictam*" of the Vulgate and Erasmian Latin as the seemingly more objective, and thus less controversial, "punishment," rather than the seemingly
more subjective "revenge."[31]

But the problem, and its antidote, is made far more explicit in commentaries and other treatises, which carefully clarified that vengeance on the
self was a sign or effect of repentance, the "grateful response to the assurance of the free gift of salvation," rather than its cause or means.[32] More
important, they insisted unequivocally that vengeance on the self was neither compensatory nor satisfying to God. English theologians inherited
formulas for this insistence from Continental Reformers, who explained
that although Protestants "grant that revenge or punishment is necessary for
penitence," it is not to be understood "as a merit or price, as our opponents
imagine satisfactions to be. But in a formal sense revenge is part of penance
because regeneration itself takes place by constantly mortifying the old
life."[33] William Perkins is deliberately polemical when he reproaches Catholics for interpreting 2 Corinthians 7:11 to imply that the "*revenge*, wherby
repentant persons punish themselves" can "satisfie Gods justice for the temporall punishment of their sinnes."[34] Instead, he says, Protestants believe that
"a repentant sinner must take revenge of himselfe, & that is onely to use all

meanes which serve to subdue the corruption of his nature, to bridle carnall affections, and to mortifie sinne."[35] Daniel Dyke, exhorting his audience to make their "zeale appeare in . . . *revenge* uppon the *flesh*, which wee must wound and daily mortifie," names a concrete economy of self-punishment: "this revenge consists in converting those very things, which have beene the matter, or object of sinne, and abused by the flesh to sinne, to the service of God." He knows the stakes of such calculations, which, he admits, may "seeme to approve of the popish exercises of penance." So he fiercely contrasts the two kinds of penitential vengeance, identifying one as carnal, the other as spiritual: "Our revenge is upon our *sins*, directed against the *flesh*, that is, against the corruption of our nature, theirs is against their *skinnes*, directed against their persons, and their outward man."[36] Such Protestant distinctions were noted disparagingly by Romanists; the Douai New Testament maintained that the sorrow or contrition which produced "indignation, yea feare, yea desire, yea emulation, yea *revenge* . . . is a thing exceedingly requisite and much praised, the fruites whereof are these that the Apostle reckeneth, working salvation." This doctrine, it emphasizes, "is farre distant from Luthers, and Calvins, and such wicked Libertines, that teach contrition to be altogether a meanes to make sinners either hypocrites, or to put them in despair."[37]

The Protestant realignment of the meritorious, satisfactory nature of the revenge-repentance nexus is one of the most significant, and overlooked, sources of the theatrical and psychological complexity of early modern revenge tragedy.[38] (The oversight is shared by both the theologically-oriented discussions of the genre, from Eleanor Prosser's *Hamlet and Revenge* to Thomas Rist's *Revenge Tragedy and the Drama of Commemoration in Reforming England*, as well as political, socioeconomic, or legal accounts, from Fredson Bowers to Ronald Broude to Catherine Belsey to Linda Woodbridge.)[39] But the doctrinal pressures on penitential satisfaction are central to the dramatic power of the period's most vibrant revenge dramas, and not only because they affect the revenger's role as "scourge and minister" by buttressing with fresh semantic urgency the idea that revenge, as a "kind of wild justice," could never satisfy.[40] They also shape the revenger in his role as penitent. The revenge protagonist, as I show below, assumes such a role because the call to retribution against others incites him to turn his vengeful energies on himself. The result is that the genre's conventional strategies— its highly symbolic violence, its elaborately meta-theatrical devices, its misogyny, and, most important here, its confessional impulse—become spirals of retributive activity against the other deeply tangled with the revenger's repentance for himself.

The Sins of the Revenger

Pursuit of their own as well as others' sins is a signal feature of three of the periods' most influential stage revengers: Hieronimo, Hamlet, and Vindice. Their faults include, of course, the quest for vengeance itself. Revenge ranked as a species of sin, most often tucked into anatomies of vices under the heading of anger.[41] It was also understood as an irrational emotion (Primaudaye famously encourages the noble mind to "master such a violent passion") and as a usurpation of God's prerogative in punishing offenders (Anthony Copley's *Fig for Fortune* warns that revenge mistakenly "aimes to defeat God of his interest").[42] Indeed, the whole structure of the revenge project—including its postponement[43]—was itself an occasion for the avenger's repentance.

But for the characters I treat here, their sense of criminality clings not (only) to their vengefulness, by which they "turn . . . into the image of those they hunt down, growing less and less distinguishable from them."[44] It also targets an abiding sense of personal corruption. This sense, what the period understood as original sin, is the great violation governing Elizabethan revenge tragedy and its penitential pursuits. As I have argued elsewhere, an engrained conviction in an original taint is brought to life by the circumstances of revenge, and it catapults revenge protagonists imaginatively or psychically back to what Hamlet calls the "unweeded garden that grows to seed," the scene of their own corrupt and corrupting patrimony which began with the primal transgression in Eden and which continues to inform their every day.[45] Early modern revengers, as Margreta de Grazia reminds us, certainly pursue manifest enemies for the kinds of crimes which may involve real land,[46] but at the same time they also "take vengeance on themselves" for the taint of an original sin which harkens back to the biblical garden. And according to Reformed theology, this original sin is a violation so calamitous that it both precludes atonement and makes atonement for actual sins impossible. The formula lies at the heart of the doctrinal disavowal of penitential satisfaction which we have been tracing.

The doctrine of original sin grew out of second- to fourth-century exegeses on Romans 5:12 ("In Adam we all die, because through one man sin entered into the world and through sin death, and thus it has passed unto all men . . . His guilt, therefore, is the death of all") and was strongly associated with Augustine's writings against the Pelagians.[47] It taught that humans inherited both the taint of Adam and Eve's initial wrongdoing in Eden as well as the corruption that was its result, so that, as Paula Fredriksen writes, "all humanity is condemned; indeed, condemnation is all anyone deserves."[48]

The doctrine was a centerpiece of both Catholic and Protestant theologies of redemption, justification, and repentance. But Reformers had put fresh pressure on the principle, since a version of both the necessity and radicality of original sin underwrote their Christology as well as their understanding of the enslaved will.[49] They stressed original sin as the source of a human depravity so complete as to be unrectifiable by baptism: the human concupiscence that remained after the sacrament was truly sin itself, and not, as maintained by the Council of Trent against Luther specifically, an inclination to sin.[50] Competing definitions of original sin thus marked a primary, distinguishing difference between Catholic and Protestant; the Roman theologian Robert Bellarmine commented that "all the controversy between the Catholics and Lutherans is about knowing whether the corruption of nature and especially of concupiscence in itself, insofar as it resides in just and baptized people, is strictly speaking original sin."[51] The Reformed opposition agreed: William Perkins, for instance, condemned Catholics for denying that original sin is "sinne properly [after baptism]" and for affirming that man "may fulfill the lawe of God, and doe good workes voide of sinne." In contrast, he claimed, Protestants "teach otherwise, that though [original sin] be taken away in the regenerate in sundry respects; yet doth it remaine in them after baptisme."[52]

Among its many consequences, this doctrine calls special attention to the transgenerationally infectious consequences of the Fall, emphasizing both the permanent, deadly nature of parental fault and the sexuality that is both its punishment and source. These emphases rely upon and reinforce a vocabulary of legacy, of the transmission and propagation of initial concupiscence from the first parents to the rest of mankind. "We are dead," Richard Sibbes tells us, for instance, "first by the sin of Adam, in whose loins we were all damned; there was a sentence of death upon all Adam's rotten race, as we say, *damnati antequam nati*, we were damned before we were born; as soon as we had a being in our mother's womb."[53] In a sermon on Psalm 38 preached at Lincoln's Inn, John Donne is especially animated:

> We are all born to a patrimony, to an inheritance; an inheritance, a patrimony of sin; and we are all good husbands, and thrive too fast upon that stock, and upon the encrease of sin, even to the treasuring up of sin, and the wrath of God for sin. How naked soever we came out of our mothers wombe, otherwise, thus we came all apparell'd, apparell'd and invested in sin; And we multiply this wardrobe, with new *habits*, habits of customary sins, everyday.[54]

An English translation of the Italian *Il Beneficio di Christo* (1573), which contains multiple references to Luther, Melanchthon, and Calvin, admits that man has a right to "complain, that . . . he is conceived & borne in sinne, and in the wickednesse of his parents, by meanes of whome death reigneth over all men."[55]

The revenge plays I study below are not the complaints for which *Il Beneficio* calls. But their plots and dialogue are animated by the vocabulary and logic of this doctrine of original violation and inherited taint, as their characters respond to an extreme situation (the questionable death of a son, father, or lover) which recalls for them an enduring violation and a recurring sinfulness for which they both are and are not immediately responsible. In early modern drama, then, the demand to revenge prompts a vexed demand to repent—and thus a vexed demand to "take vengeance on the self." In the process, the protagonists' elaborate revenge strategies on the other become fully integrated with revenge strategies on, and thus repentance for, the self.

These strategies both seek and elude satisfaction. We are accustomed to thinking about the dissatisfactions of revenge tragedy, about the ways in which its imitative structure "makes action problematic" and the way its vengeful plots "begin as carefully regulated exaction of eye for eye [but] often veer into uncontrolled excess."[56] The *locus classicus* of this sentiment is the great Senecan insight in *Thyestes* that "Thou never dost enough revenge the wronge / Exept [*sic*] thou passe" ("*scelera non ulcisceris, / nisi vincis*").[57] Atreus's claim, which implies that the demand for commensurate, eye-for-an-eye justice is only realized in the hyperbolic production of punishment and pain, is a dramatic denial of the possibility of "enough" as something one makes or feels in matters of revenge. It is echoed in a raft of early modern commentary that worries about the power of vengeful emotions to increase uncontrollably, capturing and transforming the personality: "What travaile, and payne, there is in the conception, & breeding of mischiefe, & nourishing of a revenging *thought* . . . . What disease can so disfigure the *bodie* and consume it? What losse can so take away the benefit of *Riches or honour*? Or what canker can so infect and poyson the *soule*, as an envious thirst of *vengeaunce*, and a desire to cry *quittance* with our enimies [*sic*]?"[58] And it is a convention of contemporary scholarship on Renaissance revenge drama: "Revenge tends to overflow, inflicting collateral damage on by-standers, ruining the logic of redressed grievance and the aesthetic of restored symmetry."[59]

We are less familiar, however, with thinking about the dissatisfactions of early modern repentance, about the conscientious Protestant re-scripting of penitential revenge as something that does not—is not supposed to—make or feel like enough. It is Elizabethan revenge tragedy's great theological and theatrical contribution to the dramatic tradition to combine the two positions: to accommodate the contemporary theological suspicion about doing and feeling enough in the punishment of an offending self to the classical Senecan impossibility of doing and feeling enough in the punishment of an offending other. But if the Senecan revenge tragedy, as Gordon Braden has shown, offered early modern playwrights a compelling form for dramatizing "the retaliatory prerogatives and imperatives of offended dignity,"[60] it also provided them with a form for investigating these imperatives in the absence of both vengeful and penitential "enough." The result is a genre that reveals increasingly baroque continuities between revenge on the other and repentance for the self under the banner of an unavailable satisfaction.

Sins of the Father and the Son: *The Spanish Tragedy* and *Hamlet*

Hieronimo, the hero of Thomas Kyd's *The Spanish Tragedy*, discovers the slaughtered body of his son Horatio hanging in his own garden.[61] It is a murder for which Hieronimo finds himself not only seeking redress but also shouldering blame. He hints obliquely at this blame even before he recognizes his son's hanged body: stumbling from his "naked bed" to his garden, he finds "a man hanged up and all the murderers gone, / And in my bower to lay the guilt on me."[62] This initial reaction to the as-yet unrecognized body—that he might somehow be, or seem to the world to be, responsible for it—quickly yields to Hieronimo's focus on finding the criminals and penalizing them: "To know the author were some ease of grief, / For in revenge my heart would find relief" (2.5.40–1). But his sense of responsibility lingers, reinforced by the deliberate anchoring of the scene of the son's death in the father's garden, the emblem *par excellence* of both the paradise and death associated with the biblical Eden.[63] Kyd has installed the image of the Fall and original sin at the heart of the play, so that Hieronimo's pursuit of vengeance for his son cannot be separated from his own responsibility for creating a life bound, from its very conception, to the death it has just suffered.

In the middle of the twentieth century, Fredson Bowers inventoried under the heading the "Kydian formula" the activities involved in Hieronimo's commitment to revenge: dissembling, spying, testing evidence, acting (going) mad, encountering ghosts, and plotting plays.[64] More recent critics have explained these activities in terms of their cultural or psychological functions: Christopher Crosbie has explored their basis in an Aristotelian account of the vegetative soul dedicated to its own flourishing; and John Kerrigan has discussed their role in memorializing his son, of "publish[ing] Hieronimo's bond with Horatio."[65] In these approaches revenge provides a kind of coping mechanism, a way of accommodating or relieving bitter pain and grievous loss. But Hieronimo's retributive tactics are designed not only to spend or purge his sorrow in the wake of the crime but also to atone for it, to address his own place in its cause. And part of this atonement involves the manufacture of more—of penitential—suffering. Of course, the aftermath of a son's murder and the impossibility of prosecuting the villains (Lorenzo and Balthazar, the murderers, are children of Spanish and Portuguese royalty) are already unrelenting sources of pain for Hieronimo.[66] So too is his vengeful passion, from *patior*, to suffer, which only contributes to his sense of paternal guilt (Thomas Wright, the famous chronicler of early modern emotion, explains that the source of such passion is the first transgression: "the inordinate motions of Passions, their preventing of reason, their rebellion to virtue are thornie briars sprung from the infected roote of original sinne.")[67] But Hieronimo's explicit revenge stratagems on Lorenzo and Balthazar, as they take on forms of "outward mortifications" of his own flesh, start to look like Hieronimo's penitential revenge on himself.[68]

The anguish of Hieronimo's special penitential economy lies most dramatically in his engagements with hell. A classically derived but broadly Christianized underworld is one of the most prominent features of the play, which begins with Don Andrea's long description of his visit to the judgment seat of Pluto and Proserpina and closes with his plans to accommodate friends and foes in either the Elysian fields or the boiling pits past Acheron.[69] But for the bulk of play the torments of hell belong to the protagonist, who suffers them even as he calls them up, in a cherished Senecan convention, upon his enemies. Hieronimo first encounters the underworld in the scene after he discovers Horatio, when he claims that "the ugly fiends do sally forth of hell, / And frame my steps to unfrequented paths, / And fear my heart with fierce inflamed thoughts" (3.2.16–8). And if Hieronimo simply watches and announces the approach of the fiends in 3.2, he deliberately seeks them out in later scenes. He proposes to go "down by the dale that flows with purple gore," since there

> Standeth a fiery tower; there sits a judge
> Upon a seat of steel and molten brass,
> And 'twixt his teeth he holds a fire-brand,
> That leads unto the lake where hell doth stand.
> Away, Hieronimo, to him be gone.
>
> 3.12.7–12

He intends, as he tells the royal court some moments after, to "marshal up the fiends in hell, / To be avenged on you all for this" (3.12.77–8). Later he promises that he will go

> Down to hell, and in this passion
> Knock at the dismal gates of Pluto's court,
> Getting by force, as once Alcides did,
> A troop of Furies and tormenting hags
> To torture Don Lorenzo and the rest.
>
> 3.13.109–13

Hieronimo's increasingly intense search makes both generic and narrative sense: legal redress (justice) is unavailable for Horatio, and following his ancient models he must call upon forces from another world to exercise his claims. But his undiminished desire to travel underground and his seeming delight in envisaging the journey also make psychological and theological sense: they expose him to the same punitive torment he imagines for his enemies and worries about for his son.

The height of the torment is the arrival of Bazulto, the old man who comes to Hieronimo to get justice for his own slain son. Seeing and speaking with Bazulto serves Hieronimo as a self-inculcated penalty: the confrontation reminds him that he is guilty of postponing his revenge. Earlier in the scene he had justified this postponement as a strategic maneuver, but now, as Bazulto presents to him "the lively portrait of my dying self" (3.13.85), Hieronimo begins to experience the delay as a disgrace. The old man provides a manifest reason for the self-punishments and recriminations associated with a penitential "readi[ness] to shame our selves."[70] "See, see, O see thy shame, Hieronimo," the protagonist exclaims, "See here a loving father to his son!" (3.13.95–6). Thus Hieronimo recognizes the old man as the purest representation possible of hellish vengeance come for *him*: "a Fury . . . / Sent from the empty kingdom of black night / To summon me to make appearance / Before grim Minos and just Rhadamanth, / To plague Hieronimo that is remiss, / And seeks not vengeance for Horatio's death" (3.14.153–8).

Bazulto's appearance prompts Hieronimo to invent a specific means of revenge, the sensationally violent playlet of "Soliman and Perseda" that wipes out the next generation of Spanish and Portuguese royalty. The inset play that he designs for the marriage feast, which he claims to have composed while a student decades before, recasts the narrative of his son's death: the Turkish Sultan Soliman (to be played by Balthazar), in love with the beautiful Perseda (Bel-Imperia), has her lover Erasto (Lorenzo) killed by his bashaw (Hieronimo) so that he can have her to himself. Long admired by scholars for the extraordinary way in which it exposes the permeable boundaries between life and art (since Lorenzo, Balthazar, and Bel-Imperia actually endure the deaths they are supposed simply to enact), the inset play also represents the climax of Hieronimo's particularly self-inculcating approach to revenge. For he implicates himself in his drama: in his role as the bashaw, adopted so that he can kill his son's murderer, he also becomes, according to the allegory of the play, the murderer of his son, Erasto, the lover of Bel-Imperia. In the first role he seeks revenge on Lorenzo, in the second he seeks revenge on himself.[71] Vengeance is now, in the famous divine injunction Hieronimo takes from Deuteronomy and Romans, truly "to him": "*Vindicta mihi*" (3.13.1).

Hieronimo's explanations and exultations before the stunned royal audience that has witnessed the bloodbath make clear the theological as well dramatic stakes of his revenge. Displaying Horatio's dead body, Hieronimo names Lorenzo and Balthazar as the primary killers and thus the focus of his vengeance:

> They murdered me that made these fatal marks.
> The cause was love, whence grew this mortal hate,
> The hate, Lorenzo and young Balthazar,
> The love, my son to Bel-imperia.
>
> 4.1.97–100

But with a last look back, Hieronimo re-attaches himself to the scene of the crime, to *his* "garden-plot":

> But night, the coverer of accursed crimes,
> With pitchy silence hushed these traitors' harms
> And lent them leave, for they had sorted leisure
> To take advantage in my garden-plot
> Upon my son, my dear Horatio.
>
> 4.4.101–5

Thus he intends that the Duke of Castile and the Viceroy of Portugal should suffer as well:

> Speak, Portuguese, whose loss resembles mine:
> If thou canst weep upon thy Balthazar,
> 'Tis like I wailed for my Horatio.
> And you, my lord, whose reconciled son
> Marched in a net, and thought himself unseen
> And rated me for brainsick lunacy
>
> . . . .
>
> How can you brook our play's catastrophe?
>
> 4.4.114–21

Hieronimo devised the elaborate play-within-a-play to kill Lorenzo and Balthazar, sons of a Spanish noble and a Portuguese king, but the true objects of his fury, this passage suggests, are their fathers. His revenge pursues a stunningly personal principle of commensuration which, fueled by his own sense of paternal sin, deliberately surpasses any strict equivalence of blood for blood. Instead it multiplies the objects as well as audience of his revenge, forcing the royal patriarchs to confront, as he has done, his central insight: fathers are at the origin of the death of their sons and must repent for it in variously vicious ways.

Hamlet shares Hieronimo's final insight, only he recognizes that it is the son, not the father, who must do the repenting for the corruption he has inherited, the "incurable infirmitie" nourished in his "motheres womb" and "received through yᵉ infection of our first fathers."[72] This sense of taint, whether discussed in psychoanalytic terms as the result of Oedipal and pre-Oedipal wishes or in terms of the aesthetics of complaint satire,[73] has a deeply doctrinal sensibility that draws directly on Hamlet Senior's death. Hamlet gestures to it first, with his famous pun on "too much in the sun," but Claudius spells it out clearly, when he berates Hamlet for the latter's excessive mourning:

> Fie, 'tis a fault to heaven,
> A fault against the dead, a fault to nature,
> To reason most absurd, whose common theme
> Is death of fathers, and who still hath cried,
> From the first corse till he that died to-day,
> "This must be so."[74]

Claudius's insistence that death is "common" is meant to minimize Hamlet's grief. But it only reinforces the devastation: in reiterating death's genealogical tree—from father to father to father ("your father lost a father, / That father lost, lost his")—Claudius's rhetoric pushes Hamlet back to the scene of the Fall, to the first father who lies at the root of this "common" theme. Such a configuration underwrites Hamlet's pervasive sense of personal as well as universal wrong-doing, which he articulates well before he has encountered the Ghost: "O that this too too sallied flesh would melt, / Thaw, and resolve itself into a dew!" (1.2.129–30). He pursues this kind of thinking into his explanation of Claudius's misguided revelry, "so, oft it chances in particular men, / That for some vicious mole of nature in them, / As in their birth, wherein they are not guilty / (Since nature cannot choose his origin)," and he uses it later in his rebuke to Polonius: "Use every man after his desert, and who shall 'scape whipping?" (1.4.23–6, 2.2.537).[75]

Hamlet cannot escape his own whipping. Most often it takes the form of consistent self-inflicted exposure to scenes of the very parental sexuality that grounds his bitter sense of contamination. These scenes emerge as early as act 1, scene 2, as he conjures images of his father and mother embracing:

> But two months dead, nay, not so much, not two.
> So excellent a king, that was to this
> Hyperion to a satyr, so loving to my mother
> That he might not beteem the winds of heaven
> Visit her face too roughly. Heaven and earth,
> Must I remember? Why, she should hang on him
> As if increase of appetite had grown
> By what it fed on, and yet, within a month—
> Let me not think on't!
>
>   1.2.129–45

Hamlet fervently wishes *not* to remember, *not* to "think on't," where the "it" dangles ambiguously between his knowledge of what has happened "within a month" (his father's death, his mother's remarriage and its consummation) and the vision of his mother "hanging on" Hamlet Senior with growing ardor. Yet, as Stephen Greenblatt notes, Hamlet cannot stop thinking on either scenario, cannot "keep the images from pressing themselves vividly upon him, experiencing them as a strange form of compulsion."[76] But this compulsion is not strange: it has clear penitential roots and designs, and it punishes Hamlet with scenes of parental sexuality that simultaneously remind him of and compensate for his own sinful mortality.

Hamlet's revenge strategies take shape from these scenes. His strategies have been seen by scholars as both oblique to the task of revenge for his father's murder as well as deeply indicative of Hamlet's characteristically vengeful thoughts and desires.[77] But they should also be seen to be fueled by the doctrinal association of revenge and repentance. Hamlet's famous delay, for instance, which allows him to "work himself into the bloodthirsty rage that would stun and craze an audience," also affords him multiple opportunities for self-incrimination and chastisement.[78] "O, what a rogue and peasant slave am I!" (2.1.55) is perhaps the most blatant, but such self-accusations pepper the entire play, so that he echoes the same lament again in the fourth act: "How all occasions for inform against me, / And spur my dull revenge"

(4.4.32–3). They take a distinctly misogynistic turn in his attack on Ophelia, in which Hamlet takes aim not only at what he considers the indiscriminating sexuality of women but also at its transfer through the male line, through a stock (see *OED* I.3.a) of begetters: "You should not have believ'd me, for virtue cannot so [innoculate] our old stock but we shall relish of it," he tells her. Thus his continuing assaults on her include recitations of his own failures: "Get thee to a nunn'ry, why wouldst thou be a breeder of sinners? I am myself indifferent honest, but yet I could accuse me of such things that it were better my mother had not borne me: I am very proud, revengeful, ambitious, with more offenses at my beck than I have thoughts to put them in, imagination to give them shape, or time to act them in" (3.1.116–27). A similar pattern is visible, though clearly complicated, in the meta-dramatic Mousetrap performance. Ostensibly meant to "catch the conscience of the king" and thus to verify the ghost's accusation against Claudius, the dumb show and the spoken dialogue, with their florid repetitions of parental coupling and sibling murder, seem better calculated to torment Hamlet, to catch *his* conscience.

The Mousetrap confirms in a public forum the connection between techniques of revenge on the other and penitential penalties targeted at the self. The chamber scenes that follow it—Claudius at prayer, then Gertrude in her closet—do so in private venues, a move inside that presents both the increasing circularity of revenge and repentance and the question of their satisfactions. The expressions of guilt and contrition displayed in these scenes belong to Claudius and Gertrude. But they take shape against Hamlet's own penitential program, extending and tangling his remorse and retaliatory fury in new, revealing ways. The twist begins with Claudius, whose response to the Mousetrap actually exceeds Hamlet's expectations. The Prince had hoped that Claudius, "strook so to the soul" by the playlet, would "proclaim his malefactions," thus reassuring Hamlet of the Ghost's veracity and the righteousness of his cause (2.2.589–92). But he did not anticipate the complicated sentiments of shame and regret which his uncle takes into his soliloquy. The spiritual status and efficacy of Claudius's speech, an enigma for him as well as for recent critics,[79] is surprisingly uncontroversial for Hamlet. Supposing Claudius to be "fit and season'd for his passage," Hamlet is immediately convinced that Claudius's posture is genuine and effective (3.3.86). So although he may delay an attack on Claudius, Hamlet does not hesitate to assume the sincerity and sufficiency of Claudius's repentance. Such uncharacteristic swiftness suggests a peculiar form of projection by Hamlet—the attribution to Claudius of the penitential as well as retaliatory satisfaction unavailable to him. As an avenger, he is thus dissatisfied with the imbalance Claudius's supposed atonement presents: "A villain kills my father, and for that / I, his sole son, do this same villain send / To heaven. / Why, this is [hire and salary], not revenge" (3.3.76–9). But as another penitent, he is particularly vexed by what he perceives as Claudius's accomplishment at prayer—the self-castigation that is enough to "relish of salvation" (3.3.92). This only feeds his vicious commitment to the endless violence promised by "trip[ping] him, that his heels may kick at heaven, / And that his soul may be as damn'd and black / As hell, whereto it goes" (3.2.93–4).

His treatment of Gertrude—showing her the "counterfeit presentment of two brothers"—also exacerbates his own suffering as he endures unmitigated exposure to the very reminders of sexual taint he wished to avoid: the "rank sweat of an enseamed bed, / Stew'd in corruption, honeying and making love / Over the nasty sty" (3.4.54, 92–4). Indeed, Gertrude becomes a much clearer objective correlative when she is seen as the manifest object of the punishment Hamlet aims at himself.[80] The scene is further energized by the compatibility of this self-scourging with the punitive shriving of Gertrude. The oft-remarked misogyny of this scene, then, makes particular sense as a deeply gendered and sexualized channeling of the unsatisfying circuitries of revenge and repentance: Hamlet gets revenge on his mother by demanding her penitence for the contamination he understands as his own as well as hers.[81] If he assumed this penitence of Claudius in act 3, scene 3, he insists on it for Gertrude in act 3, scene 4. Hamlet may shoulder the burden of Polonius's murder, a grave but uncomplicated error for which he has a clear compensatory equation: "For this same lord, / I do repent; but heaven hath pleas'd it so / To punish me with this, and this with me" (3.4.172–74). But that is not sufficient for the violation that most plagues him, the parental sexuality for which Gertrude has come to stand. So even after saying good night three times, Hamlet returns again to the theme that tortures him in a confusion of negatives which simultaneously invites and prohibits his mother to do "not this, by no means, that I bid you do, / Let the bloat king tempt you again to bed, / Pinch wanton on your cheek, call you his mouse, / And let him, for a pair of reechy kisses, / Or paddling with his damn'd fingers, / Make you to ravel all this matter out" (3.4.181–86).

Sins of the Confessant: *The Revenger's Tragedy*

Vindice, the protagonist of Thomas Middleton's *The Revenger's Tragedy*,[82] also punishes himself and his mother by making her repent. His approach to Gratizna represents one of the ways in which the play, with parodic exuberance, multiplies revenge conventions and obsessions learned from *The Spanish Tragedy* and *Hamlet*. Its hallmark, in addition to its misogyny,[83] is Vindice's insistence on announcing his own role in his various revenge plots. After each successful trick or murder, that is, he boasts either to the victim or to a cohort his responsibility for the deed. Vindice's retributive tactics are thus conditioned, in a much more precise and technical way than the other plays, by a specific penitential practice, that of *confession*. For Vindice revenge for his dead father and fiancée becomes an occasion to announce his own guilt, his embedded sense of the taint of original sin which haunted our other revengers. He transgresses, we might say, in order to confess.[84] And, since disclosing his identity to his victims furthers their torment, Vindice's self-revelations serve as a means as well as a goal of vengeance. Their double business is bound to the Protestant reconfiguring of confession and its satisfactions.

Auricular confession to a priest was a central concern for Reformers, who were deeply invested in dismantling its sacramental status. As chapter 1 suggested, over the course of the late eleventh to thirteenth centuries (and institutionalized by the Fourth Lateran Council in 1215, when yearly confession to a priest was made obligatory), contrition and confession had become more and more integral to atonement than public or private acts of expiation. Indeed, as Thomas Tentler suggests, enduring the pain and shame of contrition and confession *became* a form of expiation.[85] Confession, then, was a specific stage in the sacrament of penance, a prelude to satisfaction; but it also was, in a way, satisfaction itself, a unique combination of anguish and consolation. It "made enough" because it was accusatory, punitive—vengeful toward the self even as it was purgational and ameliorative. And it "felt [like] enough" because its rewards—what we now recognize as psychological relief as well as mercy and absolution—were great. As Peter Lombard's classic analysis explains, "for the mind labors when it suffers shame; and since a feeling of shame is great punishment, he who is ashamed for the sake of Christ becomes worthy of mercy."[86] The Tridentine formula, which emphasizes the importance of a complete confession of all known mortal sins, is equally clear: "Now, the very difficulty of a confession like this, and the shame of making known one's sins, might indeed seem a grievous thing, were it not alleviated by the so many and so great advantages and consolations, which are most assuredly bestowed by absolution upon all who worthily approach to this sacrament."[87] The demand is made fantastically clear in the anonymous *Short and Absolute Order of Confession* (1576), which captures the intimate texture of confessional punition as vengeful, as pleasing in its pain: "Our sinnes must be spoken with such a mynde, that delyts in accusing of one his selfe, and that in such sort, that we are desirous to be revenged of our selves therefore."[88]

Continental Reformers rejected the satisfactory as well as satisfying nature of sacramental confession expressed here, dismissing it on scriptural, doctrinal, and ultimately affective grounds. For them it smacked of notions of free will and the possibility of human cooperation in the remittance of sin; it also privileged the role of the priest in a way that they believed denied the centrality and power of Christ's sacrifice. They also rejected the demand, central to medieval and Tridentine principles, of a full confession, the solicitation of which was the motive force behind the intricate confessional literature of the later Middle Ages and Counter-Reformation.[89] Complete confession, Reformers such as Luther maintained, was by definition impossible, so requiring it resulted in a debilitating burden that "serve[d] only to frighten hearts into confessing often," rather than to promote the kind of faith that assured forgiveness.[90] Although the historian Lawrence Duggan has argued strenuously that, for a broad swath of late medieval Europe, the prospect of a complete confession before a priest did *not* "inspire intolerable fear," Luther's concerns were echoed bitterly by Swiss Reformers like Calvin, Martin Bucer, and Zwingli; the former dismissed it as a "butchery of conscience."[91]

English Reformers picked up the charge. Although the Ten Articles of 1536 affirmed that "auricular confession is expedient and necessary to be retained and continued, used and frequented in the Church of God,"[92] early evangelicals such as William Tyndale and John Bale, in the remarkably vitriolic play *King Johan* (1538), railed against the practice. By the end of the

1540s, after Henry's death in 1547 and the accession of the "hotter" Protestant Protectorate of Edward VI, confession to a priest was essentially written out of liturgical and devotional practice. For the next eighty years, a wide range of Protestant theologians routinely scorned the demand for full, complete confession; the role of the priest in hearing it and granting absolution; and, most important for us, its sacramental and efficacious status. Their language was meant to sting in rhetorically familiar ways: Thomas Becon complained "under the cloke of thys auriculare confession, much mischiefe was wrought"; Samuel Harsnett called it "that poysonable engine of hypocriticall Confession."[93] And in a marvelous moment of synesthesia, Richard Hooker singled out for special condemnation the role of the clergy as the "eye of auricular scrutinie" in confession.[94]

At the same time, however, English theologians followed those on the Continent by preaching—indeed, insisting—on the advantages of *desacramentalized* confession.[95] Scholars have chronicled the persistence of various forms of confessional practice in the Tudor and Stuart church,[96] and a stream of reformed primers, handbooks, and other treatises make clear that the dominant Protestant position taught that "a man ought to examine his owne conscience and to confesse his sins privately to God" as well as to the pastor, friends, or neighbors.[97] In addition, ecclesiastical courts ensured that those convicted of wrongdoing had to appear either in church and/or the marketplace to offer "a public apology ... to God and to the parish," an apology specifically referred to as confession and thus associated with ritual shaming.[98] Extracts from the late-Elizabethan Consistory Court at Ely, for instance, show that both male and female offenders were required to appear clothed in white sheets, to kneel for extended portions of the service, and, after the reading of the appointed gospel portion, to turn to the congregation and "with a lowde voice say and confesse" their sins.[99] Henry Holland gestures to the retention of modified forms of both private and public confession when he suggests that a truly penitent Protestant must "not onely to cease from committing of sinnes past, and to forsake them, but also to confesse them: publique sinnes ... to God and his Church publiquely: private sinnes unto God privately."[100]

But in the polemical reflex so integral to Protestant self-definition, the appropriation of a revised form of confession was accompanied by careful distancing from, and continued degradation of, Catholic practice. The homily on repentance, for instance, approves unmediated confession to God or one's neighbor on the basis of 1 John 2 ("If we confess our sin, God is faithful and righteous to forgive us our sins"), while it attacks the institutional power of the keys ("Whereas the adversaries go about . . . to maintain their auricular confession withal, they are greatly deceived themselves, and do shamefully deceive others: for . . . priests are as much bound to confess themselves unto the laypeople . . . and the laity . . . hath as great Authority to Absolve [as] the priests.")[101] Thomas Wilson, in his *Christian Dictionarie*, defines the verb "to confess" as "to lay open our sinnes and offences, either unto God in private or publicke confessions, or to our Neighbour . . . or to some godly persons, at whose hands we looke to receive comfort . . . or finally, to the whole Congregation." He specifically distinguishes this from Catholic practice: "Touching Popish confessing of our particular sinnes . . . in the eares of a Massing-Priest upon necessity of Salvation, there is no one word in all the Booke of God. For it is a meere devise."[102] Richard Pilkington, under the pressure of debate raised by the Synod of Dort in 1618, insisted that a Protestant "at all times may resort to his pastour to open and disburden his conscience of such sinnes as doe disquiet him, and crave both his prayers, comfort, and counsell." He differentiates, however, between Catholic and Protestant approaches in an extended comparison that is worth citing at length:

> But here is the difference betwixt yours, and [ours]. First, that yours is of necessity, and such as without it sinnes cannot bee forgiven: [ours] is voluntary and not exacted . . . . Secondly in yours is required an exact and most diligent enumeration of all sinnes, which is impossible . . . . Thirdly, yours is full of superstition, as if it were the chiefest part of Gods service, and by the worke wrought, that is, for this confession of the sinner, and absolution of his Confessour, his sinnes were forgiven, when as in ours there is no remission, but by the free grace of God alone.[103]

In these distinctions, and in the "loss of confession on the Catholic model without the gain of effective Protestant discourse" which they signify, scholars such as Patrick Collinson discern fresh theological and psychological complications for early modern believers.[104] Among these complications, I want to suggest, were those made on the idea of confessional "enough."

Vindice's self-revelations represent a fantastically antic rehearsal of the effects of this complication. They are made possible by his program of disguise, his transformation from Vindice into "that strange-composèd fellow" Piato and then back again in the fourth act into Vindice (1.1.96). His efforts to "turn [himself] into another" seem designed to eliminate his given, worldly self, replacing it with another entirely of his own devising (1.1.134). Of course, complete replacement is illusory: each disguise only calls attention to the *original*, and originally sinful, Vindice. Having donned the mask of Piato, for instance, Vindice asks his brother and collaborator Hippolito "am I far enough from myself?" Hippolito answers as we might anticipate, "as if another man had been sent whole / Into the world," suggesting that Vindice is now completely unrecognizable, truly someone new (1.3.1–3). But Hippolito misses the paradox that fuels Vindice's program. The unavoidable fact of Vindice's mask is that it allows him to inhabit one figure while maintaining a co-existence with an earlier and more fundamental persona, the "myself" of "am I far enough from myself?". Thus by the fourth act Vindice can relinquish his disguise as Piato and "turn myself," turn back to Vindice, who is now hired to assassinate his alter-ego (4.2.32). "I'm hired to kill myself" he realizes in the play's most splendid moment of reflexive explanation, as he becomes both the subject and the object of his own villainy (4.2.203). Vindice is truly the self-revenging revenger, whose vengeance depends upon the constant reiteration of an original, and originally sinful, self.

The rest of the play is strewn with moments that are even more explicitly confessional than these instances of self-assertion. In the "testing women" sub-plot, so integral to the play's obsession with "both the virtuous enclosure of female chastity and the 'false forms' of deceptive womanhood," Vindice, disguised as Piato, tries to seduce his sister Castiza on behalf of Lussurioso.[105] Though his sister does not waver, Vindice tempts his mother to prostitute Castiza with the promise of great riches, and, having precipitated Gratiana's sexualized vices, he returns home, undisguised, in act 4 to oversee her shrift. His vicious accusations against his mother, obviously indebted to the closet scene in *Hamlet* and meant, like its predecessor, to secure the mother's lost purity and thus the protagonist's own, ultimately serve as an opportunity for him to explain his performance as the seducer Piato—to explain, that is, his own perjured role in the seduction. When Gratiana refuses to admit her failing, he informs her that "I was the man . . . / In that disguise, I, sent from the duke's son, / Tried you, and found you base metal" (4.4.28–32). If Hamlet took on the role of his mother's scourge and minister to cultivate his own as well as her contrition, Vindice takes it on to allow for his own spiritual unburdening and its pleasures: "Our hearts wear feathers that before wore lead," he tells his brother (4.4.88).[106]

Such unburdening looks less and less spiritual in Vindice's truly ostentatious confessional scenes, which accompany his murders of the Duke and Lussurioso. The murder of the former, in act 3, is the play's *coup de théâtre*, in which Vindice tricks the Duke into kissing the poisoned skull of the deceased Gloriana. Designed to enforce a symmetrical punishment on the Duke (he poisoned Gloriana; her skull poisons him back so that "the very ragged bone / Has been sufficiently revenged" [3.5.153–4]), it becomes an exercise in excess, as Vindice nails down the Duke's tongue and forces him to watch his wife in an adulterous, incestuous embrace with his bastard son, Spurio. Critics have discussed the ways in which the plan testifies to the idiosyncratic investments informing Vindice's special calculus of adequately superfluous vengeance: Peter Stallybrass has explained the misogynistic psychology behind his manipulation of the skull of his former fiancée, who died to prevent the very kiss he forces upon her, while Karin Coddon has suggested that the scene "parodies the genre's, and the culture's, own governing symbolics of death."[107] But at the center of Vindice's program is the prospect of self-revelation as a tactic of vengeance, the prospect of deploying a strategy of revenge on the self as a way of getting revenge on the other. When the Duke, feeling the poison creep into his lips, asks "what are you two?", Vindice delights in declaring "villains all three" before he cavorts in front of the dying Duke, exclaiming " 'Tis I, 'tis Vindice, 'tis I!" (3.5.152–3, 167). Vindice goes on to torment the Duke further, but the crowning achievement of the scene is his ability not only to kill the Duke, but to kill the Duke while telling him about it—that is, to kill him while telling him that he, Vindice, is the murderer.

Torturing a victim with information is a long-standing revenge convention, one that provides the avenger with his ultimate prize: witnessing his victim's horrified recognition of the avenger's activity. Seneca displayed it in the closing moments between Atreus and Thyestes: "This is my true reward. My wicked work / Would have been wasted, if I had not heard / Those cries of agony," Atreus exclaims after he shows Thyestes that "you, you yourself have dined on your sons' flesh!"[108] In *The Revenger's Tragedy* this traditional retributive tactic is colored by its connection to confessional exculpation. *The Spanish Tragedy* gestured to this connection in its final scene, when Hieronimo detailed for the shocked royal fathers what had just transpired in the inset play. But, whereas Hieronimo's account is a rich narration of the multiple plots and agents leading to the deaths of the royal children, Vindice focuses on himself and on his ingenuity in the Duke's demise. In so doing, he darkly and thoroughly parodies the transactional model of pre-, post-, and Counter-Reformation confession, according to which admission of guilt to the injured party was meant to make satisfaction—if not to God then to the individual offended. Vindice's confession deliberately does *not* satisfy the Duke: it turns his last dying moments into a paroxysm of anger and cursing that, Vindice assumes, ensures his damnation. More important, in killing the Duke twice—first his body, then his soul—Vindice extends his own sin. Gleeful with this turn of events, Vindice is indeed satisfied: "The very ragged bone / Has been sufficiently revenged" he exclaims to the Duke (3.5.153–4). But—and this is Middleton's irony—this is only, or precisely, because his confession has not, in the doctrinal sense of the term, made satisfaction. Its satisfaction, in other words, is based in its perversion of the confessional process.

Vindice's repetitive behavior suggests that he is not satisfied for long. He recycles the confessional pattern in his vendetta against Lussurioso, which reaches its peak in the murderous rampage of the closing masque, famous for its "powerfully self-conscious image of the physically and spiritually corrosive effects of the theater."[109] After stabbing Lussurioso during his installation banquet as the new duke, Vindice gives him a full recapitulation of the play's plot, chronicling all his revenge activity and making a full disclosure: "'twas Vindice murdered thee! . . . Murdered thy father! . . . And I am he!" (5.3.93–6). Vindice's revelation here, like the one in front of the Duke, is calculated to enrage Lussurioso at the moment of his death, guaranteeing that his end, like his father's, is spiritually compromised. It serves as an instrument that both tortures the other and targets the self—or, more precisely, tortures the other *by* targeting the self.

The special interpenetration of self and other in Vindice's confessional tactic is the logical climax of Hieronimo's and Hamlet's programs, in which their revenge strategies against others were enlisted in service of their own repentance, even to the point, as we saw with Hamlet and Gertrude, that orchestrating someone else's contrition became a form of self-punishment as well retribution. But unlike his predecessors, Vindice revels in, rather than suffers from, his self-disclosures. They are a form of self-punishment—

rooted in a deep experience of personal corruption—that produces a manic kind of delight. And it is a delight that only incites the pursuit of more, making it impossible for Vindice to keep quiet. So although he swears Lussurioso to secrecy (easily accomplished since he dies), Vindice cannot stop himself from announcing to the new duke, Antonio, that it was he who had "somewhat witty carried" the plot (5.3.117). This final confession turns back on Vindice, as Antonio sentences him to execution. Vindice himself recognizes the deep structure of the recoil: "'Tis time to die when we are ourselves our foes" (5.3.130). Even on his way to the hangman, Vindice cannot stop talking, congratulating himself publicly for his accomplishments: "Our mother turned, our sister true / We die after a nest of dukes. Adieu!" (5.3.127–8).

The Ends of Satisfaction/The Satisfaction of Ends

Vindice's compulsion to confess, which perverts a stage of penance into a surer means of death and damnation for himself and others, could be seen as part of Middleton's Calvinist agenda, intended to parody the practice as a hollow, ineffectual performance, as dangerous and damning as revenge itself.[110] Such a reading would be perfectly consistent with other moments in Middleton's oeuvre, including his satiric assault on auricular confession in *A Game at Chess* (1624), which depicts the confessional as the venue for the seduction by the Black Bishop of the innocent White Queen's Pawn. But it could also be seen as a mockery of the Protestant dismantling of confession, a dramatization of what happens when the practice is detached from its sacramental as well as satisfying status. The viability of both interpretive possibilities epitomizes the revenge genre's broad, protean entanglement with the early modern problem of satisfaction, and thus the difficulty of pinning down any play to a particular doctrinal position.

In the case of revenge, I have argued, that entanglement is rooted in the Protestant exegesis of 2 Corinthians 7:11, according to which vengeance on the self, a staple of penitential performance, no longer has the status of an activity that "makes enough" or merits "feeling enough." So when an injunction to revenge, with its intimate links to original sin, calls forth a corresponding impulse to repent, the protagonists embark on increasingly elaborate revenge designs that bring together Senecan conventions of vindictive excess with the doctrinal suspicions of Protestant soteriology. The resultant assimilation—of programs for revenge on the other with programs for revenge on the self—challenges the benign premises of a theology that requires penitential mortification as the consolatory effect, rather than the cause of, satisfaction. For in the merger, penitential vengeance, like Senecan revenge, gets stuck in a cycle of physical and emotional violence alienated from any model of the very closure and certainty promised in Protestant penitential theories.

In the plays' final moments the characters seem to "unstick" things. Hieronimo, having assassinated his son's murderers and explained his actions to the court in vivid detail, claims that his "heart is *satisfied*" (4.4.129, my italics). Vindice, as he is being led to his execution, proposes that "We *have enough*, i'faith," before he delivers his closing lines (5.3.123, my italics). Hamlet is neither so explicit nor so unequivocal; it is Laertes, not the Danish Prince, who calls himself "satisfied in nature" (though not in honor, which requires him to step up to the duel) (5.2.244). Nevertheless, scholarly tradition identifies a shift in Hamlet's mood from the end of the third act to the beginning of the fifth which may signal something akin to the hero's content or "composure."[111] Hamlet himself implies a kind of contentment when, implicitly distinguishing himself from his survivors, he tells Horatio to "report me and my cause aright / To the unsatisfied" (5.2.339–40).

This recovery of satisfaction has depended, in Senecan fashion, on substituting *more* for *satis*. It has come, that is, at the cost of enough. In his final scene Hamlet not only battles his "brother" Laertes, repeating the "primal eldest curse," but turns on Claudius with sword and cup so as to ensure what the latter had earlier termed "superfluous death" (5.2.244, 3.3.37, 4.5.96). Hieronimo has deliberately gone beyond the "vulgar wits of men" in his murderous masque, after which he goes on to kill the Duke of Castile and then himself. And even these deaths are revealed, in the play's final scene, to be no more than the prelude to Revenge's "endless tragedy" in the underworld.[112] Vindice, of course, has heaped brutality upon brutality to achieve what he calls, in his final speech, enough.

Such escalation in the pursuit of enough was, of course, one of the Protestant critiques of Catholic penance. The plays, then, could be seen as Reform-minded critiques of sacramental satisfaction and its tendency to infinite regress, particularly since they are set in overtly Catholic countries (Spain, Italy) or feature characters aligned with Catholic doctrine (the Ghost from purgatory). But these dramas, I maintain, resist this kind of unequivocal reading. Rather, they turn the critique back on Reformed economies of repentance, depicting their suspicion of penitential satisfaction not as a theological triumph but as the opening up of a conceptual vacuum. The power of this vacuum, the plays demonstrate, is to turn cherished mechanisms of repentance into forms of aggression, so that the possibility of atonement by taking vengeance on the self always includes turning on the other— and vice versa. One's own repentance, in these cases, is never enough.

Chapter 4

As Good as a Feast?

Playing (with) Enough on the Elizabethan Stage

Given the conceptual centrality in the early modern period of *satis*, enough, in organizing various systems of obligation and recompense, it should not surprise us to see the term emerge as a character in the mid-Tudor interlude, a genre intimately concerned with "the spiritual implications of wealth and social conduct."[1] In the 1570 play *Enough Is as Good as a Feast*, for instance, "Enough" doubles with "Hireling" and serves as the protagonist's chief ally as well as his chief antagonist, reciting all the while the proverb that gives the play its title and its didactic coloring, its homiletic message about the importance of economic moderation.

The character of "Enough" also appears, closer to the end of the sixteenth century, on Shakespeare's stage.[2] Only in Shakespeare's theatrical universe, his name is Shylock. At least this is what the clown of *The Merchant of Venice*, Launcelot Gobbo, suggests when he explains his desire to exchange his present employment with the Jew Shylock for work with the Christian Bassanio. As he tells his new master, "you have the grace of God, sir, and he hath enough."[3] Launcelot, whose dialogue is usually spiced with unwitting malapropisms, is here fully conscious of the rhetorical division he performs on the maxim. "The old proverb is very well parted," he warns Bassanio, before parceling grace and enough between the Venetian aristocrat and the Jewish moneylender (2.2.149).[4]

This chapter explores the migration of "Enough" from its place in Elizabethan homiletic drama to its seemingly ironic lodging in the figure of Shylock, the Jewish moneylender whose profession and religion were customarily among the period's preeminent symbols of *excess*, the ever-increasing "overplus" associated with illicit commerce as well as the general acceleration of early modern England's domestic and international economies.[5] This acceleration, and the kinds of financial instruments and ideologies it involved, is inextricable from the enormously complicated intersection of economic practices and Reformation religious beliefs.[6] Here I identify a discrete aspect of this juncture as a crucial moment in the history of satisfaction, a moment when the ethical and affective values assigned to *satis* by the strong voices of economic morality stood in striking contrast to (but also in inevitable contact with) the values associated with penitential "enough."

As we have been chronicling, in matters of repentance Reformers understood "enough" as the prohibited proportion between human penitential activity and divine receptivity. But in matters of worldly wealth they considered it, as well as its affective companion "contentation," to be Christian ideals. The juggling of these two definitions came under special pressure, this chapter suggests, at points where penitential and commercial exchange were most closely interwoven at conceptual as well as literal levels. One of those points was in the notion of "salvific economy" or the "salvation market," the more or less benign practices of commutation, alms-giving, and the purchasing of indulgences roundly rejected by Reformed theologians and moralists.[7] Another of those key points was in the potential for worldly economic activity to become an occasion of sin.[8]

Didactic and sermonic traditions drew on a number of gospel examples to dramatize this potential: Judas's selling of Jesus for thirty pieces of silver, or Dives's denial of Lazarus's plea for alms. But the general vices of pride and envy and greed for which these examples stood took shape in concrete commercial practices most often associated with merchants. A rich body of penitential literature evolved over the course of the Middle Ages to combat "the temptation to profit by dishonourable means lurk[ing] at every crossroads, threatening to steal [the merchant's] virtue."[9]

The goal of this literature, as Odd Langholm has shown, was to indicate precisely what—and how much—men and women had to do to atone for their particular financial sins (as well as what—and how much—counted as financial sin). Early modern Reformers, however, insisted that there was nothing—and no amount—that humans could do in such cases. They maintained this position even as they called routinely and passionately for repentance in matters of economic transgression.[10] They thus introduced a new semantic complication into the perennial problem of commercial sin. They maintained that although "enough" was something that men and women were obliged to make and have in the conduct of their economic and social lives, it was not something that they could do or feel in matters of atonement. At the same time, atonement was central to the conduct of moderate, "contented" economic and social life.

The first half of this chapter demonstrates the ways in which the mid-Tudor interlude, with its focus on economic practices that threatened the commonwealth, literally dramatizes the problem of enough, playing with its elusive, abyssal status as well as with the semantic complication between its economic and penitential values. In the second half of the chapter I discuss how Shakespeare's *Merchant of Venice* reconfigures, for cosmopolitan Venice and its world of international credit and debit, the interlude's simultaneous celebration and suspicion of *satis*. Shakespeare's contribution in this play, suggested in Launcelot's quip, is to orchestrate the term's divergent values around the figure of Shylock, thus carving out a unique—and ultimately disavowed and degraded—role for the Jewish moneylender in the world of Christian repentance.[11]

Enough Is as Good as a Feast

Determining the contradictory contours of "enough"—as a principle of either exactitude or estimation, as a measure of either sufficiency or plenitude—is a fraught, tendentious undertaking. Indeed, enough and its indeterminacies were precisely what Reformers had abandoned in penitential matters. Yet they remained deeply attached to the idea as a socioeconomic standard. Despite the inherent difficulties of its quantification, they clung to it in the face of the broad economic changes of the mid-sixteenth and seventeenth centuries, all of which—from rising prices to population expansion,

from rapid development of foreign and domestic trade to increased circula-
tion of consumer goods and financial instruments, and from growth of commercial farming to aggressive estate management—posed for them the threat
of excess or exorbitance.[12]

To counteract this threat, which represented potentially uncontainable violations of social as well as cosmic order and degree, Elizabethan ecclesiastics
and social critics offered the idea of enough and its conceptual variants: moderation, equity, balance, necessity. In a cascade of treatises they offered broad
jeremiads attacking the vice of greed, staking their claims not against wealth
itself but rather the "wicked using or evil spending" of it, which included ac-
quiring riches beyond one's social station.[13] Against it they opposed a general,
and naturalized, notion of order, balance, degree, and moderation, all neatly
summed in Thomas Lodge's insect fable: "The laboursome Ant gathereth
not in excesse, but sufficient provision for the Winter."[14] But their critiques
could be far more specific and technical, fully engaged with increasingly sophisticated financial practices and instruments. These concerns are especially
clear in their discussions of usury and interest, which were "the burden of
more sermons and passages in sermons on social wrong of the time than any
other single factor in contemporary life."[15] In these they struggled with both
long-standing questions about the propriety of taking more than the principal
for certain loans as well as long-standing distinctions between intent and action in determining economic sin.[16] Thus they recoiled from the "multipl[ying]
or breed[ing] beyond al measure" which they associated with usury and of
which, according to David Hawkes, they had a "metaphysical terror."[17] But
they asserted the possibility of collecting "above the principall, answerable
to the damage . . . suffered," which they called *interest* and even, in some
instances, our own word of choice. "This is no usurie," wrote Roger Fenton,
"but due and just *satisfaction*."[18] Indeed, the definitional challenge of usury
serves as a synecdoche for the dilemma of enough at the heart of economic
morality. "All good Christians agreed that usury was wrong," explains Norman Jones in his seminal *God and the Moneylenders*, "but they could not agree
on what it was and when it occurred."[19] Or in the terms offered by Elizabethan parliamentary debate: the "mischief [of usury] is of the excess."[20]

But moralists also tackled a range of other economic practices in addition
to usury that they wished guided by principles of moderation and the mean.
William Perkins, for instance, invokes equity as a synonym for these principles, so that by its "rule and direction"

men may know how to guide themselves, *in suing bondes, and taking forfei-tures*: and how men may with good conscience, carrie themselves in *surety-ships, in taking of fines, in letting of leases* . . . By vertue of this, a man may see how to frame all these and such like actions, in such sort, as himselfe shall reape credit, *and gain ynough* (italics mine), & his neighbour helpe and suc-cour him.[21]

Perkins is clearly familiar with contemporary financial instruments. But his real interest is not simply proper or moderate economic *behavior* but rather its matching economic *disposition* or *affect*. That disposition he calls "con-tentation," the privileged state of mind in which the minimum—assumed to be one's present condition—is experienced as plenty. Such a state of mind was the opposite of the vice of covetousness, "the disease which we cal the Woolfe, that is alwaies eating, and yet keepes the body leane."[22] Contenta-tion, explained as a sign of election by contemporary moralists, was the an-swer to any kind of ambition—but particularly economic ambition—that threatened established hierarchies. Like the idea of "enough," it was cham-pioned by clergy and others committed to the doctrine of callings, the so-cially conservative application of predestinarian theology that reinforced vocational and class order in the service of a peaceful commonwealth.[23] The preacher John Carpenter offered his *Preparative to Contentation* (1594) as

an argument most necessary to be urged, and a thing in earnest expectation of all good mindes, within whom the holy spirit of discipline is made sad and sorrowfull, through the consideration of the manifold disorders and huge inconveniences of noysome *Discontentation*, to whose good natures, the true *Contentation*, is every way both profitable and acceptable, in the feare of God, and honour of the Prince.[24]

Spokespeople for this basic economic morality were not at all confined to churchmen. The Elizabethan lawyer and historian William Fulbecke used a Ciceronian model to advance the Christian promise of enough in his *Booke of Christian Ethicks or Moral Philosophie* (1587):

If to be choaked and strangled with the cares of this world, be an infinite torment: if to see the conscience besieged with an hundred hels, and to feele the racking and renting thereof, as it were with a thousande fleshhookes, be an intollerable griefe, then happie and thrise happy is the mortified Christian that *is satisfied* with the sweete content of a meane estate, and the moderate portion that God hath allotted him.[25]

John Wheeler, author of a history and defense of the Merchant Adventurers Company, condemns non-company retailers who trade outside licensed precincts for showing "an exorbitant, and unsatiable desire, and greedines of gaine"; at the same time he praises his company as perfectly moderate in the ways it governs members from monopolies: "There is a stint, and reasonable proportion alloted, and set by an ancient order & manner, what quantitie either at once, or by the yere every man may ship out or transport, which he is not to goe beyond nor exceed."[26] Even Gerard Malynes, the early modern merchant and writer best known for his treatises on the intricacies of trade balances and the technicalities of exchange rates, couched many of his arguments about monetary exchange in extensive moral allegories that insisted each member of the commonwealth "should live *contented* in his vocation and execute his charge according to his profession."[27]

Such expressions pose a pressing semantic tension for their Protestant authors and audience: between a Christian economic moralism that prescribed "enough" as a social and affective goal, and a Christian penitential structure built around the rejection of making or feeling *satis*. This tension is perfectly visible in treatises such as Philipp Caesar's *A General Discourse against the Damnable Sect of Usurers* (1578), which maintained that although repentant usurers were required to supply *restitution* to those whom they had wronged ("a sinne is not remitted, except the thing stolen be restored"), this restitution should not be understood as compensatory but as "a parte of contrition, and . . . not that canonicall *satisfaction,* whiche they [Romanists] define to bee woorkes not commaunded."[28] But it is more vibrantly and consistently on display in the mid-Tudor economic interlude. A descendant of the medieval morality play,[29] this genre, under the broad banner of schooling its audience in the path to a distinctly Reformed salvation, addresses a range of topical concerns, including "religious issues [and] the growing concern with the effects of a cash economy."[30] It thus brings together the pressures of enough presented by economic sin and repentance, pressures which were to be rendered more nuanced, secular, and sophisticated in later Renaissance city comedies and tragicomedies.[31]

These interludes tackle head-on the elusive, ever-receding structure of *satis* that frightened preachers: "Every word may be defined, & every thing

may be measured, but *enough* cannot be mesured [*sic*] nor defined it changeth every yeare: when we had nothing wee thought it *enough* if wee might
obtaine less then we have: when we came to more we thought of an other
enough: nowe we have more wee dreame of another *enough*, so *enough* is alwayes to come though to [*sic*] much be there already."[32] In *The Trial of Treasure*, whose "Everyman" protagonist Lust is tempted to worldly indulgence
by vices such as Inclination, a figure named Contentation delivers a series of
orthodox warnings against the lure of material excess. She reminds the audience, for instance, that "those that are contented with their vocation, / Be
thankefull to God, this is a true consequent, / And those that be thankefull
in their conversation, / Can not but please the Lorde God omnipotent, / But
those that be sturdie proude, and disobediente, / The Ruler of Rulers will
them confounde."[33] The play's Prologue worries that wealth "is demed /
to be the originall and fountaine of pleasure, / [which] causeth luste to raigne
without measure"; the figure Just says that the demands of greed and lust
"resembleth Hydra the serpent, / Whose head being cut off, another riseth
incontinent: / So, one of Lust's cogitations being cut away, / There riseth up
another, yea, many, we may say."[34] Meanwhile the vices thrive on, rather
than castigate, increase, promising Lust that if he embraces Lady Treasure
"you shall have mirth by measure and overplus."[35]

The play is obviously designed to disparage the lure of excess while extol-
ling the virtues of moderation, with the intention of shocking its viewers to
repent for their own crimes of financial indulgence. In so doing it also displays with aplomb the definitional as well as affective obstinacy of enough,
the way it inevitably cedes to more. The same is true of Thomas Lupton's
All for Money, which neatly turns the abyssal problem of enough into the
play's dramaturgical design. The Prologue enumerates the cascading consequences of the pursuit of money—murder, perjury, adultery, folly, loss of
virginity—all of which lead, he reminds the audience, to "endless damnation" in hell.[36] But the high spectacle of the play's opening scenes *enact* the
problem, as the character Money (relying on the "fine conveyance" called for
in the stage directions) vomits up Pleasure, Pleasure vomits up Sin, and Sin
vomits up Damnation.[37] The final scene reinforces the threat of money's
lure and the need for atonement: it features ascents from the underworld by
Judas and Dives, both of whom yearn "one halfe houre to live" to repent for
their attachment to money (Judas, the Prologue had recalled, "for money
his master Christ betraye[d]").[38] Sandwiched between these moments is an

explicit conversation about *satis* by Learning with Money, Learning without Money, and Money without Learning, in which the former two characters cite classical philosophers (including Cicero, Sallust, Cato, Pliny) to defend the gospel position that "godlines is great gaine, if a man be content with that he hathe" (1 Timothy 6:6).[39]

Both the allure and intractability of this gospel proverb are comprehensively explored in William Wager's *Enough Is as Good as a Feast*.[40] The drama focuses on Worldly Man who, in a series of conversion scenes, rejects, embraces, and then again rejects the principle of enough and the contentment attached to it. Having entered onto the stage announcing that he has "riches and money at my pleasure, / Yea, and I will have more in spite of them all," Worldly Man is converted by the evangelical persuasions of Heavenly Man and Contentation, learning that "enough is as good as a feast. / Good Lord, how your words have alter'd my mind; / A new heart methinks is enter'd in my brest, / For no thought of mine old in me I can find" (94–5, 267–70). But the play's strength—what makes it more than a simple "demonstrat[ion] of the truth of [Wager's] chosen proposition"—is that it sees into the difficulty for Worldly Man, despite his best intentions, of living out the commonplace, of experiencing enough as a feast.[41]

This difficulty is personified by the Vices, who emerge to win Worldly Man back to their side. Led by their ringleader Covetous, who renames himself "Policy," the characters Inconsideration, Temerity, and Precipitation go in disguise to "get the Worldly Man hither by some shift" (520). The two sides face off when Worldly Man, accompanied now by the character Enough himself, encounters Covetous and his companions. Worldly Man has been championing his newly converted condition: "I am content myself for to stay / With Enough which bringeth me to quiet in body and mind," and Enough has been reinforcing this conviction: "Enough is as good as a feast, well you wot, / More than enough, a man needeth not; / Whether it be lands, money, friends or store, / If he have enough, what needeth he any more?" (662–3, 789–92). But his reassurances are drowned out by the appeals of Covetous and Precipitation, who convince Worldly Man that he can do more good for others if he has more for himself: "Enough is not enough without us two, / For having not us, what can Enough do?" (807–8). Worldly Man is thus captured, "plucked back" according to the delightful stage directions, by the Vices and their privileging of mundane wealth over its heavenly counterpart.

Ineke Murakami suggests that Covetous's commonwealth logic—that one can or will be a better neighbor or citizen if one has more resources—is part of Wager's sophisticated political critique of the problem of acquisitiveness, one that exposes "the ease with which policy, which is starting to denote any devious, self-interested activity of Elizabethan authorities, can be naturalized and excused in the name of the very commonwealth it undermines."[42] But Wager, a church rector with various pastoral responsibilities, also exposes the theological grounds of this dilemma.[43] Part of what he reveals so shrewdly is the ways in which the traditional imprecision of the meaning of enough has left it open to the kinds of violations Covetous and his friends perform upon it ("There is another Enough which is invisible," Precipitation says, "Which Enough, to want is impossible" [813–4]). An even more important part of what he reveals is the deep appeal of "more" even to the champions of enough. Like so many moral treatises, the play's Virtues, the ones who endorse *satis*, rely on the promise of increase in heaven to promote moderation on earth. Heavenly Man and Contentation, for instance, encourage Worldly Man to refuse the "treasure of this world" in favor of the rewards of the next (200). They specifically invoke, that is, the principle of spiritual usury, *foenus spirituale*, according to which "him that is mercifull to the poore [can] most assuredly expect that the thinges which hee layeth out shall be rendered againe of God *with a most liberall increase*."[44] Enough is as good as a feast, they explain, not only because a peaceful mind is the equivalent of riches but also because contentment signifies predestined glory and the "heavenly treasure" which "God hath prepared for his dear elect" (211, 220–1). Such reasoning may seem to attack the idea of increase, but it only relocates it to the afterlife, moralizing and postponing it. Although entirely orthodox according to a range of Christian understandings, which were bolstered by the numinous rhetoric of 1 Corinthians 2:9, it can nevertheless be understood as the source of Worldly Man's vulnerability to the persuasions of Covetous and his crew, his difficulty of experiencing enough as a feast. For enough is *not* as good as a feast, the theology acknowledges; rather, it guarantees one later, for the saved. Worldly Man, taken in by Covetous's lure that there are "a thousand, thousand, thousand ways . . . / To fetch in double as much as you have spent," gives way to the kinds of economic sins with which Tudor moralists were most concerned: usury, rent-racking, enclosure, denial of wages. Worldly Man abuses an old tenant and refuses to pay a servant, thus becoming a model of "what early Elizabethan preachers and play-makers saw as the widespread practice of fraud, oppression, and injustice arising from a surge in the growth of commerce and wealth."[45]

More crucial than the exposure of the ironies of *foenus spirituale*, however, is the presentation of Worldly Man's faltering repentance for his economic sins, a faltering to which Wager was especially sensitive.[46] Indeed, Wager's play forces into full view the pain of an economic morality narrative governed by the absence of penitential satisfaction. The pain of the morality play governed by an unrelenting Calvinist belief in predestination has long been noted; David Bevington, for instance, in his seminal *From* Mankind *to Marlowe*, traces a shift from late medieval to Elizabethan homiletic drama which transformed "a struggle for the soul of a universal man to a series of contrasts between those who are unquestionably saved and those who are irreparably damned."[47] But the link between this sense of impending damnation and the distinct inability to make enough remains to be clarified. This is the inability with which Worldly Man grapples.

The late medieval morality play depended upon the possibility that its characters could atone for their misdeeds and sins;[48] the Tudor homiletic drama depends upon the assumption that its characters cannot.[49] The belief that gives consistency to this assumption, as we have been charting, is that human repentance is not itself compensatory or satisfying. Wager dramatizes this position as a point of confusion for Worldly Man. Just as the protagonist starts to triumph that his "riches doth increase," a loud voice sounds from without, proclaiming the words of Jeremiah: "O thou earth, earth, earth! hear the word of the Lord; / Know thyself to be no better than clay or dust" (1164, 1185–86). Then the Prophet himself appears on stage, with a gospel-infused warning of future condemnation: "But that servant that liveth idly without care . . . / The portion of hypocrites shall be his; / Into utter darkness cast him out will [his master] / Where weeping and gnashing of teeth shall be" (1195–1208).[50]

Worldly Man's response to this speech is instructive. He knows that "these be the words of the Holy Scripture / Declaring the difference between the just and unpure" (1211–12). But he does not know what to do with them in the absence of mediation: "Good Lord, I would know what these words do mean," he admits (1213). Such foggy spiritual semi-recognition characterizes Worldly Man for the remainder of the scene, as he grows sicker and sicker from God's Plague. This sense of helplessness and hopeless inefficacy darkens the satire of Worldly Man's covetousness into what Craik aptly calls "sinister comedy."[51] Worldly Man, for all his attachments to his goods (a source of critique both within the play and for scholars), has some spiritual awareness: he knows that "there is no remedy" for him (1280). There is poignancy to this recognition, as well as to Worldy Man's tremendous fear of hell and even to his reluctance to forego his estate: "What a goodly turret I have made in my hall! / But yet my banqueting house pleaseth me best of all. / O, O, alas what a pang is this at my heart" (1327–29). (The fact that the play was likely performed in a banqueting hall only sharpens the cry.)[52] Covetous mocks him for this focus: "Lo, see you not how the Worldly Man showeth his kind? / As sick as he is, on his goods is all his mind" (1324–25). These are conventional moral sentiments meant to justify Worldly Man's impending doom, but Wager has put them in the mouth of Covetous, twisting their provenance and thus challenging the easy condescension and judgment they imply.

At this point the play gives way to broad, anti-Catholic comedy, as Ignorance, a caricature of a Catholic priest, arrives to try to heal Worldly Man but proves himself—along with his garbled Latin—to be a laughingstock, completely ineffectual. The parodic appearance of Ignorance the priest to help Worldly Man decipher the situation makes clear that Wager has no nostalgia for the sacrament of penance and its promises of satisfaction. But it also reinforces how helpless Worldly Man remains in both making sense of Scripture and in resolving what to *do*: "O, I would if I could," he murmurs to himself, "but now it is too late" (1277).[53] Reformers wrote off such hopelessness as a sign of damnation, but Worldly Man's terse assumption that he cannot *do* anything toward his salvation actually echoes Calvinist penitential orthodoxy. The educated audience around him—the audience that has listened to the titular proverb repeated some thirteen times—knows that what he cannot do is do *enough*.[54]

The play's doctrinal lesson thus insists on human inefficacy. Like its fellow Elizabethan moralities, then, *Enough Is as Good as a Feast* reveals the extent to which Protestant penitential logic and economic morality are at cross-purposes in their understanding of *satis*, enough. As something one *should* make and have in commercial and social transactions, enough was supposed to be experienced as plenty, more, a feast. As something one *should not* do or feel in matters of penitence, enough was supposed to be experienced as *not even* enough, *never* enough—and thus, ironically, to be scan-

dalously excessive. (The irony is condensed in a metatheatrical gesture by
the Prologue, who explains that the actors will "rhetorically amplify" the
title's proverb—a proverb whose very message warns against increase or amplification [Prologue, 80].) This conceptual disjunction, I suggest, fuels the
very problem of insatiable materialism which the interlude documents in
figures like Worldly Man, Lust, and Money-without-Learning. Of course,
the plays' obvious target for the problem is a human soul shaped in original
sin, a version of an argument about inherent, transhistorical covetousness
which has returned today in books such as Robert and Edward Skidelsky's
How Much Is Enough: Money and the Good Life. In it they propose that economic insatiability, while exacerbated by capitalism, "is rooted in human nature—in the disposition to compare our fortune with that of our fellows and
find it wanting."[55] But the interludes suggest the specific theological forces
governing this materialism. These forces are related to but not the same as the
predestinarian commitments identified in Max Weber's famous thesis that
early modern acquisitiveness was driven by the belief that worldly success
represented the "surest and most evident proof of rebirth and genuine faith."[56]
Rather, they suggest that, given the conceptual as well as material imbrication
of penitential practices with economic ones, the problematizing of *satis* in the
former problematized it in the latter. Or, more precisely, the rejection of *satis*
in the former rendered its fundamental ambiguity in the latter that much
more unstable. Although Reformed moralists might insist on the dignity of
enough in the realms of worldly acquisition and status, their theology of repentance undermined this value. The result, these plays suggest, was that in
neither of the two realms—financial or penitential—could enough be experienced either as sufficient or as a feast. Tudor interludes as a genre thrive on
this paradox as their characters, like Worldly Man, suffer from it.

In *The Merchant of Venice*, Shakespeare pursues this paradox as he re-
works the homiletic plays that heralded it. He redistributes the issues, turning from the crimes of covetousness which characterize the interludes to sins
of debt and vengeance, the transgressions which preoccupied sixteenth-
century dramatists in their encounters with "the underside of commercial
growth, namely the expansion of credit relations and with that expansion
enhanced possibilities both for default on proliferating debts and also for
imprisonment."[57] He resets them in a cosmopolitan *entrepôt* with a special
place in the English imagination: Venice served as a model of opulence with
its "magnificent and gorgeous buildings, and inestimable Treasures" and as

a model of political and religious liberty—but also as an example of decadence and imminent decline.[58] He also uses a plot derived from a sixteenth-century Italian novella, thus making possible the "especially dense set of erotic, economic, and spiritual transactions" which characterizes the play and its complicated set of relationships.[59] And finally, he organizes the problem so that it is displaced from the allegorical caricature of "worldly man" and absorbed by the figure of the Jew.[60]

"My extremest means"

Several of the play's characters struggle to identify enough, to distinguish between the exact and the excessive, between the lowest common denominator and pure bounty. Such a struggle informs Bassanio's early parable, with which he tries to persuade Antonio to "shoot another arrow that self way / Which you did shoot the first" so that he can either retrieve the bounty of both arrows or at least "bring your latter hazard back again" (1.1.148–9, 151). Portia, in a scene that risks displaying the conceptual struggle over adequation and superfluity as a deeply manipulative one,[61] proclaims to her new husband:

> You see me Lord Bassanio where I stand,
> Such as I am; though for myself alone
> I would not wish myself much better, yet for you,
> I would be trebled twenty times myself,
> A thousand times more fair, ten thousand times more rich,
> That only to stand high in your account,
> I might in virtues, beauties, livings, friends
> Exceed account.
>
>   3.2.149–57

And Morocco rejects the silver casket for the gold one by attempting to estimate both alongside, and beyond, accuracy: "If thou [the silver casket] beest rated by thy estimation / Thou dost deserve enough, and yet enough / May not extend so far as to the lady" (2.7.27–9). His reasoning and choice do not fit the model of Christian "hazarding" the lottery will eventually reward. But he shares with the Venetians their sensitivity to the pressures placed on "enough" as signifier of the simultaneously apt and inadequate in spiritual, romantic, and financial matters.

Antonio, the merchant, is the character most afflicted by these pressures. From the first scene he voices an abiding concern with identifying the parameters of enough and more. "My purse, my person, my extremest means," he tells Bassanio when the latter asks him for money, "lie all unlocked to your occasions" (1.1.138–9). Critics have focused on Antonio's unsettling equation between purse and person, a commodification of identity that prefigures Shylock's "my ducats, my daughter" even as it echoes the exclamations of that earlier stage Jew, Marlowe's Barabas.[62] But the (perhaps) unwitting oxymoron of "extremest means" best captures Antonio's dilemma: his gesture of self-effacing amity represents both the appropriate and the excessive simultaneously.

This gesture is tied to Antonio's characteristic urge to self-mortification and self-display. In Barbara Lewalski's classic account of the play, this yearning is the "embodiment of Christian love" and the sacrifice such love entails.[63] More recent scholars, recognizing the triumphalist Christian assumptions of this reading, have emphasized these yearnings as masochistic and punitive: responses to the guilt not only of unspoken homoerotic desire (his "already-existing shame and sexual taint") but also of his place in the historical course of Christian supercessionism.[64] We can thus see the particularly melancholy shape of this longing,[65] as well as its confusion of extremes and means, as penitential, developing from the absence in his world of an identifiable, reliable structure of sacramental satisfaction.

"I know not why I am so sad," he announces in the play's opening line, inciting from Salerio and Solanio interpretations that he will then disavow (1.1.1). In the *Anatomy of Melancholy* (1620) the consummate early modern theorist of the disease, Robert Burton, explained that a great generator of religious melancholy was the human tendency to feel sinful and to "have to [*sic*] great an opinion of our own worth that we can *satisfy* the law."[66] Burton, like the Protestant theologians we saw in chapter 1, was concerned that the demand to *make enough*, which included, he lists, "auricular confession, satisfaction, penance, [and] Peter's keys," could "terrify the soul of many a silly man."[67] The result was the untreatable melancholy he describes. But these distinctly Catholic practices are alien to Antonio's Venice.[68] The absence is visible in the striking contrast between this play's setting and that of Shakespeare's other Mediterranean cities, commercial or romantic, which feature a figure of the confessional or keys. There is no abbey in Venice as there is in cosmopolitan Ephesus, for instance, and no friars as there are in Messina or Verona. So if today we understand melancholy as the classic symptom of the loss of someone

or something whose idealized image continues to exert its power, then Antonio's sadness is a struggle not with the demands of a sacramental program
(à la Burton), but rather with its absence.[69] His efforts to avoid both debt (his
"ventures are not in one bottom trusted, / Nor to one place") and usury ("I
neither lend nor borrow / By taking nor by giving of excess") may be meant to
insulate him from this absence.[70] But they cannot counteract or cover over the
entirety of his guilts and longings (1.1.42–3, 1.3.61–2).

Antonio's activities across the play can thus be seen as the pursuit of his
own idiosyncratic system of expiation, one that bypasses or disavows observable contrition and confession to proceed directly to the "doing" of self-
punishment. The program first takes shape in his promise to Bassanio, as
he smuggles the language of penitential (even inquisitorial)[71] suffering and
self-exposure into his financial practices: "Try what my credit can in Venice
do; / That shall be *racked* even to the uttermost" (1.1.180–1, emphasis mine).
In Antonio, then, Shakespeare gives us a merchant whose vocation provides
both the occasion for and the means of his repentance. Such a compensatory
logic was always fully integrated into penitential strategies which legislated
alms and donations to chantries as methods of atonement. But Antonio's
particular embodiment of the logic indicates a fresh desperation in the face
of competing systems and priorities for satisfying for sin and crime.

"And he hath enough": Shylock and the Promise of *Satis*

This desperation underwrites his relation to Shylock. In the Jewish money
lender Antonio has found the only figure that can assess him in the very
language he cannot, as "sufficient" (1.3.17). And in the flesh bond, Antonio
finds the instrument and supervisor of a compensatory punition otherwise
unavailable to him. Shylock's proposal comes only after the two characters
argue over their commercial practices. Antonio, activating the conventional
equation that distinguishes between interest and excess in matters of usury,
insists that he neither lends nor borrows "upon advantage" (1.3.65). Shylock
answers Antonio's charge with his exegesis of the Jacob and Laban story
from Genesis 30 ("When Jacob graz'd his uncle Laban's sheep"), using biblical precedent to finesse the equation. As Shylock admits, Jacob did not "take
interest, not as you would say / Directly int'rest, mark what Jacob did"
(1.3.71–2), and he goes on to explain his ancestor's manipulation of the

birthing of sheep as a matter of divinely sanctioned thrift: "This was a way to thrive, and he was blest: / And thrift is blessing if men steal it not" (1.3.84–5). Shylock has effectively introduced into the discussion a new vocabulary of appropriate recompense: "thrift" (1.3.98).

Bassanio has already used this term in the first scene, when he tells Antonio that if he can participate in the lottery for Portia, "I have a mind presages me such thrift / That I should questionless be fortunate" (175–6). It conveys his hope of fortuitous, almost magical—though carefully plotted—prosperity or success (*OED* I.1.a). But the term also carried the sense of a "careful expenditure of means" (*OED* I.2.a) which could easily shift into a pejorative sense of niggardliness (*OED* I.3.a). Shylock's use of the term combines the two meanings, projecting a sense of earned bounty as well as gesturing to his deliberation—as well as his damnation—in achieving it. It allows Antonio to identify him both as a demon ("the devil can quote Scripture") and as a figure of fiscal and theological *enough*—enough as plenty, as "blessed," *as a feast* (1.3.98).

This double sense of Shylock's thriftiness is consonant with his separation from the Venetian Christians, what Julia Lupton describes as his "habitation in a community apart, defined by its own hermeneutic patterns and forms of social congregation."[72] Shylock embraces the imposed ghettoization of his community, for instance, which he understands as a kind of spiritual autonomy: "I will buy with you, sell with you, talk with you, walk with you, and so following: but I will not eat with you, drink with you, nor pray with you" he tells Bassanio (1.3.30–3). He actively preserves the enforced personal and religious isolation that, in Benjamin Nelson's seminal reading, distinguishes him from the Christians, with their embrace of a "universal brotherhood" as well as their obtrusive profligacy.[73] "Hear you me Jessica, / Lock up my doors, and when you hear the drum / . . . / But stop my house's ears, I mean my casements, / Let not the sound of shallow fopp'ry enter / My sober house" (2.5.20–36).

Such a portrait of sobriety differs from contemporary depictions of Venetian Jews as "*out of measure* wealthie in those parties [parts]."[74] But it finds a relevant non-fictional echo in Thomas Coryate's description of the Jewish enclave in his portrait of Venice: "I was at the place where the whole fraternity of the Jews dwelleth together, which is called the Ghetto, being an Iland: for it is inclosed round about with water." Coryate reads the Jews' geographical situation onto their features: some, he says are "such goodly and proper men, that then I said to my selfe our English proverbe: To look like a Jewe (whereby is meant sometimes a weather beaten warp-faced fellow, sometimes a phreneticke and lunaticke person, sometimes one discontented) *is not true*."[75] (Recent historical discussions of the Venetian Ghetto reinforce Coryate's impression: the Ghetto, Robert C. Davis explains, represented an "almost oriental culture thriving and seemingly self-contained in the heart of this Catholic city.")[76]

For Antonio, Shylock is Coryate's contented Jew. Indeed, Shylock's verbal repetition, which packs into one word multiple significations; his highly contained revenge fantasy of "feed[ing] fat the ancient grudge" on a single pound of flesh, keeping Antonio on his hip and in his gullet in a closed circuit of violence; and his ability to consider three thousand ducats "a good round sum," with the sense of measured perfection that the circular image offers: these are all distinctive characteristics central to the presentation of the Jew as a creature who has enough, who may even experience enough as plenty (1.3.46, 1.3.103).[77] Early modern commentators such as John Foxe certainly interpreted this kind of contentment or sufficiency as a sign of the Jews' spiritual degeneration: "Being otherwise a people most abhorred of God, & men, they ... neverthelesse most arrogauntly vaunt them selves to bee more esteemed, and more precious in the sight of God, then all other nations, people, and tongues: and that they were his only darlings."[78] Such a view of Jews, as Sharon Achinstein has shown, allowed English Protestants to channel "age-old stereotypes about the cultural or racial other" through topical political frameworks.[79] But for Antonio, despite his flagrant hatred for Shylock, Jewish "vaunting" has an appeal, a magnetic pull that attracts him to the flesh bond as an emblem of sufficient penalty, of punitive satisfaction that makes enough for him and plenty for Bassanio.

Antonio has already been imagining Shylock as a source of apt punishment, calling himself an enemy "who if he break, thou may'st with better face / Exact the penalty" (1.3.131–2), when Shylock introduces his plan:

> I would be friends with you, and have your love,
> Forget the shames that you have stain'd me with,
> Supply your present wants, and take no doit
> Of usance for my moneys, and you'll not hear me—
> This is kind I offer.
>
> 1.3.134–38

The persuasive force of Shylock's term "kind" rests not simply in its meaning of "natural" or of "gentle" but of "naturally pertaining to, or associated with, a person or thing; *proper, appropriate, fitting*" (*OED* I.1.c, italics mine). For Antonio, Shylock's "kindness" hints at the prospect of a penalty that might represent symbolic rather than fiscal sufficiency.[80] Shylock goes on to name the physical price he will exact in the case of forfeit, to which Antonio is strikingly quick to agree:

> Go with me to a notary, seal me there
> Your single bond, and (in a merry sport)
> If you repay me not on such a day
> In such a place, such sum or sums as are
> Express'd in the condition, let the forfeit
> Be nominated for an equal pound
> Of your fair flesh, to be cut off and taken
> In what part of your body pleaseth me.
> 1.3.140–47

Scholars have connected the flesh bond to various anti-Judaic beliefs circulating during the early periods: beliefs about the Jews' role in the Crucifixion, about Host desecration, about circumcision of Christian boys and men, and about ritual murder of young Christian boys for their blood—all of which involved accounts about Jews "told by Christians, to Christians, to make Christians act and redefine that which made them Christian."[81] Their various resonances are all active here, working to underline Antonio's sacrificial and potentially satisfying relationship to Shylock.[82] In the radical purity of its approach to repayment, in its claim to reduce all exchange not just to the flesh but to a precise pound, the "merry bond"—the very opposite of Antonio's boundless melancholy—serves as the embodiment of a punitive "enoughness."[83] Indeed, extending James Shapiro's insights about the role of the Jew in embodying for Reformers the Catholic ritualism and legalism they rejected but could not avoid, Shylock's bond represents the principle of calculation and proportionate adequation that marks the lost penitential satisfactory.[84] Far from being an instance of Shylock's usurious need for excess, the bond, which seems to promise "to circumscribe contingency by contractual stipulation, and to submit the incalculable energies of natural creation to strict quantitative accounting,"[85] represents exactly enough for the Jew, precisely what does and will "pleaseth me" (1.3.151). It heralds for Antonio the special affective profit that he has been lacking: "Content, in faith" (1.3.152).

By sealing to the bond, Antonio is connected to Shylock in interlocking circuits of economic and penitential satisfaction according to which he promises to make enough for the Jew who, in turn, "hath enough." In so doing, Antonio hopes also to have enough, to have the fulfillment of suffering on his own as well as Bassanio's behalf. According to the terms of the bond, in other words, Shylock supervises for Antonio the possibility of a penance the latter sees no other way of making. Bassanio is not only horrified but suspicious of this prospect; a master of exchange himself, he senses the way in which the exacting bond might become boundless, too much. But Antonio's desperation for missing expiatory closure makes the prospect of Shylock's potential vindictiveness attractive to him. It is as if the challenge leveled at penitential satisfaction as a result of Reformation theology makes the threat of Jewish punishment the most plausible, appealing approach to repentance for the melancholy Antonio. Shakespeare, that is, portrays the potential for the doctrinal pressures of Reformation debate to throw the Christian, even or especially the Venetian Christian, into a special relationship with the Jew as the figure of enough.[86]

The shock of this situation drives the energies of the play, which are dedicated largely to extricating Antonio from his entanglement with Shylock. And Antonio can only be split from Shylock when the Jew's unique relation to enough is publicly discredited and detached from the promise it seems to offer Antonio of plenty, of grace. Launcelot's parting of the proverb announced this separation; it disconnected enough from its partner grace and assigned it, in its newly suspect form, to stand for the Jews' fundamental failure of faith. The *dramaturgical* models for this jest, as we have seen, are the economic interludes and the tradition of proverbial wordplay they represent.[87] But its *conceptual* grounds, I want to stress, lie in the semantic challenge precipitated by Reformation theologies of repentance: theologies that denigrated the idea of enough, not only recognizing the difficulties inherent in determining its contours but also rejecting altogether its possibility as a human endeavor. The work of Shakespeare's drama, then, is to play out Launcelot's premise, convincing Antonio of the poverty of Shylock's version of penitential enough even as the Jew's material sufficiency is taken away to supply Venetian coffers.[88]

This is a multipronged process. It depends upon, and begins with, Jessica's elopement with the Christian Lorenzo, a plot direction not in Shakespeare's Italian source. As Shakespeare portrays it, the escape is an assault precisely on Shylock's sense of content. He understands this "loss upon loss" as alien both to him and to his people: "The curse never fell upon our nation till now; I never felt it till now" (3.1.85–6). The violation of Shylock's self-sufficiency, of the sense of containment represented in the earlier image of his "sober house," takes shape as the stripping from his world of principles of enough, content, restoration: "[t]he thief gone with so much, and so much to find the thief, and *no satisfaction*, no revenge!" (3.1.92–4, italics mine). The most resonant portrayal of this experience is the famous "hath not a Jew eyes?" monologue, in which Shylock's effort to establish equivalencies between Jew and Christian is a symptom of his sudden loss of *satis*:

> Hath not a Jew eyes? Hath not a Jew hands, organs, dimensions, senses, affections, passions? Fed with the same food, hurt with the same weapons, subject to the same diseases, healed by the same means, warmed and cooled by the same winter and summer, as a Christian is? If you prick us, do we not bleed? If you tickle us, do we not laugh? If you poison us, do we not die? And if you wrong us, shall we not revenge? If we are like you in the rest, we will resemble you in that. (3.1.59–68)

As we saw in chapter 3, the satisfactions of revenge are exceptionally fragile. Shylock acknowledges this problem in his desire for a vengeance beyond sheer equivalence: "The villainy you teach me I will execute, and it shall go hard but *I will better* the instruction" (3.1.71–3; italics mine). But even before Shylock voices the drive of revenge toward addition or multiplication, his whole speech has been a long, plangent record of his loss of "enough." The Shylock who closed his literal and metaphoric mouth and ears against the Venetians now exposes himself to direct comparison with them. First he pleads for the humanity of the Jew: he is like all others with "hands, organs, dimensions, senses, affections, passions." Then he pleads for the Christianity of the Jew: he is "[f]ed with the same food, hurt with the same weapons, subject to the same diseases, healed by the same means, warmed and cooled by the same winter and summer, as a Christian is." Shylock had drawn strict boundaries between himself, his tribe, and the Venetian world in a way that signaled his sufficiency or wholeness; he now dissolves them.[89] The "hath not a Jew eyes" speech, then, far from being a universalist, humaniz-ing plea on behalf of a maligned race,[90] is the beginning of a conversion predicted for him at the end of act 1 and demanded from him at the end of act 4. It marks his own, unsolicited assimilation to the terms and orienta-tions of the Christians. Most of all, it announces a loss of satisfaction until now represented most vividly in Antonio's melancholy and in his ship-wrecks.

Shylock's pursuit of the flesh bond is designed to restore to him this loss. The repetition of his claim gestures to what is at stake: "I'll have my bond," Shylock repeats. "I will not hear thee speak. / I'll have my bond, and there-fore speak no more. / I'll not be made a soft and dull-ey'd fool, / To shake the head, relent, and sigh, and yield / To Christian intercessors" (3.3.12–6). The Venetians diagnose in his efforts the resonances of an innate Jewish disposition, vengeful and unholy from its inception: Shylock is a "stony ad-versary," the Duke tells Antonio, "an inhuman wretch / Uncapable of pity, void and empty / From any dram of mercy" (4.1.4–6).[91] But Shylock's pur-suit emerges only when he becomes like the Venetians, when he takes on the Venetians' sense of loss.[92] What the Venetians understand as the sheerest expression of Shylock's "Jewishness"—his commitment to the precise terms of his bond—is a new, desperate assertion of that "Jewishness" when its privileged relation to sufficiency has begun to dissolve. Antonio's submission to Shylock, his willingness to "follow him no more with bootless prayers," is of a piece with this assertion, promising that Shylock will have, and the merchant will make, enough to compensate for losses whose material and spiritual aspects are inextricable.

The bitter rhythm of the ensuing trial scene, in which Shakespeare's dra-matization of the vicissitudes of atonement reaches its crescendo, prevents this outcome. Satisfaction as a spiritual and psychological pursuit is denied to both men and given instead, in a juridical and incipiently sexual form, to Portia in her disguise as Balthazar. "He is well paid that is well satisfied, / And I delivering you, am satisfied" she says as the trial closes (4.1.434–5).

What has Portia done, and how exactly is it satisfying? She arrives in the courtroom well after the Venetians have assembled to plead, cajole, and ul-timately threaten Shylock, who refuses to cede to their demands even against the promise of more money. "For thy three thousand ducats here is six!" Bassanio offers, to which Shylock performs this astonishing math: "If every ducat in six thousand ducats / Were in six parts, and every part a ducat, / I would not draw them, I would have my bond!" (4.1.84–7). In the face of these multiplying ducats Shylock insists solely on the idea of precise, symbolically satisfying adequation embedded in the bond. That idea remains appealing to Antonio, who attacks Shylock's entrenched Judaism but ultimately embraces its demands: "Let me have judgment and the Jew his will" (4.1.83). So if Portia cannot tell "which is the merchant here? And which the Jew?" it is because by the time of the trial their notions of and search for spiritual as well as material satisfaction have become so deeply entwined (4.1.174). We hear the depth of this connection when Antonio reassures Bassanio: "Repent but you that you shall lose your friend, / And he repents not that he pays your debt. / For if the Jew do cut but deep *enough*, / I'll pay it instantly with all my heart" (4.1.274–77, italics mine).

Portia prevents the Jew not only from cutting Antonio but also from locating, somewhere in Antonio's interior, the site of this "enough." Her procedure depends upon judging in a way that enforces Launcelot's quip. She begins by insisting on the utter, unearned surplus of forgiveness: "The quality of mercy is not strain'd" she says famously (4.1.180). But when Shylock will not relent, and when Antonio prepares himself for the knife, Portia must actively sever the relationship between gratuitous mercy and the adequations of the law, between plenty and enough. Ironically, this requires her own species of highly refined accounting. As Shylock moves towards Antonio, she warns: "Shed thou no blood, nor cut thou less nor more / But just a pound of flesh. If thou takest more / Or less than a just pound, be it so much / As makes it light or heavy in the substance, / Or the division of the twentieth part / Of one poor scruple" (4.1.321–6). Portia, a merchant as well as a judge, is a master of accelerating fractions, and she uses her acumen to demonstrate the impossibility of the "enough" for which both Antonio and Shylock yearn.

Scholars have read her ruling as a gloss primarily on *Shylock's* legalism.[93] But it is a gloss on *Antonio's* as well. Or, perhaps more accurately, it is a gloss on Antonio's commitment to legalism as an avenue to a missing penitential plenitude. Portia's threats to Shylock are really reminders to Antonio that he too cannot—and cannot be allowed to—make enough. "Shed thou no blood," she says, a directive that could be leveled at Antonio as well as at the Jew. If, as I have been arguing, the "pound of flesh" has served both Shylock and Antonio as the sign of a perfectly compensatory satisfaction, Portia has shown not only that a pound is never "just a pound,"

but that, in its vulnerability to an ever-receding horizon of ever-finer incre-
ments ("the twentieth part / Of one poor scruple"), it has no special relation
to spiritual fulfillment. It is Portia who thus definitively parts the proverb,
permanently separating a now degraded "enough" from grace and mercy.
The detachment deprives both Shylock and Antonio of the kinds of *satis*
they had sought.

"Dropping manna": Christian and Jewish Excess

But only Shylock is publicly penalized, and in a way that reclaims a purified, redefined "enough" for all the Venetians. Again the work is left largely
to Portia, who relies upon a familiar scrupulosity of financial detail. Since
Shylock, the stranger, sought the life of a Venetian citizen, he must face the
death penalty and pay up: "The party 'gainst the which he doth contrive, /
Shall seize one half his goods, the other half / Comes to the privy coffer of
the state," she orders (4.1.348–50). The flavor of her rulings is repeated in
the Duke and Antonio's additional requirements: "I pardon thy life before
thou ask it," the Duke tells Shylock, with some qualifications: "For half thy
wealth, it is Antonio's / The other half comes to the general state, / Which
humbleness may drive unto a fine" (4.1.365–8). Antonio concludes the deal
by performing the only kind of sacrifice left to him: he quits half of his part
of the penalty as long as Shylock "will let me have / The other half in use, to
render it / Upon his death unto the gentleman / That lately stole his daughter" (4.1.378–81). Then Antonio adds "[t]wo things provided more": "he pres-
ently become a Christian: / The other, that he do record a gift / (Here in the
court) of all he dies possess'd / Unto his son Lorenzo and his daughter"
(4.1.382–6). When it comes to Shylock's possessions, then, as opposed to Antonio's body, it is possible to calculate to, and give away, the last scruple.

    That allows Portia, who has dismantled a penitential calculus according
to which people *make* enough, the ability to reinstall an economic morality
according to which people—at least her people—*have* enough, enough as a
feast.[94] And her people have enough when the Jew no longer does. Shylock's
initial response to her sentence suggests a lack of material sufficiency entirely new to him, one that strikes at the heart of his being: "Nay, take my
life and all, pardon not that— / You take my house, when you do take the
prop / That doth sustain my house: you take my life / When you do take

the means whereby I live" (4.1.370–3). When he finally agrees to Antonio's terms he first presents himself as "content," a term that now rings with Launcelot's sense of lack and degradation. Thus when he leaves the stage he is ill: "I pray you give men leave to go from hence, / I am not well" (4.1.391–2). Shylock exits the play as Antonio entered it: sick and sad.

This image of Shylock is, in Fisch's terms, a dual one. One side of the image is of a Christian: although his conversion is not shown, the end of the trial scene suggests his incorporation into—or, more accurately, his dependence upon—the Christian community. In the series of symbolic losses that the divvying up of his goods represents, the Hebrew has turned, or been turned, Christian; the sufficiency that defined his Judaism from the play's opening has been entirely compromised. But the other side of that image is of the unconvertible Jew. As Portia's parting shot indicates ("Art thou contented, Jew?" she asks), his commitment to and need for his goods as a source of self only reinforces the early modern stereotype of the Jew as dissatisfied. In a move that makes explicit Launcelot's earlier disdain, the court ruling allies the Jew with a spiritually impoverished "enough," an enough shorn of its connection to blessing and grace. At the same time it insists that the Jew is incapable of having or appreciating the material as well as spiritual goods with which he has been left. Portia has thus overseen Shylock's loss of sufficiency and then established dissatisfaction as his "natural" disposition.

The other side of this proof is that the Christians are capable of having, though not of making, enough. The implication is realized in the final scene's resonant vocabulary of *manna*. Back in Belmont, Portia and Nerissa present "some good comforts," including the "special deed of gift," to Lorenzo and Jessica, the eloped lovers (5.1.289, 292). Lorenzo, rather than Jessica, responds: "Fair ladies, you drop manna in the way / Of starved people" (5.1.294–5).[95] Manna, the special food which God miraculously provided for the hungry Israelites in Exodus 16, is a privileged symbol of satisfaction, of enough as personalized plenty. John Donne captures its essence when he uses it as a metaphor for the psalms: "As Manna tasted to every man like that he liked best, so doe the Psalmes minister Instruction, *and satisfaction*, to every man, in every emergency and occasion."[96] It is also the privileged symbol for Christians of Jewish ingratitude, of the inability of the Israelites to trust or value properly the blessings of God. (According to the scriptural account, God warned the Jews neither to hoard it nor to search for it on the Sabbath; they did both, and it rotted and did not appear, respectively.) The manna of act 5 of *Merchant* is the only instance of the word in the Shakespeare canon, and it carries with it the referential richness that accrues to a well-established type of the Eucharist and a well-established example of Jewish failure to respect God's gifts. Indeed, the typological and historical meanings coincide in Christian exegesis; as Henry Smith warns in his *Treatise of the Lords Supper* (1591), Christ calls the bread his body "to make us take this Sacrament reverentlie, because we are apt to contemne it, as the *Jewes* did their Manna."[97] When Lorenzo takes Shylock's deed of gift and calls it manna, he suggests that, unlike the proleptically dead Jew whose wealth he will inherit, he values it appropriately, recognizes it as more because it is enough. In Andrew Willet's words, Lorenzo knows that "the Lord signifieth the great abundance of this heavenly bread, which should overflow, and fall every where that both poore and rich *might have enough*."[98]

By the close of the play, then, Shylock has been converted into "enough": enough as manna, as a (perversely Eucharistic) feast properly appreciated by the Venetian Christians but under- and over-estimated by the Israelites for whom he stands; and enough as the debased opposite of spiritual plenitude. His conversion coincides with both the rescue of Antonio from his fantasies of satisfactory self-abasement and the restoration of Antonio's fortune. These accomplishments, all at Portia's hands, can be read as an allegory of the Protestant dismantling of the sacrament of penance and the place of *satis* within it. That is, over the course of the play, Portia invalidates the penitential satisfactions symbolized in the flesh bond; releases Antonio from its material and emotional circuitry; redefines enough as the mis-measure of human penitential activity; and establishes "unstrained" mercy as the only basis or standard of repentance, forgiveness, and reward. But given the kinds of calculations her judgments have involved, the allegory seems ironic. Shakespeare exposes not only the conditionality of supposedly unconditional mercy but also the lingering attraction to and reliance on the economies of satisfaction in the face of their disavowal. Insofar as that disavowal depends upon Shylock, *Merchant* is our best witness to the place of the Jew as the scapegoat for the problem of "enough" at the heart of Reformation theologies which had claimed to bid it "adew."

Chapter 5

"Wooing, wedding, and repenting"

The Satisfactions of Marriage in Othello *and* Love's Pilgrimage

Satisfaction, as we have charted over the course of the preceding chapters, is a qualitative as well as quantitative principle that organizes various categories of exchange: of transgression and redemption, of violation and vendetta, of debt and repayment. In Shakespeare's *The Merchant of Venice*, these categories converge in the famous "flesh bond," which trammels up the characters' financial as well as religious and emotional interdependencies.

Those interdependencies share their syntax with an additional category of interpersonal exchange: marriage. Karen Newman, for instance, suggests that the intersection of the erotic and the economic in marriage grounds the play's other relations. "The exchange of Portia from her father via the caskets to Bassanio is the ur-exchange upon which the 'main' bond plot is based," she explains, offering a bracing reminder that the institution of marriage, given its role as a socioeconomic as well as affective and sexual transaction (nowhere made more explicit than in the commonplace of "rendering the marriage debt"), is implicated in the history of satisfaction.[1]

But the place of marriage in this history, I suggest, is not necessarily originary or paradigmatic, as Newman's language of "ur" suggests. Rather, like the other activities, vocations, and desires we have been tracking, marriage's place is determined by its conceptual and instrumental proximity to repentance. This proximity, as I discuss below, is observable in the shared status of marriage and penance as sacraments dismantled in the course of the Protestant Reformation. But it is more deeply enabled by the ways in which marriage served as an *occasion* as well as an *object* of repentance. Matrimony and marital satisfaction, this chapter suggests, were thus especially sensitive to the period's reconfiguration of penitential "enough."

The Merchant of Venice, with its threats of cuckoldry and bawdy puns on intercourse, touches in a comic vein on the reparative as well as punitive resonances of marital satisfaction. It is Shakespeare's other Venetian play, *Othello*, which dwells on them in tragic length and detail, forcing its protagonist to confront as sheer loss the transvaluation of satisfaction in the early modern period. As I explore in this chapter, Othello's lament, "Would I were satisfied!" records a comprehensive sense that "enough" is no longer available in the realm of matrimonial love, where the sacred and secular (and specifically sexual) meanings of our term converge most intimately. This sense, I suggest, marks the climax of the early modern history of satisfaction, as the shock of the term's theological reorientation reverberates in one of the most private spaces of shared human experience.[2]

The denouement of this history can be traced in the theatrical descendants of *Othello*, which had an exceptional afterlife in court revivals throughout the early Stuart period.[3] Echoes of the play's treatment of marriage and penitence sound across a range of Jacobean and Caroline "sex tragedies" that revel in the excesses and incompatibilities of female and male desire in relation to the bonds of marriage; they achieve maximum intensity in John Ford's *Love's Sacrifice* (1633), a text that is so explicitly indebted to Shakespeare (although in this version the Desdemona and Cassio characters do fall in love) that Martin Butler suggests the characters "must have seen *Othello*."[4] But I focus here on a romance, Francis Beaumont and John Fletcher's *Love's Pilgrimage* (1613–1614), a close retelling of Cervantes's "Las Dos Doncellas (The Two Damsels)" whose Spanish setting gives the dramatists nostalgic as well as parodic access to the possibility of penitential and erotic satisfaction.

"Increase and multiply"

The vicissitudes of satisfaction structure early modern accounts of marriage as a sexual, emotional, and communal bond.[5] Wedlock's specifically erotic component—sexual gratification or "due benevolence"—was itself called satisfaction and was subject to its vocabularies of enough and more.[6] Thus the literature of marital advice and commentary, having accepted the Pauline admission in Corinthians that it is "better to marry than to burn," endorses and even celebrates sexual activity as the "well-spring of marital plenitude, the primary means by which two become one"—as long as it remains rooted in a principle of restraint and self-control.[7] William Perkins warns in a familiar formulation that "[the] performance of special benevolence one to another" is "to be done in moderation. For even in wedlocke excess in lusts is no better then plaine adulterie before God."[8] William Gouge, in his *Domesticall Duties*, clarifies that "*excesse* [in due benevolence] is either in the *measure* or in the *time. In the measure*, when husband or wife is insatiable; provoking, rather than asswaging lust, and weakning their naturall vigor more then suppressing their unnaturall humor."[9]

Satis provides the measure for other conjugal categories: of affection, devotion, and sociality between partners.[10] Indeed, marriage may be said to turn on the pivot of "enough," insofar as enough could serve paradoxically as both a principle of moderation *and* of augmentation, of "increase and multiply." Such a demand for increase referred not only to the reproduction of offspring but also to the amplification of the marriage bond in its widest sense, as the "chiefe ground & preservation of all societies . . . a communion of life betweene the husband and the wife, extending it selfe to al the parts that belong to their house."[11] The pursuit of contentment, and then of additional contentment, was a conventional aspect of marital exchange. Heinrich Bullinger offers perhaps its most influential articulation in the oft-reprinted treatise *The Christen State of Matrimony*, first published in English translation by Miles Coverdale in 1541. As Bullinger explains, the proper Christian couple strives "faythfully [to] kepe and *increace* the love and dewty of mariage."[12] The wife's contribution to this increase is her obedience: "Every honest wyfe [must] submit her selfe, to serve her husband with all her power, and gyve herselfe over frely [*sic*] and wyllyngly . . . to hold her content with her husbande, to love hym onely, to harken unto hym."[13] At the same time the husband "ought not . . . to be satisfyed, that he knowethe what matrimoniall love is & how he shuld [*sic*] love his spouse, but he must apply hymselfe to love her in dede, as ye lord hath commaunded hym & not that only, but also endevour hymselfe ever more and more, to kepe & increace the same love."[14] Gouge, working specifically from Ephesians 5, echoes the same terms: "*Husbands must come as neare as they can to Christ in loving their wives. In which respect, because they can never love so much as Christ did, they must never thinke they have loved enough.*"[15]

These logics of mutual reinforcement have roots in classical as well as medieval theories of marriage; they were reoriented for the period by divines who emphasized afresh the "virtues of marital love . . . as the *sine qua non* of marriage."[16] And as feminist and other scholars have articulated so carefully, they are deeply colored by—as well as productive and reinforcing of—patriarchal and even misogynist assumptions about female subjection on which constructions of companionate love and partnership as well as marital hierarchies were grounded.[17] My concern here is the way these gendered asymmetries, and the facts and fantasies about marriage they underwrite, depend upon the precariousness of satisfaction, upon the way "enough" in matrimony ultimately becomes synonymous with more. According to this semantic and experiential calculus, the wife is to be content with the husband's content, and the husband's content is to make his spouse content, to "make enough" for her and himself by making more. Fran Dolan has persuasively suggested that this equation, and the imagined marital union and fulfillment it represents, functioned as a reassuring "cover story" for the fact that marriage was actually "an economy of scarcity in which there is only room for one full person."[18] But this "cover story" did not simply provide ideological comfort. The demand for a marital satisfaction that was also a surplus—and yet a surplus which did not violate the "difference between healthy sexual pleasure and the dangers of brutish lust"—returns us to the threats and pressures of *satis* which we have explored in earlier chapters.[19] On its own, such a demand was anxiety-provoking, turning erotic desire into "a sign of human inadequacy" and threatening a "male collapse under the burdens of economic responsibility."[20] I suggest here, however, that the problem of marital and sexual satisfaction was uniquely inflected by the period's rescripting of penitential satisfaction. Because to talk of marriage in this period, as a digression in Richard Snawsel's popular *A Looking Glasse for Maried Folkes* reminds us, was to talk about repentance.

"Wooing, wedding, and repenting"

In his address to readers, Snawsel notes that his treatise, derived from Erasmus's *Encomium Matrimonii*, expands on its model by adding a discussion of *"the substance of faith and repentance,* with divers other particular poynts and examples . . . which being practised, are sufficient to life eternall."[21] He goes on to pepper his tract, a multi-part conversation in which the virtuous wife Abigail instructs her neighbors in proper marital relations, with reminders that seeking forgiveness from God is inextricable from sympathy and tenderness towards one's spouse: "The long patience and goodnesse of God, ought to leade us to repentance, and to deale favourably and in tender compassion one with another."[22] Other aspects of the *Looking Glasse* mark it as a concentrated expression of specifically Puritan practical piety,[23] but the weaving of marital and penitential behaviors and affects is congruent with a broad sectarian range of discourses that recognized a special connection between marriage and repentance.

The most obvious connection between the two is their status as Catholic sacraments rejected as sacramental in Protestant theology. The story of the "entrenchment" of marriage as a sacrament in the twelfth century, and its Reformation rejection (along with its Tridentine stabilization) in the sixteenth and seventeenth centuries, is vast and complex.[24] The enormous historiography records important theological distinctions between confessions and denominations both on the Continent and in England, particularly in terms of their understandings of the validity of wedlock privately contracted.[25] But it also records significant lines of confessional continuity, including a commitment to mutual consent as both a theoretical ideal and a practical requirement. Eric Carlson has documented for the early modern English church a process of both transformation and conservation of marital theology: The transformation was made possible by a critique of Catholic sacramental theology that denied marriage's status as an avenue of grace (even as it insisted wedlock was not inferior to celibacy); the conservation was made possible by a commitment to the spiritual centrality of the marital relation and the continuation of the ecclesiastical court's jurisdiction over marriage. (In fact, the English ecclesiastical courts hewed to pre-Tridentine canons so that, after "significant changes in marriage law" at Trent in the 1560s, the English system remained in some ways "more 'Roman' than the Roman church.")[26] As Carlson suggests, the English church "shap[ed] both a new theology of marriage which exalted it above celibacy and a ritual which endued marriage with dignity while stripping it of its sacramentality."[27] In this way the English church clung to wedlock as an institution "signifying unto us the mystical union, that is betwixt Christ and his Church," even as it officially refused marriage sacramental status in the Thirty-Nine Articles.[28] Carlson doubts whether anyone other than the "theologically savvy" would have detected the discrepancies between marriage as a Catholic sacrament and marriage as a Reformed "holy ordinance," the term used in the service of matrimony in the *Book of Common Prayer*. But this seems to underestimate the way in which the language of the service insists on the distinction between the two views: between marriage as an efficacious channel of grace and marriage as a blessing instituted by God in Eden and as a sign of Christ's sacrificial love for the church.[29] As a dismantled sacrament whose spiritual content was redefined and preserved in a new form, the structural analogy between marriage and penance is a distinct and pressing one.

It also points to other connections between repentance and marriage. They both share the prospect and promise of redemption, of both a return to a state of innocence and the potential of a heavenly afterlife. James Grantham Turner has described the exegetical tradition, beginning with the patristics and continuing into the early modern period, which "filled [Genesis 1–3] with redemptive possibilities, and reconstruct[ed] a pre-lapsarian happiness whose traces can still be felt in fallen sexuality."[30] These "redemptive possibilities" inform a wide range of early modern English commentaries on marriage, which recall the original purity of Edenic wedlock, instituted "in the blissful place of Paradise, where was no sinne: and when Man was in his chiefe perfection."[31] And if such praise had to admit that this primal version of holy matrimony was a prelude to the Fall, the violation of God's commandment that permanently altered all relations among humans and between human and divine, it still celebrated post-lapsarian wedlock precisely as an antidote for the expulsion. For marriage allowed fallen humans to "perceive . . . glimpses and sparkles of originall purity and felicity unextinguished."[32]

If such accounts present marriage as a means back to Eden, others trace it as a path towards heaven, the symbol or the guarantor of a future paradise rather than the restoration of a lost one. The simplest view of this promise is the commonplace that marriage was a "remedy against sin," offering an acceptable outlet for sexual activity which, if practiced out of wedlock, would be understood as mortal for the soul. But writers had more sophisticated ways of making this connection. For this they had at their disposal the language of Ephesians, which established concretely the analogy of the marriage of husband and wife with Christ's "espousal" to his bride the church. They also turned to the language of Proverbs to explain the holy household as the scene of religious thanksgiving and instruction as well as sorrowing and forgiveness. John Wing puts the two together in his *Crown Conjugall*, in which he reads Proverbs 12:4 ("A virtuous woman is a crown to her husband") as a prompt to prayer, since a good wife is "a more speciall gift of God, whose love is more extraordinary in *this one*, then in *all other.*" Furthermore, she is an emblem of his even more ineffable grace: "Loe, she is the Lords favour, and none of his common kindnesses, (*such as houses, and riches*, and such like, *which descend upon us from progenitors*) but a mercy, wherof he only, wil be the giver."[33]

Circulating alongside the paradigm of the redemptive marriage are models of wedlock more intimately as well as explicitly connected to penitence. The marital relation had long been viewed as the scene of potential wrongdoing and thus an *occasion for* repentance. Adultery, abuse, abandonment—these were only the most extreme of a range of activities that required atonement to the disappointed spouse as well as to God. Medieval theology and canon law treated marriage and sexual relations as categories of everyday life that generated sin and required confessional policing; in the early modern period these categories remained within the scope of ecclesiastical jurisdiction and could result in penitence performed publicly.[34] But an equally pervasive—and less frequently noticed—connection was established in early modern discourses that understood marriage as an *object* of penitence. That is, the prescriptive as well as imaginative literature of the period frequently cast wedlock as a choice and condition that could be repented as a grave spiritual error.

The potential for this repentance is a staple of misogynistic satires such as Thomas Dekker's *Batchelars Banquet* (1603), an anthology of cautionary tales for men to discourage them from the horrors of women and marriage. The young man—"the jolly yonker," Dekker calls him—pursues a conjugal union despite all advice to the contrary and eventually "begin[s] to see his follie, and *repent* as well his fondnes . . . but all too late."[35] The context here suggests that the youth's "repentance" be read as an ironic shadow of the real thing, a self-regarding regret for his current state which lacks the genuine sorrowing associated with true contrition. But the idea of marriage as the cause of emotions assimilable to the feelings and procedures associated with repentance sounds in more orthodox discourses—sermons, treatises, commonplace books—which use the term to worry that husband, wife, or both will feel a uniquely powerful remorse about their union and its effect on their own and their partner's salvation. In these depictions the repented marriage is not simply parodic; it assumes the shape of a mistake or even sin which its participants wish ideally to rectify.

The problem of the repented marriage hinges on a hallmark of early modern marital theory, a precept inherited from a long line of medieval theology and canon law: that the necessary ground of a valid marriage is the mutual consent of the partners.[36] Developed "primarily to ensure freedom from positive compulsion," this priority, when it led to clandestine contracts or secret solemnizations, presented legal as well as moral confusions and uncertainties; these uncertainties are the subject of legal proceedings and spiritual sermonizing in the period as well as its popular literature.[37] But theologians and moralists as well as the weight of popular custom maintained the conviction that the "marriage bond was to be formed by a free consensual union between two parties."[38] "Wedlocke is a lawefull knotte and unto God an acceptable yokinge together of one man and one womanne with the good consente of them both, to the intent that the two maye dwell together in frendeshype & honesty," Bullinger insisted in the first half of the sixteenth century.[39] At that century's end Convocation "reasserted the traditional principle that 'consent in marriage is the matter specially to be regarded, and credit of kindred, honour, wealth, contentment and pleasure of friends be rather matters of conveniency than necessity in matrimony.'"[40] The transparency of such "free consent" was, of course, mitigated by external and internalized social pressures—economic conditions, family and community expectations—as well as the unconscious drives which govern romantic attraction and marital interest.[41] But constraining complications seem only to have fueled reminders that the agreement of the marrying partners was a governing condition of marital harmony.

Mutual consent implies knowing assessment, deliberate choice, willed agreement. A range of early modern commentators, as David Cressy points out, "observed that the selection of a marriage partner was one of the most important decisions in life."[42] But their writings make clear that, even as they invite this active agency, they also fear the way that it opens up for bride and groom the possibility of later regret and remorse. Thus their focus—often with a predictably masculinist emphasis—on the careful selection of a mate as a means to avoid future compunction. Edmund Tilney, for instance, encourages a slow, steady courtship since "hastie love is soone gone. And some have loved in post hast, that afterwards have *repented* them at leysure."[43] Robert Cleaver, in his massively popular *Godly Forme of Household Government*, warns that much care must be taken—by bride and groom as well as their parents or friends—in selecting a mate, "least afterwards with much griefe and sorrow of heart, he doe too late *repent*."[44] Henry Smith, a champion of the benefits of marriage, still prefers the single life to a misguided decision based on superficial liking: "Choose whom thou maist enjoy," he warns, "or live alone still, and thou shalt not *repent* thy bargaine."[45] In his long exegesis of the Book of Ruth (another frequent proof text on marriage), clergyman Richard Bernard reminded his readers that "nothing . . . so much concern[s] the welfare, or downefall of man in this life" as marriage. Looks, wealth, status, and sexual desire should thus be discounted when entering into wedlock, for "these, and such like, make hastie matches, at leasure *to be repented of.*"[46] And John Bodenham's commonplace collection *Politeuphuia* warns that "in the choosing of a wyfe," the husband should find a woman who is not only beautiful but also virtuous and wise: "So shalt thou have neither *cause to repent*, nor occasion to mislyke thy choyce."[47] For Bullinger, the threat of a bad choice (seen as the fault of greedy parents rather than foolish children) assumes tragic proportions, for when parents marry off their children for money, the "whole house is fylled full of those tragedies even unto the toppe."[48] Tragedy, in other words, is the genre of the *repented* marriage in addition to the enforced one.[49]

The repented marriage becomes its own scourge, a mistake whose consequences serve as a form of painful, futile expiation. Thomas Gataker explains this rhythm on the model of Eve and Adam: "So he that gave man a wife at the first immediately, doth still give men wives by meanes, good ones in mercy, evill ones in wrath; the one for solace and comfort, the other for tryall, cure, correction, or punishment."[50] Richard Heale, who takes a uniquely sympathetic approach to women and wives, nevertheless describes marriage as "that state which either imparadizeth a man in the Eden of felicitie, or els exposeth him unto a world of miserie."[51] Although these tracts emphasize the unfortunate husband, such a "world of miserie" was also the fate of the long-suffering wife, who was told that "howsoever their husbands may deale roughly and untowardly with them, yet God will graciously respect them, if they shall patiently in obedience to his ordinance beare their husbands unjust reproofs."[52] Gouge does not specify the gender of suffering in the wake of a misbegotten choice: "Many by their preposterous and undue performing of so weightie a matter, doe not only cause great trouble and disquietnesse on the mariage day, but also much sorrow all the daies of their life."[53] So in the proverbial terms employed by *Much Ado about Nothing*'s simultaneously jaded and romantic Beatrice, marriage is for men and women the focus of fatal regret:

> For, hear me, Hero: *wooing, wedding, and repenting*, is as a Scotch jig, a measure, and a cinque pace: the first suit is hot and hasty, like a Scotch jig, and full as fantastical; the wedding, mannerly-modest, as a measure, full of state and ancientry; and then comes repentance and, with his bad legs, falls into the cinque pace faster and faster, till he sink into his grave.[54]

Wooing, wedding, and repenting: as Beatrice's dance-of-death metaphor implies, the repented marriage mocks the biblical injunction to "increase and multiply" as it races faster and faster towards death.[55] For what gets intensified and repeated in the repented marriage is precisely what marriage is supposed to redeem: a post-lapsarian condition of sin and misery. As an institution built on the demand for adequation and increase, marriage in the Reformed tradition opens onto the various crises of "making enough" we have been charting. But as an object of penitence, the repented marriage more specifically smuggles the theological problem of penitential satisfaction into the domestic world of husband and wife. Spouses repent their marriage, and the repented marriage becomes its own kind of sorrowful—but inefficacious—suffering. Put another way, the repented marriage in early Reformation England collapses into itself two desacramentalized sacraments, penance and matrimony, so that the production of conjugal "more" is devoid of satisfaction: of both consolation and of end.

The singular symptom of this painful process is jealousy, an emotion well understood during the period to be unquenchable, the experience of "hot love turn[ing] to burning coles, proving such fondnesse as wee suspecte our owne shadowes."[56] But all aspects of the repented marriage become bitter reminders of the loss of satisfaction. Looking at their espousal in retrospect, then, the regretful couple might see their wedding day as "igno-minious and reprochfull, as if it were the day of ones publique penance or execution."[57] Only the penance and execution is never complete.

Convincing Othello that this formula represents his experience—that his wedding day was really the start of his and Desdemona's public penance and execution for their choice and consent—lies at the heart of Iago's sadis-tic agenda.[58] In his capacious work on *Othello*, Daniel Vitkus describes the play as a sequence of conversions that depend upon the early modern con-flation of religious and sexual change: "The transformation of Othello, the moor of Venice, from a virtuous lover and Christian soldier to an enraged murderer may be read in the context of early modern conversion, or 'turn-ing,' with particular attention to the sense of conversion as sensual, sexual transgression."[59] I want to suggest that, alongside the conversions which Vit-kus charts so thoroughly (Christian to Turk, lover to tyrant, saved to damned), we place the transformation of the redemptive, satisfying marriage into the repented, unsatisfying—and ultimately murderous—one.

"Why did I marry!": Othello and the Repented Marriage

Defending his formerly secret marriage in the public space of the Venetian senate, the protagonist describes a special circuit of suffering and reward as the basis of his courtship with Desdemona. He

> Took once a pliant hour, and found good means
> To draw from her a prayer of earnest heart
> That I would all my pilgrimage dilate
> . . . .
> I did consent,
> And often did beguile her of her tears
> When I did speak of some distressful stroke
> That my youth suffered.[60]

The description, which culminates in Othello's "My story being done, / She gave me for my pains a world of kisses," traces a deeply idealized por-trait of marital satisfaction, an erotic *and* redemptive exchange according to which he makes enough for his wife, whose love or pity is the return on the "vices of my blood" and the "disastrous chances" of his life.[61] Such an expansive sense of the relationship is set against a strictly sexual, but at the same time "permissible," gratification when he defends Desdemona's accompaniment of him to Cyprus as a gesture not "to comply with heat— the young affects / In me defunct—and proper satisfaction / But to be free and bounteous to her mind" (1.3.260–4).[62] The liberality which Othello proposes echoes the prescriptions of marital treatises which, as we have seen, prescribed the "gain [of] a larger increase" as the register of marital satisfaction.[63]

Othello also traces for his audience an idealized portrait of mutual consent and choice. Indeed, "consent" is the word he uses to name his response to Desdemona, whose request for a story he himself has solicited. Her request points to the centrality of female agency in the depiction of consent: she asks for Othello's narrative, she "inclines" to listen to him, she gives him kisses. Shakespeare takes pains to emphasize this mutual agency even beyond Othello's description of it: Brabantio's loud objections that his daughter "is abus'd, stol'n from me, and corrupted / By spells and medicines bought of mountebanks" only provide opportunities for Desdemona as well as Othello to explain her willfulness (1.3.60–1). She does so when she tells her father, in her elaborate analogy, that she prefers her new husband to her father as her mother preferred Brabantio to hers: "So much I challenge that I may profess / Due to the Moor, my lord" (1.3.187–8). And she does so with even more force when she explains her desire to travel with Othello to Cyprus: "That I [did] love the Moor to live with him / My downright violence, and storm of fortunes, / May trumpet to the world" (1.3.248–50).

Desdemona continues to trumpet this conviction during her reunion with Othello on Cyprus. When Othello cannot imagine an increase in marital joy beyond the "content" of their meeting—"If it were now to die, / 'Twere now to be most happy; for I fear / My soul hath her content so absolute / That not another like to this / Succeeds in unknown fate"— Desdemona rebukes the death wish, pleading that "our loves and comforts should increase / Even as our days do grow" (2.1.187–91, 191–2). Her response echoes orthodox injunctions that husbands and wives should "heapeth and encreaseth love matrymoniall."[64] As a range of the play's critics have shown, this conventional demand opens onto the "full contradictoriness" of early modern marital ideology.[65] Part of the contradictoriness lies in the paradoxical logic of conjugal satisfaction itself, as its implicit anticipation of more produces a "deep current of sexual anxiety in Othello."[66] But for Othello, the more pressing concern lies in the paradoxical logic of marital consent. The issue is not primarily that the agency implied in Desdemona's agreement challenges or undermines the expectation of wifely submission to patriarchal authority. Rather it is that in her explicit choice of her partner, concretized in the secrecy of their espousal, Desdemona raises the specter that she might eventually rue her choice. The play itself announces the dilemma; as Brabantio warns Othello, "look to her Moor, if thou hast eyes to see, / She has deceiv'd her father, and may thee" (1.3.292–3). According to Brabantio, Othello should fear Desdemona's choice of him because it serves as an explicit precedent for a subsequent betrayal. But the implicit yet palpable threat—the threat that paves the way for adultery—is the possibility that she might regret or repent that choice. The production of this possibility is Iago's special handiwork.

Iago has been conjuring this idea from the play's start. Trying to soothe Roderigo, for instance, he imagines in the crudest of terms both Othello and Desdemona ruing their choices: "It cannot be long that Desdemona should continue her love to the Moor . . . nor he his to her . . . . The food that to him now is as luscious as locusts, shall be to him shortly as [acerb] as [the] coloquintida. She must change for youth; when she is sated with his body, she will find the [error] of her choice" (1.3.341–51). He repeats this model of grotesque satiation for Othello, capitalizing on orthodox emphases of the importance of parity in marriage—sameness of degree, age, religion, and now "complexion"—in order to spark Othello's concern precisely about Desdemona's choice and her capacity to regret it:

> Not to affect many proposed matches
> Of her own clime, complexion, and degree,
> Whereto we see in all things nature tends—
> Foh, one may smell in such, a will most rank,
> Foul disproportions, thoughts unnatural.
> But (pardon me) I do not in position
> Distinctly speak of her, though I may fear
> Her will, recoiling to her better judgment,
> May fall to match you with her country forms,
> And *happily repent*.
>
> 3.3.229–38

Iago introduces the prospect of Desdemona's regret for the marriage by stressing the full dimensions and potential of Desdemona's consent to Othello, the romanticized version of which dominated the first act. As Iago reminds Othello, Desdemona not only chose Othello, she also rejected others, the "proposed matches / Of her own clime." Iago clearly exploits the couple's racial difference and age disparity—he "carefully nurtures in Othello [a sense] of his own marriage as an adulterous transgression"—while emphasizing Desdemona's own willfulness.[67] But the real fear that Iago precipitates is the prospect that Desdemona has come to repent her partner precisely because she chose him. "For she had eyes, and chose me," Othello recognizes (3.3.189). Both Katherine Eisaman Maus and Stanley Cavell have written eloquently of Othello's epistemological as well as erotic predicament here, as the intensity of the marriage relation forces him to recognize in his wife a "simultaneously privileged and elusive" inwardness to which he has no access.[68] Intolerable to Othello about this inwardness is that, insofar as it enables Desdemona's choice to marry him, it also provides the space in which she can be sorry for it. For Othello such remorse is the logical middle term that bridges Desdemona's decision to marry him and her choice of another instead.

Othello thus enters an extraordinarily painful spiral in which he repents their wedlock even as he imagines Desdemona is already doing so herself. His own remorse will include explicit regret for his initial procedures of wooing: "Did Michael Cassio, when you wooed my lady, know of your love?" Iago inquires, reminding Othello of the erotic triangulation at the core of his marriage, which was customarily understood as a precursor to infidelity (3.3.94–5).[69] And it will culminate in an overt rejection of the enterprise of his marriage itself: "Why did I marry?" (3.3.242).

But the governing expression of Othello's marital repentance is his jealousy. Associated with the period's intensifying concerns about private ownership of land, goods, and knowledge,[70] for Othello the conventional mistrust and anxiety of the husband is an apt perversion of the redemptive impulses of marriage. Jealousy performs the emotional arithmetic that links regret for one choice to the pursuit of an alternative. It then turns marriage into a form of punishment for love itself: "As no sweetnesse, no pleasure, no happinesse, are so delightfull, so pleasant, nor so much desired, as that which proceedeth from Love; even so againe, those bitter pils, those untollerable Griefes, and those disastrous . . . Mischiefes . . . exceede (beyond all com-

parison,) all other Torments, and Tortures."[71] Jealousy translates Othello's
fear of marital alienation into self-laceration: "If I do prove her haggard, /
Though that her jesses were my dear heart strings, / I'ld whistle her off, and let
her down the wind / To prey at fortune" (3.3.260–3, italics mine). It turns
his marriage into the period's most commonplace of punitive diseases, plague:
"Yet 'tis the plague [of] great ones, / Prerogativ'd are they less than the base;
/ 'Tis destiny unshunnable, like death. / Even then this forked plague is
fated to us / When we do quicken" (3.3.273–7). And it manufactures for
Othello an experience of compunction akin, he tells Iago, to being "set on
the rack":

> What sense had I in her stol'n hours of lust?
> I saw't not, thought it not; it harm'd not me.
> I slept the next night well, fed well, was free and merry;
> I found not Cassio's kisses on her lips.
> He that is robb'd, not wanting what is stol'n,
> Let him not know't, and he's not robb'd at all.
>
> 3.3.338–43

Othello thus describes the way in which repenting his marriage—and imagining Desdemona repenting as well—takes shape as jealousy, a form of
punitive suffering that offers a deeply contorted image of fruitful marital
increase. "This strange maladie," warns Varchi, "engendreth a continuall
and perpetuall discontentment and disquietnesse in the minde"; it "encreaseth continually to the greater discontent of his minde."[72] If marriage is meant
to augment content, jealousy accelerates discontent, producing and repro-
ducing more pain. It is suffering devoid of the promise of satisfaction. As the
purest expression of the repented marriage, it marks the place where the
impossibility of enough in wedlock and enough in atonement converge.

Othello's famous valediction registers this impossibility as sheer loss, literally bidding good-bye to satisfaction as a feature of domestic and military
life. "O now, for ever / Farewell the tranquil mind! farewell content! / Farewell the plumed troops and the big wars / That makes ambition virtue! O
farewell!" (3.3.347–50). The speech's crescendo, when Othello announces res-
onantly that his "occupation's gone," records his related conviction that he
cannot do enough for Desdemona, and now for himself, materially, spiritually, and sexually.[73] He thus turns to Iago to protest both his suffering and

its inefficacy: "If there be cords, or knives, / Poison, or fire, or suffocating streams, / I'll not endure it: *would I were satisfied!*" (3.3.388–90, italics mine).

Othello's subjunctive and passive construction belies the real thrust of his speech: that "satisfaction" has been removed from his world as something he can accomplish or possess. Iago manipulates this mood to invent scenes of bestial sexuality that repeat the visions he once conjured for Brabantio ("Even now, now, very now, an old black ram / Is tupping your white ewe" [1.1.88–9]). Here as there, they exacerbate the hearer's sense of his own dissatisfaction:

> You would be satisfied.
> .   .   .   .
> And may, but how, how satisfied, my lord?
> Would you, the supervisor, grossly gape on,
> Behold her topp'd?
> .   .   .   .   .   .
> It is impossible you should see this,
> Were they as prime as goats, as hot as monkeys,
> As salt as wolves, in pride; and fools as gross
> As ignorance made drunk: but yet I say,
> If imputation and strong circumstances,
> Which lead directly to the door of truth,
> Will give you satisfaction, you may ha't.
>
> 3.3.393–408

In the play's opening scene, Roderigo, following Iago's lead, had told Brabantio to "straight satisfy yourself" of Desdemona's elopement by searching his house for her (1.1.137). Her absence is precisely the satisfactory proof Roderigo had anticipated, but it is deeply unsatisfying for Brabantio, as it announces the escape of his daughter, a blow to his sense of patriarchal plenty and control. Iago rehearses this same stratagem, realizing precisely what Othello's demand—"would I were satisfied!"—had tried to forestall. Iago pretends to hear in Othello's plangent lament simply the desire for empirical evidence. But the "ocular proof" that Othello demands, and which Iago so easily conjures into being in his whispered conversation with Cassio, only supplies for the protagonist the horrifying image of his own insufficient as well as hypertrophied desires. Iago exploits the inherent paradoxes of marital satisfaction to force Othello to recognize that "enough" is unavailable for him to make or do for his partner or himself. In so doing he distills the idea of *"satis"* purely to a matter of erotic capacity. He disentangles the multiple valences of marital satisfaction—legal, economic, affective, erotic, penitential, even sacramental—and reduces them to the evidentiary and orgasmic.

A rich critical tradition has adopted this perspective to explain Othello's crisis as the internalization of ideologies of female chastity and marital sexuality meant to "legitimate" sexual desire "within the bounds of propriety and orthodoxy."[74] Thus critics such as Stephen Greenblatt, Arthur Kirsch, and Edward Snow have suggested that Desdemona's paradoxically outspoken submissiveness triggers in Othello a heightened sense of his own adulterous sexual guilt—a "disgust with sexuality itself"—which in turn he projects onto his wife.[75] More recently Mark Breitenberg has explained Othello's jealousy as the product of an anxiety bred by various early modern beliefs about the proper ordering of the Protestant couple, particularly the necessity of female orgasm for conception. As he summarizes, "the husband was expected to give his wife enough satisfaction to avoid her being obliged to go elsewhere, but not to arouse her so much as to provoke extra-marital sex—a recipe for masculine anxiety if ever there was one."[76]

Such accounts are sensitive to the vexed standards embedded in the term "satisfaction" to describe the real and fantasized fulfillments of Othello's and Desdemona's sexual desire. They exploit the tremulous, even oppositional possibilities couched in the concept of "making enough"—achieving perfect fitness, supplying or wanting more—to explain the psychic joys, fears, and guilts of erotic activity. Stanley Cavell, in his reading of the play, has gone so far as to cast the puzzlements of the heterosexual encounter as the exemplary form of philosophical doubt ("the existence or occurrence of the woman's satisfaction . . . [is] the essential object or event of the skeptical question: Is she satisfied and is the satisfaction directed to me?").[77] They do not, however, recognize the profound confluence between the possibilities of sexual and penitential satisfaction. But in the history of making as well as having enough the two are inextricable.

That history, as we have charted, is oriented by the Reformed rejection of satisfying God for sin. And that rejection, *Othello* shows us, seeps into the terms and structures of holy wedlock and its premise of redemptive mutuality. Desdemona need not be seen to take the place of God for Othello (or vice versa) to understand how this denial could trouble a marriage and its economies of exchange, particularly when lives have been staked on spousal faith.[78] Iago works all along to taunt Othello with this problem. His rhetorical mode for this program is the interrogatory, which activates not only Othello's desire to get more information but also his urge to provide it. "Why dost thou ask?" Othello responds to Iago's query about Cassio. "But for a *satisfaction* of my thought," Iago tells him, opening up an onslaught of more questions that inaugurate the protagonist's sense of inadequacy (3.3.97–8, italics mine). So although Greenblatt has described Iago as a mock confessor, "lead[ing] Othello through a brutally comic parody of the late medieval confessional manuals with their casuistical attempts to define the precise moment at which venial temptation passes over into mortal sin," his role seems more accurately that of a Reformed dogmatist, initiating his mortal audience into the realization that neither he nor marriage as an institution can ever make enough to compensate penitential or erotic demands.[79]

The Reformed dogmatist was expected, of course, to supplement that realization by reminding his readers or hearers that their actions, while not compensatory or efficacious, could nevertheless be understood as signs of election and salvation. This is not, of course, what Iago does.[80] Instead he works to redirect Othello's energies into less spiritual channels. These include the "marriage" to Iago, whose love he greets "not with vain thanks, but with acceptance bounteous," as though this were still a relationship in which he could do enough, and his pursuit of revenge, the signature enterprise of the pursuit of satisfaction (3.3.470). Othello vows that his "bloody thoughts, with violent pace / Shall ne'er look back, ne'er ebb to humble love, / Till that a capable and wide revenge / Swallow them up" (3.3.464–7).

The fury of Othello's imagination returns us, of course, to the terrible irony embedded in the structure of revenge, whose promise of restitution and equivalence can only be accomplished through amplified, excessive punishment and pain. Focused on Cassio, Othello's "bloody thoughts" overflow the bounds of human capacities: "Had all his hairs been lives," he says, "my great revenge / Had stomach for them all" (5.2.75–6). But his assaults on Desdemona—verbal and physical—are particularly disturbing, since their warrantlessness underscores the illusory lure of their promised fulfillments. Even Othello senses this when he fears his "sacrifice," the privileged model of satisfactory expiation, may really be a "murder." Like revenge, the sacrifice of Desdemona is meant to reestablish Othello in a world in which precise atonement and recuperation is possible. "Be thus when thou art dead," Othello announces, "and I will kill thee / And love thee after": he imagines that her death at his hands can actually restore both of them to the lives they once inhabited (5.2.18–19). But Othello's rites are muddled (his sacrificial victim doubles as the sacrificial subject of purification), and Desdemona's "resurrection"—her brief revival during which she reports to Emilia that she has slain herself—is a mocking reminder, in its almost parodic resistance to precision, of the impossibility of exact sacrificial compensation.

The most telling anagnorosis of the final scene, then, is Othello's recognition of his inability to make or have enough in multiple dimensions: "I am not valiant neither, / But every puny whipster gets my sword" (5.2.243–4). Whatever else he fails to comprehend at the end of the play,[81] he acknowledges both the insufficiency of his deeds and the overabundance of his sins. The first is explained to Gratiano, as Othello describes a former self who, making "my way through more impediments / Than twenty times your stop," was entirely commensurate with his calling. He contrasts this former Othello to the present one, whose sins defy all punishment. When he and Desdemona "shall meet at compt, / This look of thine will hurl my soul from heaven, / And fiends will snatch at it . . . . Whip me, ye devils, / From the possession of this heavenly sight! / Blow me about in winds! roast me in sulphur! / Wash me in steep-down gulfs of liquid fire!" (5.2.263–4, 273–80). The second vision is part of his final monologue, in which Othello traces his failures back to an inability to evaluate correctly between spiritual and secular goods as well as between truth and lies. He names this confusion his "perplexity," so that, "like the base Judean," he "threw a pearl away / Richer than all his tribe" (5.2.348–9).

This perplexity has been traced to Othello's ambiguous racial and religious status as the "Moor of Venice" for an audience who would have both seen him as a figure of "uncodified and uncodifiable diversity"and increasingly associated him with Islam.[82] Recent scholars have clarified the complicated early modern English investments in Moor, Turk, and Muslim, particularly as multivalent signifiers of religious schism in the wake of the Reformation; they have also examined the widespread English fear that the "Ottoman empire was continually expanding at the expense of Christian rulers."[83] They thus continue to diagnose an English perception of the racial and Islamic other as all things excessive: tyrannous, lascivious, legalistic, and incapable of assessing worldly (and thus illusory) versus spiritual (and thus

real) value. Such a perception marks even the period's marital texts. Andrew Willet's 1613 sermon celebrating the good Protestant marriage of
Princess Elizabeth and the Elector Palatine (the festivities for which
featured a performance of *Othello*) relied, for instance, on an implicit assumption that Moors and Turks are the negative image of the good English
husband: "The subjection of the wife must not be slavish, or servile, as the
Turkes and Moores at this day use their wives as their slaves, but it must be
sociable and amiable."[84] Their assessment rotates on an axis of essentialized
insatiability, and their assumptions, as Gail Paster points out, are tragically
internalized by Othello over the course of the play.[85] The thrust of this
chapter has been to suggest that Othello's absorption of such racial and religious stereotypes, insofar as they push him to repent for a marriage he
believes Desdemona to repent as well, operates under the pressure of contemporary Protestant revaluations of penitential efficacy. Othello's final recognition of himself as "a malignant and a turban'd Turk" depends upon his
inability to get and to make enough according to a Christian world order in
which marriage, repentance, and their sacramental satisfactions were being
revised and rejected. The play's eventual installment of the stereotype of the
insatiable Islamic other (including its inevitable pun on "more") measures in
full the effects of a Reformation rescripting of satisfaction that turns "enough"
into something too little, too much, and never available.

"Do you desire to satisfie?": *Love's Pilgrimage*

Another figure of racial and religious difference is conjured during *Othello*:
the "specter of Spain" that emerges in the characters of Iago and Roderigo.
Eric Griffin suggests that the portrayal of these characters contributes to a
"new, Hispanophobic intensity" on Shakespeare's part which aims to "de-
monize the spirit of Spanish Catholicism . . . as faithless 'workes.' "[86] I have
been suggesting that the seduction and betrayal of Othello depends upon
Iago's mastery of Reformed principles and their implications for ideas of
marital satisfaction; but such mastery does not preclude either Iago's connection with Spanish Catholicism or the kind of audience suspicions and
hostilities such a connection might raise.[87] Indeed, the play invites an
allegoresis according to which Iago's Catholicism drives his deliberate
manipulation—what Richard Mallette calls his blaspheming—of Protes-

tant doctrine to secure Othello's downfall.[88] In the figure of Iago, then, the specter of Spain in its most Hispanophobic form—as a Catholic power using Protestantism against itself—governs the tragic shape of *Othello*'s repented marriage.

But the early modern English stage did not treat Spain and its specters uniformly, particularly in matters of love and marriage. Vying with the negative presentation offered in *Othello* was a long history of English "cultural Hispanophilia" which continued through the sixteenth century despite the political and military hostilities of the Reformation and Armada and which was refreshed after the peace treaty of 1604.[89] Spanish sources supplied the English literary and theatrical imagination with models of chivalric, picaresque, Byzantine, and pastoral romance, and English writers capitalized on these sources with a sense of "admiration, tinged with envy."[90] This is the tradition on which Beaumont and Fletcher rely for their *Love's Pilgrimage*, dated to 1614–15 but not published until the 1647 folio, which likely includes revisions from the 1630s.[91] A close retelling of a typically ironic novella from Cervantes's *Novelas Ejemplares* (1613), its specifically Spanish context allows the dramatists to draw on the fantasied specter as well as the real space of Spain to exploit the language of marital and penitential satisfaction in critical, parodic, and nostalgic ways.

The drama revolves around the romantic pursuit by two noble damsels, Theodosia and Leocadia, of the handsome but caddish Mark-antonio, who has wooed and proposed to—and been accepted by—both. The women are each disguised as men in order to travel unmolested across Spain (and in order to indulge the kinds of homoerotic and incestuous energies enabled by cross-dressing).[92] In the first act of the play, the fragile Theodosia (disguised as a young man, Theodoro) is discovered at an inn in Seville by her brother, Philippo, who joins the search for Mark-antonio. On their way to Barcelona, where Mark-antonio is headed in order to ship for Genoa, they encounter the cross-dressed Leocadia, whom they invite to travel with them and whom they discover is also in pursuit of Mark-antonio. When they find Mark-antonio in Barcelona he is engaged in a violent skirmish with port city locals; wounded and taken to the governor's home, he becomes contrite only after using his injury to fondle the breasts of the governor's wife. But fearful of his impending death, of which Leocadia has falsely convinced him, he offers a kind of confession:

> Oh heavens, an hour?
> Alas, it is too little to remember
> But half the wrongs that I have done; how short
> Then for contrition, and how least of all
> *For satisfaction?*[93]

To which the aggrieved Leocadia, who hopes to reunite with him, replies: "But you desire *to satisfie?*" (4.1.143, italics mine).

Mark-Antonio's sudden concern with penitential satisfaction, only moments after trying to seduce a third, married woman into an adulterous affair, is clearly the object of religious parody. So too is Leocadia's quick rejoinder—"But you desire to satisfie?"—by which the playwrights gleefully seize on the linguistic connection between the man's spiritual atonement and the woman's erotic gratification to emphasize Leocadia's emotional desperation. The deliberate irony here resembles the various kinds of polemical satire aimed at what Protestants considered the superficiality of the three stages of Catholic penance, including both the sensuality of the confessional and the superfluity of atoning works. In Leocadia's repetition of the word to express her own desire for marriage and sex, the playwrights seal their mockery of satisfaction as the recuperative premise or romantic goal of wedlock.

But the resonant punning, which continues to inform the scene, testifies to a lingering fascination with—and not just contempt or condescension for—the possibility of satisfaction in penitential and marital economies. This fascination is best observed in the most significant change made by the play to the Cervantine original: it keeps both heroines out of Mark-antonio's bed. Cervantes's "The Two Damsels" does not feature explicit scenes of lovemaking, but the logic of the novella's conclusion—in which Mark-antonio chooses Theodosia over Leocadia—depends upon the fact that former, and not the latter, has actually slept with him. As Theodosia reveals near the start of the novella, she was so smitten by Mark-antonio that, in Mabbe's 1640 translation (the first into English), his

> every word, was a Canon shot which did batter down a part of the Forte of
> mine honour; every scalding teare, was a flaming fire wherein my honesty
> was scorched and burnt; every sigh, a furious wind which did in such sort
> augment the flame, that it came to consume that vertue which untill then

had beene never touched; and lastly, having plighted his faith and truth to me to bee my husband . . . scarse had he taken of me *the possession of that which hee so much desired*, but that within two dayes after he disappeared and was gone.[94]

Given that it followed the plighting of their troth, such a consummation—as Cervantes's and Beaumont and Fletcher's audience surely knew—would constitute, at least according to "powerful cultural currents," a confirmation of their union.[95]

This is *not* the situation of Beaumont and Fletcher's Theodosia. The playwrights are at pains to demonstrate that their heroine has not allowed her Mark-antonio what Cervantes's leading lady has surrendered to him: "The obtaining of that fruit, which shee could give" (G1v). Rather, Theodosia, rehearsing her woes to her brother, discloses the complicated state of her commitment to Mark-antonio, which includes gifts and oaths but decidedly not sex or solemnization. As she tells him, they were "contracted, sir, and by exchange of rings / Our souls deliver'd: *nothing left unfinish'd / But the last work, enjoying me*, and Ceremony" (1.2.84–6, my italics). When she apologizes a few moments later to Philippo, he readily forgives her, explaining that he bears "no anger / While your fair chastity is yet untouch'd" (1.2.145–6).

The preservation of Theodosia's virginity allows her to remain what Nancy Pearse identified some years ago as a Fletcherian "mirror figure": the desirous but chaste heroine, whose passionate plight the audience is meant to understand sympathetically.[96] But it also ensures two additional things: one, that the legality and ethics of her nuptials with Mark-antonio remain ambiguous, contestable; and two, that the pro-spect—rather than the re-spect—of a wished-for consummation will govern the shape of the play. The dramatic dynamism of the situation, which speaks to the period's many concerns about the protocols of courtship and contract, is reinforced in the central, suspenseful scene between the two women. Theodosia, still dressed as a man, senses that the disguised Leocadia might really be female; she entices Leocadia to admit her gender and then to give an account of her misfortunes. These include, much to Theodosia's surprise, a relationship with Mark-antonio. As Leocadia reveals, "we grew acquainted, and from that acquaintance / Neerer into affection" until eventually "this neerness / Made him importunate; When to save mine honor, / Love having ful possession of my powers, / I got a Contract from him" (3.2.76–7, 85–8). She then admits that she "pointed him a by-way to my chamber / The next night at an hour" (3.2.93–4).

The conversation then becomes a frenzied effort on Theodosia's part to establish the status of this contract—in other words, to establish whether or not Mark-antonio and Leocadia have had sex:

> And when the night came, came he, kept he touch with ye?
> Be not so shamefast; had ye both your wishes?
> Tell me, and tell me true, did he injoy ye,
> Were ye in one anothers arms, abed? The contract
> Confirm'd in ful joys there? Did he lie with ye?
> . . . .
> Did that nights promise
> Make ye a Mother?
>
> 3.2.95–103

To which a confused Leocadia, shocked by the barrage of intimate questions, protests, "alas he never came nor never meant it" (3.2.109). Then Leocadia admits to her own fears: that Mark-antonio has run away with the beautiful Theodosia. "They are together, love together, / Past all deceipt of that side; sleep together, / Live, and delight together" (3.2.155–7).

A version of this scene features in Cervantes's model. But its stakes for the two works are entirely different. In "The Two Damsells," the conversation confirms for Theodosia her sexual distinction from Leocadia and thus her marital priority with Mark-antonio. In *Love's Pilgrimage*, it accentuates their similarity: both are virgins, and both seek marriage with the same man. More precisely, both seek consummation with—satisfaction from— the same man in order to fulfill and legitimate their conjugal contracts. And insofar as the play sponsors the women's world view, it endorses the *appeal*, and not simply the parody, of this satisfaction.

It also makes clear that in its absence, the women will become prey to sharp jealousies. Leocadia's envy is expressed in verbal attacks on Theodosia, whom she is "bound to ban for ever, curse to wrinckles . . . and aches" (3.2.127–8). Theodosia, still disguised as Theodoro, laments privately that, in helping Leocadia, she "nourish[es] a wolfe to eat my heart out . . . . O noble love, / That thou couldst be without this jealousie, / Without this passion of the heart, how heavenly / Would thou appear upon us?" (3.2.277,

289–92). Unlike Othello, however, their jealousies are not attached to repented marriages: the women, in hot pursuit of Mark-antonio, have no regrets about what they have done or about Mark-antonio as a desirable love object. Instead they are plagued by more proleptic fears: of marital satisfaction postponed or unconfirmed. Assuaging those fears depends on Mark-antonio's—not their own—penitence.

Any kind of remorse or repentance seems unlikely from Mark-antonio, the play's committed rogue. On his way to Barcelona, he boasts that he favors "variety" over steadfast love; in Barcelona, he tries, against custom, to peek under the veil of Eugenia, the governor's wife; in the governor's house, having been wounded, he pretends that he wants to speak alone to Eugenia of things that "sit heavy on my conscience" in order to seduce her. His ploy deliberately mocks penitential procedure: he laughs to think that while the other characters imagine him to be with "my ghostly Mother / To hear my sad confession" he will really be romping with Eugenia "on that bed within" (4.3.79–81). But Leocadia, still disguised as a gentleman, is convinced that she can "make him / Shew himself truly sorrowful" to Eugenia and the others (4.3.112–3).

Thus the exchange we have seen above between Leocadia and Mark-antonio, in which she persuades him that he is about to die. Having thus pricked his conscience so that he now "desire[s] to satisfy," she removes her disguise to reveal her identity to him and to insist that he sleep with her, even at the hour of his death:

> It is within your power
> *To give me satisfaction*; you have time
> Left in this little peece of life to do it:
> Therefore I charge you for your conscience sake,
> And for our fame, which I would fain have live
> When both of us are dead, to celebrate
> That Contract, which you have both seal'd and sworn,
> Yet ere you dye.
>
> > 4.1.150–7, italics mine.

Mark-antonio apologizes to all those gathered around him, including the still disguised Theodosia and her brother, and confirms Leocadia's honesty. But he insists that he cannot marry her:

> 'Tis impossible to satisfie
> *You* Leocadia, *but by repentance,*
> Though I can dyingly, and boldly say
> I know not your dishonor, yet that was
> Your vertue, and not mine, you know it wel;
> But herein lies th'impossibility,
> O *Theodosia, Theodosia*, I was betroth'd to *Theodosia*
> Before I ever saw thee; heaven forgive me,
> She is my wife this half hour while I live.
>
> 4.1.174–82, first italics mine

Mark-antonio may have jested with the terms of penance earlier, but he now displays theological seriousness as well as semantic sensitivity. He recognizes that Leocadia has conflated his penitential satisfaction with her marital and sexual one. And he moves quickly to separate them. As he says, he can give one to Leocadia but not the other.

He can give both to Theodosia, however. Renouncing both his earlier irreligion as well as his caddishness, he associates his ability to love only Theodosia with his ability to repent:

> When I make jests of oathes again, or make
> My lust play with religion, when I leave
> To keep true joyes for her, and yet within
> My self true sorrow for my passed deeds,
> May I want grace, when I would fain repent,
> And find a great and sodain punishment.
>
> 4.3.215–20

Mark-antonio's sudden conversion to a kind of spiritual as well as conjugal champion resembles Beaumont and Fletcher's characterology more generally: they delight in spectacular, seemingly arbitrary changes that sacrifice psychological consistency for emotional effect.[97] And though there is an essential element of parody here, the unexpected conversion need not undermine the authenticity of Mark-antonio's penitence or the authenticity of the Catholic penitence he represents.[98] Instead the scene, in its rewarding of the grateful Theodosia, seems to endorse or indulge in what Mark-antonio implies: that satisfaction is something he can do or make in both conjugal and penitential realms.

Theodosia now rejoices while Leocadia runs off in despair. She is eventually stopped by Theodosia's brother Philippo, who with ardent as well as extraordinarily technical pleading about the nature of marital pre-contracts, argues with a disconcerting intensity that she should love and marry him instead. She agrees, however reluctantly, and after a few unexpected delays and interruptions, including a threatened duel between Philippo and Markantonio, they pair off peacefully under their fathers' approving eyes.

In Cervantes's version, the story ends with the couples going off on pilgrimage to Santiago de Compostela. Beaumont and Fletcher leave out this ending, but indeed the entire play, which has crisscrossed Spain from southwest to southeast, has already *been* a pilgrimage, the "erotic penance" associated with the shape of the prose romance.[99] As we know from the body of their work, this generic shape—as well as its ironic double in the picaresque—had vast appeal to Beaumont and Fletcher, particularly in the genre's Spanish incarnations.[100] Critics have offered compelling accounts of the playwrights' interest in Iberian authors, particularly their attraction to what Trudi Darby and Alexander Samson call Cervantes's "ironic refashioning of romance" as well as his "oppositional politics." They suggest "Cervantine ambivalence to Spanish imperial and colonial aspirations . . . probably found a counterpart in Fletcher's political hostility to Spain, opposition to the royal policy of rapprochement, anxieties about the colonial process, and exploration of political alternatives to Jacobean absolutism."[101] Gordon McMullan explains that Fletcher, like Beaumont in *Knight of the Burning Pestle* (1607), was attracted to the "self-consciousness and anti-romance" of Cervantes's stories, a "correlative to his own generic experiments on the stage."[102]

But the extensive punning on satisfaction at the end of act 4's climactic scene suggests fresh reasons for the appeal. That is, the possibility of satisfaction—as mutually reinforcing erotic and theological goal—may offer a *doctrinal* explanation for the "ambivalent Hispanophilia" the playwrights shared with a wide English audience.[103] There is no need to label Beaumont's or Fletcher's own confessional status (Beaumont came from a family of recusants, Fletcher's father was once Bishop of London),[104] in order to see them taking up their source in a manner that some travelers to Spain did: with the "desire to live according to the overwhelming custom of the countr[y] where they founds themselves."[105] Cervantes's story licenses the playwrights to design a drama in which marriage and repentance are still sacraments and to reinforce satisfaction as a marital as well as penitential possibility—rather than, as in *Othello*, to treat it as a forsaken objective whose loss is central to the tragedy. As I have noted, there is a parodic timbre to the engagement: certainly a joke is being had at the expense of the Catholic ritual. But the delight that the playwrights take in manipulating the term suggests a sympathy and attraction to this technical feature of penance.

This sympathy has been generated by Beaumont and Fletcher's nostalgia, a sensibility that marks their unique place in the history of satisfaction that we have been tracing. That is, their particular enthusiasm for the confluence of penitential and marital *satis* derives from a basic acknowledgment that it has been, for their world, fundamentally dismantled. The Protestant theology of repentance stands behind that dismantling, and its prooftext is *Othello*. If satisfaction "exists precisely as 'impossible,'" Beaumont and Fletcher are able to reconstruct or resuscitate it in the Spanish setting of *Love's Pilgrimage* only because Shakespeare had already shown it to be so thoroughly lost.

Postscript

Where's the Stage at the End of Satisfaction?

This book began with a discussion of a distinct Reformation doctrinal change; it then traced the significance of this change as it was intuited by and fashioned for the early modern stage. It has thus been concerned largely with dramatic content, with the ways in which the theater *represented* to its audience an early modern problem of satisfaction.

But the stage also *presented* this problem, showing it to be an intrinsic element of theatrical performance and reception, a feature of theater-going.[1] How can we describe and then explain this particular instance of the the-ater's metadramatic function, and what does it suggest about the place of the stage at the end of satisfaction?

The provisional answers I offer here hinge on the highly overdetermined relationship between Renaissance drama, repentance, and satisfaction. As a business enterprise, the theater, like the systems of revenge, credit, and mar-riage we have studied, was poised upon a notion of compensatory exchange: the new and thrilling premise of the Elizabethan and Jacobean commercial stage was that patrons paid to see gratifying entertainment. This theatrical exchange shared the signature quality we have observed in other matters of satisfaction: it straddled the boundaries of enough and more, of contentment and demand. Indeed, as Susan Cerasano has eloquently written, the professional theater depended upon the ambiguity of *satis* in order to "make money. In order for a spectator to enjoy a performance, he or she had to pay for admittance to see the play; and because of the evanescent nature of the performance, the spectator was required to pay admission again if he or she wished to see either a different play or a repeat performance of the same play."[2] And Jeremy Lopez suggests that the spectator's enjoyment was bound up in theatrical excess, in the way early modern plays offered the audience a "surfeit of information."[3]

Given the theater's particular aesthetic and affective as well as business economy, then, it is not surprising that the enterprise absorbed and reproduced the period's pressures on the parameters of *satis*. We can hear this response in various theatrical and para-theatrical texts, from prologues and epilogues that try to orchestrate audience approval to antitheatrical texts tormented by the excesses not only of the plays themselves but of the entire operation of play-going. Henry Crosse's complaints about both a surfeit of contemporary plays and the class-defying extravagance of theater professionals are instructive in their rhetoric of increase:

> But if we oppose our quotidian interludes to them of former time, and consider the multitude of ours with the paucity and fewness of theirs, we shall see a great diversity as well in the method of writing, as in the time, place, and company: for now nothing is made so vulgar and common, as beastly and palpable folly; lust, under color of love, abstract rules artificially composed to carry the mind into sinful thoughts, with unclean locution and unchaste behavior.[4]

He similarly challenges the actors and dramatists who "grow rich, purchase lands by adulterous players . . . so are they puffed up in such pride and self-love as they envy their equals, and scorn their inferiors."[5]

I want to suggest that this kind of sensitivity to theatrical exchange and its threat of increase would have been exacerbated by the concrete, performative connections between the stage and repentance. One of these connections, promulgated by antitheatrical opponents of the stage, was that the theater was a source of sin and thus required repentance. As Stephen Gosson suggests in his *School of Abuse* (1579), "the abuses of poets, pipers, and players . . . bring us to pleasure, sloth, sleep, sin, and, *without repentance*, to death and the devil."[6] At the same time, various writers and commentators insisted that drama actually encouraged—rather than obliged—repentance. *A Warning for Fair Women*, a Chamberlain's Men's play from the close of the sixteenth century, offers a suggestive anecdote of this function when one of its characters recounts the way in which a woman who killed her husband responds to a play with a similar plot:

> A woman that had made away her husband
> And sitting to behold a tragedy
> At Linne a towne in Norfolke,
> Acted by Players travelling that way,
> Wherein a woman that had murtherd hers
> Was ever haunted with her husbands ghost:
> The passion written by a feeling pen,
> And acted by a good Tragedian,
> She was so moved with the sight thereof,
> As she cryed out, the Play was made by her,
> And openly confesst her husbands murder.[7]

This fabulously self-reflexive moment (the stage tells the story of another stage) promotes the relatively commonplace idea that the theater could provoke off-stage penitence. It also reinforces the idea that off-stage penitence could promote theater. Indeed, Elizabethan contemporaries, like recent critics, consistently recognized the theatricality of repentance: its dynamic, dialogic structure of guilt and confession as well as its dependence upon staging and audience for successful completion. This phenomenon looks back to the public exposure and punishments of the early church; for our period it was manifest in the non-sacramental, communal penances enforced by the ecclesiastical courts as well as in the public execution of felons approved by the state. These forms of public justice, both spiritual and secular, involved what Arthur Golding, best known as a translator of Ovid, aptly termed an "open Theater."[8] Spiritual courts—the "bawdy courts"—sentenced those in violation of sexual, devotional, or defamatory regulations to ritualized, exemplary shaming that echoed earlier forms of public penance and explicitly invoked the stages of confession and satisfaction.[9] The offender, dressed symbolically in a white sheet and carrying a white rod or taper, would stand at the parish church door during Sunday or holiday services until ushered inside for the sermon or homily, which would often be chosen to address his or her particular sin. At this point he or she might be required to make a confession in front of the gathered community.[10] Such confessions, meant both to humiliate the offender and warn the onlooker, were equally central to public executions, the violent punishment meted out to felons to "set the world to rights."[11] As Peter Lake explains, admissions of guilt and expressions of repentance were the focal points of juridical scenes directed at an on-site and then a print audience. These "last dying speeches" aimed to insure—and to assure witnesses of—"the salvation of prisoners' souls," but they answered other motives such as "bolster[ing] the cause of order and obedience in church and state."[12]

The theatricality of these penitential practices opens onto a host of epistemological and ontological quandaries about the motives and intentions of penitents as well as the ideological aims of the practice itself.[13] Indeed, scholars suggest, such uncertainties were exploited by offenders who chose to "ruin" the supposedly edifying goals of public repentance by displaying not sorrow but rather "despair or light-hearted defiance or unconcern."[14] Both Katherine Maus and Ramie Targoff have explored the ways in which the early modern stage incorporated both these practices and these quandaries, particularly those concerning the authenticity and efficacy of the movement between the penitent's "external practice and inward will."[15]

The stage also reproduced a set of quandaries specific to the theatricality of penitential *satisfaction*. As Martin Ingram suggests, public penance was "supposed to work for the health of the culprit's soul, to deter others and *to give satisfaction to the congregation* for the affront of public sin."[16] Protestant theology, as we have seen, had dispensed with the believer's satisfaction to God (and thus his or her own satisfaction as a result), but it had never abandoned the potential and importance of making satisfaction to others. Compensatory works made by the penitent to specific fellow humans were discussed by Reformers (as they had been for centuries) in the terminology of "restitution," which distinguished these works from those made to God. But when discussing the relation between a sinner and the neighborhood or community *in toto*, Reformers returned to the vocabulary of satisfaction. Thus records from Ely document a case in which a husband and wife who slept together before they were married "have *for and in satisfaction of* theire said offence given and paid into the hands of us the Churchwardens . . . to the use of the poore of our said parishe the full summe of sixe shillings and eight pence of good and lawfull monie of England."[17] F. E. Emmison records an instance in which the offending William Gyon of Coggeshall had "made competent penance *to the satisfaction* of the congregation in the presence of . . . one of the churchwardens."[18] In *A Warning for Fair Women*, a gentleman convicted of murder is told in his final moments *"to satisfie the world,* / and for a true and certaine testimonie, / of thy repentance for this deed committed . . . freely confesse what yet unto this houre, / against thy conscience . . . thou hast concealed."[19] Satisfaction, as restitution was recognized as something due unto—and to be experienced by—others.

The staging of repentance—that is, the staging of the *staginess* of repentance—makes clear that the satisfaction at stake in restitution is the satisfaction of the theater. The dramatic parlance for this satisfaction is pleasure; as numerous prologues and epilogues attest, the Horatian goal of the theater was to teach and delight, "to mix profit with your pleasure."[20] The prologue to *The Knight of the Burning Pestle*, famously disliked and rejected by its early audience, had nevertheless hoped to "move inward delight . . . and to breed (if it might be) soft smiling."[21] Shakespeare concludes *Twelfth Night* with the promise that "we'll strive to please you every day."[22] Some forty years later, just before the closing of the theaters at the start of the Civil War, Richard Brome articulated principles of audience approval based on decades of experience with the stage, regretting in his *Jovial Crew* (1641) that "jovial mirth is now grown out of fashion" and hoping that "dullness may make no man sleep, / Nor sadness . . . any woman weep."[23] But it is antitheatrical discourse, ironically, that provides us with a more precise vocabulary for the components and ideological dimensions of this pleasure, including imitation, moral recognition, aesthetic appreciation, and erotic seduction.[24] As Crosse lists, when exposed to plays "the ear is tickled with immodest speeches, the mind imprinted with wanton gesture, and the whole affections ravished with sinful pleasure."[25] Other antitheatrical tracts describe—in the process of criticizing, of course—the pleasures of vicarious violence and revenge the theater affords when it teaches "how to murder, how to poison, how to disobey and rebel against princes."[26]

If these are the satisfactions of the theater, then, public penance—repentance in an "open Theater"—shares them and offers them to its onlookers. John Parker makes a similar observation when he writes that "the historical crucifixion offered no less 'satisfaction' than if God had hung a

fine painting—or staged a tragedy."[27] For Parker the audience of this tragedy is—theologically, at least—the Creator himself, who is then associated
with the emotional and aesthetic investments that accrue to the mundane
spectator. My concern at the very end of this book is with that mundane
spectator: the early modern witness to both on- and off-stage penance who
stood at the receiving end of a penitential satisfaction disallowed by Protestant theology to God and the penitent but available to him or her. And that
satisfaction borders on the pleasures of a play. At the end of satisfaction,
then, the stage reminds us that it has preserved for its audiences what was
displaced, over the course of the Reformation, from the relation between
God and sinner.

NOTES

Introduction

1. William Shakespeare, *Othello*, in *The Riverside Shakespeare*, ed. G. Blakemore Evans, 2nd ed. (New York: Houghton Mifflin, 1997), 3.3.395–406.

2. See Katherine Maus, *Inwardness and Theater in the English Renaissance* (Chicago: University of Chicago Press, 1995), 104–27; Stanley Cavell, *Disowning Knowledge in Six Plays of Shakespeare* (Cambridge: Cambridge University Press, 1987), 125–42.

3. For a similar discussion about the dynamism of "moderation," and the difference between "late modern conceptions [that] tend to stress its passivity" and early modern understandings of moderation as "by definition *active*," see Ethan Shagan, *The Rule of Moderation: Violence, Religion and the Politics of Restraint in Early Modern England* (Cambridge: Cambridge University Press, 2011), 36.

4. Desire is that which, Catherine Belsey reminds us, "repeatedly seek[s] out impediments to satisfaction" (*Desire: Love Stories in Western Culture* [Oxford: Blackwell, 1994], 53). See William Kerrigan, "*Macbeth* and the History of Ambition," in *Freud and the Passions*, ed. John O'Neill (University Park: Pennsylvania State University Press, 1996); and Robert Watson, "Tragedies of Revenge and Ambition," *The Cambridge Companion to Shakespearean Tragedy*, ed. Claire McEachern (Cambridge: Cambridge University Press, 2002). For a recent corrective, see Joanne Diaz, "Grief as Medicine for Grief: Complaint Poetry in Early Modern England, 1559–1609," PhD dissertation, Northwestern University, 2008.

James Simpson, Debora Shuger, and Richard Strier discuss the reformation of penance in literary contexts: James Simpson, *Burning to Read: English Fundamentalism and Its Reformation Opponents* (Cambridge, MA: Belknap Press, 2007), esp. 69–87; Debora Shuger, "The Reformation of Penance," *Huntington Library Quarterly* 71.4 (2008): 557–71; Richard Strier, *The Unrepentant Renaissance: From Petrarch to Shakespeare to Milton* (Chicago: University of Chicago Press, 2011), esp. 207–29.

5. For this use of the term as a measure in psychoanalysis and economics, see Todd McGowan, *The End of Dissatisfaction: Jacques Lacan and the Emerging Society of Enjoyment* (Albany: State University of New York Press, 2004), 1–38.

6. It is "difficult to exaggerate," Judith Anderson reminds us, "the extent to which recourse to literal or etymological signification contributes to meaning in the early modern period" (*Translating Investments: Metaphor and the Dynamic of Cultural Change in Tudor-Stuart England* [New York: Fordham University Press, 2005], 12).

7. Thomas Wilson, *A Christian Dictionarie* (London, 1612), 2E3v.

8. See *The Theory of the Atonement: Readings in Soteriology*, ed. John R. Sheets, SJ (Englewood Cliffs, NJ: Prentice-Hall, Inc., 1967); and Stephen Finlan, *Problems with Atonement* (Collegeville, MN: Liturgical Press, 2005), 1–38.

9. Thomas Cooper, *Thesaurus Linguae Romanae & Britannicae* (London, 1565), 3T2t1r.

10. Thomas Elyot, *Bibliotheca Eliotae* (London, 1545), 2H1r.

11. Robert Cawdry, *A Table Alphabeticall* (London, 1604), H4v.

12. Thomas Kyd, *The Spanish Tragedy*, ed. J.R. Mulryne, 2nd ed. (London: A&C Black, 1989), 3.6.24–6.

13. Ben Jonson, *Volpone*, in *The Complete Plays of Ben Jonson*, ed. G.A. Wilkes (Oxford: Clarendon Press, 1982), v. 3: 3.7.121–2.

14. Francis Beaumont, *The Knight of the Burning Pestle*, ed. Michael Hattaway (London: A&C Black, 1989), 3.1.84–91.

15. Raymond Williams, *Keywords: A Vocabulary of Culture and Society*, 2nd ed. (New York: Oxford University Press, 1985), 14.

16. William Ian Miller, *Eye for an Eye* (Cambridge: Cambridge University Press, 2006), 140.

17. Reinhard Zimmerman, *The Law of Obligations: Roman Foundations of the Civilian Tradition* (Cape Town, South Africa: Juta and Co., 1990), 222.

18. Jill Mann, "Satisfaction and Payment in Middle English Literature," *Studies in the Age of Chaucer* 5 (1983): 18, 35.

19. See Book II of Aristotle, *Nichomachean Ethics*, ed. Hugh Treddenick (New York: Penguin, 2003), esp. 34–41.

20. Mann, "Satisfaction and Payment," 30.

21. Joshua Scodel, in *Excess and the Mean in Early Modern English Literature* (Princeton, NJ: Princeton University Press, 2002), examines the ways in which "the notion of a virtuous mean between two vicious extremes figured crucially in the writings of educated early modern English authors" (1). Scodel's focus, on the inheritance of Renaissance humanists of the classical mean, is nevertheless significantly different than my focus on the Christian model of *satis* being reworked by Reformers.

22. A.W. Moore, *Infinity* (Brookfield, VT: Aldershot, 1993), xvii.

23. Henry Smith, *The Benefit of Contentation* (London, 1590), B7r.

24. Adolf Berger, *Encyclopedic Dictionary of Roman Law* (Philadelphia: American Philosophical Society, 1991), 690.

25. *Dictionnaire de Théologie Catholique* (Paris: Librarie Letouzey et Ané, 1939), 14.1: 1135.

26. Hugo Grotius, *A Defence of the Catholick Faith Concerning the Satisfaction of Christ*, trans. W.H. (London, 1692), 136–7.

27. *"Offrir satisfaction n'etait pas s'acquitter totalement de la dette ou accepter de subir le châtiment mérité, c'était cependant reconnaitre le droit, confesser son tort, accepter le principe d'une reparation, par là se conformir à la justice, tout en faisant appel à la bienveillance et en s'appliquant à obtenir, par l'aveu de sa dette ou de sa culpabilité, de n'être point traité selon toute la rigeur des lois"* (*Dictionnaire*, 14.1: 1135).

28. *Black's Law Dictionary*, ed. Bryan A. Garner, 9th ed. (St. Paul, MN: West, 2009), 1370.

29. John Bossy, "Practices of Satisfaction, 1215–1700," in *Retribution, Repentance, and Reconciliation: Papers Read at the 2002 Summer Meeting and 2003 Winter Meeting of the Ecclesiastical History Society*, ed. Kate Cooper and Jeremy Gregory (Suffolk, UK: Boydell & Brewer, 2004), 106.

30. Gail Kern Paster, Katherine Rowe, and Mary Floyd-Wilson, "Introduction: Reading the Early Modern Passions," in *Reading the Early Modern Passions: Essays in the Cultural History of Emotion* (Philadelphia: University of Pennsylvania Press, 2004), 18. For satisfaction as the state sought by the passions, consider Thomas Wright: "the wyll, by yeelding to the passion, receiveth some little bribe of pleasure, the which moveth her to let the bridle loose unto inordinate appetites, because she hath ingrafted in her two inclinations, the one to follow reason, the other to content the sences: and this inclination (the other being blinded by the corrupt judgement, caused by inordinate passions) heere she feeleth *satisfied*" (*The Passions of the Mind in General* [London, 1601], 99, italics mine).

31. The notion of satisfaction thus provides a model for traversing a *subjective-objective* division of experience rather than the materialist *subject–object* binary popular in recent materialist criticism. See, for instance, *Subject and Object in the Renaissance*, which proclaims its methodological intention to "insist that the object be taken into account" (Margreta de Grazia, Maureen Quilligan, and Peter Stallybrass, introduction to *Subject and Object in Renaissance Culture*, ed. Margreta de Grazia, Maureen Quilligan, and Peter Stallybrass [Cambridge: Cambridge University Press, 1996], 5).

32. *Everyman,* in *Everyman and Medieval Miracle Plays*, ed. A.C. Cawley (London: Everyman's Library, 1974), ll. 535–6, 769–70. V.A. Kolve argues, however, that this satisfaction has less to do with confession and scourging than with the sacrament of the altar: "[Five Wits] names the change as though Everyman were its agent; but of course the facts are otherwise. Christ alone could make true satisfaction for sin—He is the great restitution—but it is available to any man through the sacrament of the altar. Everyman makes satisfaction in the only way possible for man fallen and forlorn: he satisfies justice by accepting Christ's body into his own" ("Everyman and the Parable of the Talents," *Medieval English Drama: Essays Critical and Contextual*, ed. Jerome Taylor and Alan H. Nelson [Chicago: University of Chicago Press, 1972], 333).

33. Consider Luther on Genesis: "Original sin really means that human nature has completely fallen; that the intellect has become darkened, so that we no longer

know God and his will and no longer perceive the works of God; furthermore, that the will is extraordinarily depraved, so that we do not trust the mercy of God and do not fear God but are unconcerned, disregard the word and will of God, and follow the desire and the impulses of the flesh; likewise, that our conscience is no longer quiet but, when it thinks of God's judgment, despairs and adopts illicit defenses and remedies. These sins have taken such deep root in our being that in this life they cannot be entirely eradicated," (*Lectures on Genesis, Chapters 1–5*, trans. George Schick, vol. 1 of *Luther's Works*, ed. Jaroslav Pelikan [St. Louis: Concordia Publishing, 1958], 114).

34. See Brad Gregory, *The Unintended Reformation* (Cambridge, MA: Harvard University Press, 2012).

35. Deal W. Hudson, *Happiness and the Limits of Satisfaction* (Lanham, MD: Rowman and Littlefield, 1996), 7. For the banalization of happiness itself in the eighteenth century into "a mere feeling . . . void of all ethical or political content," see Vivasvan Soni, *Mourning Happiness: Narrative and the Politics of Modernity* (Ithaca, NY: Cornell University Press, 2010), 9. Consider also Howard Mumford Jones, who notes regretfully "how far" the twentieth century "ha[s] drifted from either the Horatian, the Stoic, or the Christian doctrine of happiness as resignation" (*The Pursuit of Happiness* [Ithaca, NY: Cornell University Press, 1953], 155–6). For one of several recent efforts to recover the rich philosophical potential of happiness, see Julia Annas, *The Morality of Happiness* (New York: Oxford University Press, 1993).

36. They also insisted that men and women *could* compensate—satisfy—other people: "if we have done any man wrong, to endevour our selves to make hym true amendes, to the uttermoste of our power" ("Homilic of Repentance," in *Certaine Sermons or Homilies* [Gainesville, FL: Scholars' Facsimiles and Reprints, 1968], 269).

37. Although I do not rely on psychoanalytic theory for the language or model of the experience of satisfaction, a useful comparison for the doctrinal loss of satisfaction is offered by the Lacanian account of the loss of *jouissance*, enjoyment, as a developmental phenomenon. See Jacques Lacan, *The Other Side of Psychoanalysis: The Seminar of Jacques Lacan Book XVII*, trans. Russell Grigg (New York: W. W. Norton, 2007). The point is usefully clarified by Alenka Zupančič: "The loss of the object, the loss of satisfaction, and the emergence of a surplus satisfaction or surplus enjoyment are situated, topologically speaking, in one and the same point: in the intervention of the signifier" ("When Surplus Enjoyment meets Surplus Value," in *Jacques Lacan and the Other Side of Psychoanalysis*, ed. Justin Clemens and Russell Grigg [Durham, NC: Duke University Press, 2006], 156). Her aphoristic gloss is especially useful: "Repetition is, in its essence, the repetition of enjoyment as impossible (which is not to say as nonexisting: *enjoyment exists precisely as 'impossible'*)" (171, italics mine).

38. These various socioeconomic contexts are the conditions that Norbert Elias, in his classic account of the "civilizing process," suggests were responsible for making the early modern subject "much more restricted in . . . his chances of directly satisfying his drives and passions" ("Power and Civility," *The Civilizing Process*, vol. 2, trans. Edmund Jephcott [New York: Pantheon Books, 1982], 241). See also Jonathan Hall: "The *deferral of satisfaction* (whether of consumption, of consummation, or of revenge) becomes socially desirable, and hence largely internalized by the subject" (*Anxious Pleasures: Shake-*

spearean Comedy and the Nation-State [Madison, NJ: Farleigh Dickinson University Press, 1995], 56).

39. Debora Shuger, *Habits of Thought in the English Renaissance: Religion, Politics, and the Dominant Culture* (Toronto: University of Toronto Press, 1997), 6.

40. For an overview of the legal and theological history of the word, see *Dictionnaire* 14.1: 1129–1210.

41. "The economy of salvation and the economies of worldly goods could become entwined in penitential efforts," Abigail Firey, introduction to *A New History of Penance*, ed. Abigail Firey (Leiden, Netherlands: Brill, 2008), 13.

42. Quotation from Jean-Joseph Goux, *Symbolic Economies: After Marx and Freud* (Ithaca, NY: Cornell University Press, 1990), 2. For the relation of currency and language in terms of their symbolic or "tropic" functions, see Marc Shell, *Money, Language and Thought: Literary and Philosophical Economies from the Medieval to the Modern Era* (Berkeley: University of California Press, 1982); for the relation of double-entry bookkeeping and penitential accounting, see James Aho, *Confession and Bookkeeping: The Religious, Moral, and Rhetorical Roots of Modern Accounting* (Albany: State University of New York Press, 2005).

43. Patricia Parker, *Shakespeare from the Margins: Language, Culture, Context* (Chicago: University of Chicago Press, 1996), 18.

44. Andrew Pettegree surveys this shift in his introduction to *The Reformation World* ("The Changing Face of Reformation History," *The Reformation World*, ed. Andrew Pettegree [New York: Routledge, 2000], 1–8). For the historiographical basis for this approach, see J. J. Scarisbrick, *The Reformation and the English People* (Oxford: Basil Blackwell, 1984); Christopher Haigh, *English Reformations: Religion, Politics, and Society under the Tudors* (Oxford: Clarendon Press, 1993); and Eamon Duffy's influential *Stripping of the Altars: Traditional Religion in England 1400–1580* (New Haven, CT: Yale University Press, 1992). See also Eric Josef Carlson's useful summary of a "strong case for the unambiguous protestant and predestinarian character of the English church" based on a "slow, untidy" process of change that "involved propaganda and polemic, exposure to skilled pastors and preachers, and a host of reconstructions of familiar institutions such as guilds to accommodate the new realities" ("Cassandra Banished? New Research on Religion in Tudor and Early Stuart England," in *Religion and the English People, 1500–1640: New Voices, New Perspectives*, ed. Eric Josef Carlson [Truman State University Press, 1998], 4, 6).

45. See Thomas Tentler for a measured approach to Reformed repentance that notes that "the penitential systems of the Reformation represent, simultaneously and paradoxically, a continuation of medieval mentalities and practices and a revolutionary break with them" ("Postscript," *Penitence in the Age of the Reformation*, ed. Katharine Jackson Lualdi and Anne T. Thayer [Aldershot, UK: Ashgate, 2000], 240).

46. *The Apology of the Augsburg Confession*, in *The Book of Concord*, ed. Theodore G. Tappert (Philadelphia: Muhlenberg Press, 1959), 184.

47. R.N., *The Christians Manna* (St. Omer, 1613), B4r.

48. David Matthews and Gordon McMullan, "Introduction: Reading the Medieval in Early Modern England," in *Reading the Medieval in Early Modern England*, ed. Gordon McMullan and David Matthews (Cambridge: Cambridge University Press, 2007),

2. For a theoretically compelling discussion of the remnants of medieval religious and literary forms in the early modern period, see Julia Reinhart Lupton, *After-Lives of the Saints: Hagiography, Typology and Renaissance Literature* (Stanford, CA: Stanford University Press, 1996).

49. Millar MacClure, *The Paul's Cross Sermons* (Toronto: University of Toronto Press, 1958), 57.

50. Alexandra Walsham, *Providence in Early Modern England* (Oxford: Oxford University Press, 1999), 32.

51. See Anthony Milton, *Catholic and Reformed: The Roman and Protestant Churches in English Protestant Thought* (Cambridge: Cambridge University Press, 1995).

52. Peter Lake, *Anglicans and Puritans? Presbyterianism and English Conformist Thought from Whitgift to Hooker* (London: Allen & Unwin, 1988), 24. For a succinct introduction to the Calvinist consensus as well as its proponents and opponents, see Peter Marshall, *Reformation England, 1480–1643* (New York: Oxford University Press, 2003). See also Brian Cummings on the "the fundamental dissentiousness of sixteenth-century religion" (*The Literary Culture of the Reformation: Grammar and Grace* [Oxford: Oxford University Press, 2002], 13).

53. Jesse K. Lander, *Inventing Polemic: Religion, Print, and Literary Culture in Early Modern England* (Cambridge: Cambridge University Press, 2006), 34. For a sharp observation of how the early reformers were "drawn into" what they had "considered to be tangential theological discussion," leading ultimately to "divisions in the reformers' camp" as a result of printed debate with Sir Thomas More, see David Birch, *Early Reformation English Polemics* (Salzburg, Austria: Institut fur Anglistik und Amerikanistik, 1983), 64.

54. Lawrence M. Clopper, "English Drama: From Ungodly *Ludi* to Sacred Play," *The Cambridge History of Medieval English Literature*, ed. David Wallace (Cambridge: Cambridge University Press, 1999), 759. Although I do not trace a trajectory from medieval to early modern in a way that would present a *dramatic* history of treatments of repentance—I focus on plays of the sixteenth and seventeenth centuries—the following chapter charts the development of penitential theory and practice from the medieval to early modern periods in order to make possible a *semantic* history of satisfaction and the theater's historical place in it.

55. Sarah Beckwith, *Shakespeare and the Grammar of Forgiveness* (Ithaca, NY: Cornell University Press, 2011), 7, 28.

56. Quotation from Jeffrey Knapp, *Shakespeare's Tribe: Church, Nation, and Theater in Renaissance England* (Chicago: University of Chicago Press, 2002), 28. For the Renaissance stage as an "emergent commercial entertainment that was still imbued with the heritage of suppressed popular and religious traditions," see Louis Montrose, *The Purpose of Playing: Shakespeare and the Cultural Politics of the Elizabethan Theater* (Chicago: University of Chicago Press, 1996), 39. Ken Jackson and Arthur F. Marotti offer an important critique of how these approaches hew too closely to a "secularization thesis" that turns the theater into a site of charismatic appropriation ("The Turn to Religion in Early Modern English Studies," *Criticism* 46.1 (2004): 167–90.

57. Jane Hwang Degenhardt and Elizabeth Williamson, introduction to *Religion and Drama in Early Modern England: The Performance of Religion on the Renaissance Stage*, ed. Jane Hwang Degenhardt and Elizabeth Williamson (Burlington, VT: Ashgate, 2011), 4, 15. See also Anthony Dawson, "Shakespeare and Secular Performance," *Shakespeare and the Cultures of Performance*, ed. Paul Yachnin and Patricia Badir (Burlington, VT: Ashgate, 2008), 83–100.

58. Quotation from Huston Diehl, *Staging Reform, Reforming the Stage: Protestantism and Popular Theater in Early Modern England* (Ithaca, NY: Cornell University Press, 1997), 3–4. See also Bryan Crockett, *The Play of Paradox* (Philadelphia: University of Pennsylvania Press, 1995); Elizabeth Mazzola, *The Pathology of the Renaissance* (Boston: Brill, 1998); Michael O'Connell, *The Idolatrous Eye: Iconoclasm and Theater in Early Modern England* (New York: Oxford University Press, 2000); and Adrian Streete, *Protestantism and Drama in Early Modern England* (Cambridge: Cambridge University Press, 2008).

59. Bossy, *Christianity in the West*, viii; John Parker, *The Aesthetics of Antichrist: From Christian Drama to Christopher Marlowe* (Ithaca, NY: Cornell University Press, 2007), x. Consider also Alister McGrath's position that doctrinal formulations "do not merely *generate* conflict but *transmit* it as an essential constituent element" (*The Genesis of Doctrine: A Study in the Foundations of Doctrinal Criticism* [Oxford: Basil Blackwell, 1990], 3).

60. Kevin Sharpe, *Remapping Early Modern England: The Culture of Seventeenth-Century Politics* (Cambridge: Cambridge University Press, 2000), 12. I am indebted to Jackson and Marotti for calling my attention to this book.

61. I do not advocate interpretations of early modern drama that look for the reinforcement of specific doctrinal positions in plays (for such approaches see Roland Mushat Frye, *Shakespeare and Christian Doctrine* [Princeton, NJ: Princeton University Press, 1963]; David Beauregard, *Catholic Theology in Shakespeare's Plays* [Newark: University of Delaware Press, 2008]).

Chapter 1

1. Thomas Wilson, *A Christian Dictionarie*, 372.

2. Timothy Gorringe, *God's Just Vengeance: Crime, Violence and the Rhetoric of Salvation* (Cambridge: Cambridge University Press, 1996), 131.

3. Lydia Whitehead, "*A Poena et Culpa*: Penitence, Confidence, and the *Miserere* in Foxe's *Actes and Monuments*," *Renaissance Studies* 4 (1990): 288.

4. Quotation from David Myers, *Poor Sinning Folk: Confession and Conscience in Counter-Reformation Germany* (Ithaca, NY: Cornell University Press, 1996), 16. Richard Strier underestimates the Protestant emphasis on justice, but his summary is instructive: "The Roman Church insisted on merit and on pain—indeed, on the merit of pain. It celebrated God's mercy but also took heed of His justice. It saw God as exercising His mercy in allowing man to satisfy His justice. The Protestants, on the other hand, insisted on mercy alone, on mercy *rather than* justice," ("Herbert and Tears," *ELH* 46.2 [1979]: 229).

5. Dewey Wallace, *Puritans and Predestination: Grace in English Protestant Theology, 1525–1695* (Chapel Hill: University of North Carolina Press, 1982), 11.

6. Wietse De Boer, "At Heresy's Door: Borromeo, Penance, and Confessional Boundaries in Early Modern Europe," *A New History of Penance*, ed. Abigail Firey (Leiden, Netherlands: Brill, 2008), 345.

7. See John McNeill, *History of the Cure of Souls* (New York: HarperCollins, 1977). For recent revisionist approaches to the histories of penitential doctrine and practice in the late medieval and early modern periods, see the essays in *A New History of Penance*, ed. Abigail Firey; Mary C. Mansfield, *The Humiliation of Sinners: Public Penance in Thirteenth-Century France* (Ithaca, NY: Cornell University Press, 1995); and Ronald K. Rittgers, *The Reformation of the Keys: Confession, Conscience, and Authority in Sixteenth-Century Germany* (Cambridge, MA: Harvard University Press, 2004).

8. Abigail Firey, introduction to *A New History of Penance*, 1.

9. Alexander Nowell, *A Catechism, or First Instruction and Learning* (London, 1570), N3v, italics mine. For the relatively non-polemical tone of early modern catechisms, see Ian Green, *The Christian's ABC: Catechisms and Catechizing in England, c. 1530–1740* (Oxford: Clarendon Press, 1996), 39.

10. For an overview of the range of *logics* of atonement, beginning with Paul, see *The Theory of the Atonement*, ed. John R. Sheets; and Stephen Finlan, *Problems with Atonement* (Collegeville, MN: Liturgical Press, 2005), 1–38. My account of *satisfaction theory* specifically is heavily indebted to Gustaf Aulen, *Christus Victor; An Historical Study of the Three Main Types of the Idea of the Atonement*, trans. A.G. Herbert (New York: Macmillan, 1951), supplemented by the important qualifications and critiques offered by Gorringe, *God's Just Vengeance*; John Bossy, *History of Christianity in the West, 1475–1700* (Oxford: Oxford University Press, 1985); Rene Girard, *Things Hidden Since the Foundation of the World* (Stanford, CA: Stanford University Press, 1987); and, most recently, Theodore Jennings, *Transforming Atonement* (Minneapolis, MN: Fortress Press, 2009).

11. "St. Paul does not quite say why God could not remit the penalty of sin without the death of His Son. But it cannot be denied that those theologians who declare that this would be incompatible with God's justice—the justice which requires that somehow sin should be punished—or with the consistency which demands the infliction of the particular punishment which God had threatened, namely death—are only bringing out latent presuppositions of St. Paul's thought" (Hastings Rashdall, *The Idea of Atonement in Christian Theology* [London, 1920], 91–2). For the way in which the "influence of Roman law over the world in which the early theology of the Latin-speaking church was forged made it inevitable that Roman understandings of the *nature* of justice would be projected on to the term [*iustitia*] as and when it occurred in holy scripture," see Alister McGrath, *Luther's Theology of the Cross: Martin Luther's Theological Breakthrough* (Oxford: Blackwell, 1985), 101.

12. For an alternative tradition, best exemplified by Abelard, that stresses Christ's exemplary rather than propitiatory status in the Crucifixion, see Rashdall, *Idea of Atonement*, 360.

13. Consider Peter Stallybrass's clearly parodic version of the correspondences: "A man and a woman steal from their landlord. He discovers their theft, and so, until they

can make restitution, they are in his debt.... Eventually a benefactor intervenes. He takes over the couple's debt and 'pays the price.' This benefactor pays off the debt; he pays with his own body.... In fact, so valuable is this man's body that he *more* than pays the debt, setting up a bank account that others can use to pay off *their* debts.... If this narrative now looks like a travesty of Christianity, it is in part because we have been profoundly shaped by the attempt to drive the economics out of belief" ("The Value of Culture and the Disavowal of Things," *The Culture of Capital: Property, Cities, and Knowledge in Early Modern England*, ed. Henry S. Turner [New York: Routledge, 2002], 279–80).

14. Cited in Jean Delumeau, *Sin and Fear: The Emergence of a Western Guilt Culture, 13th–18th Centuries* (New York: Palgrave Macmillian, 1990), 194, italics mine.

15. "To the extent that any formulation could be called "definitive" for this doctrine in the Latin West, it would be the understanding of the work of Christ set forth by Anselm of Canterbury, which had both systematized the doctrinal development preceding him and shaped the development after him," (Jaroslav Pelikan, *Reformation of Church and Dogma*, in vol. 4 of *The Chrisitan Tradition: A History of the Development of Doctrine* [Chicago: University of Chicago Press, 1984], 23).

16. Michael O'Connell, *Idolatrous Eye: Iconoclasm and Theater in Early Modern England* (New York: Oxford University Press, 2000), 47; Rashdall, *Idea of Atonement*, 351.

17. Anselm of Canterbury, *Cur Deus Homo*, in *The Major* Works, ed. Brian Davies and G. R. Evans (New York: Oxford University Press, 1998), 349.

18. Gorringe, *God's Just Vengeance*, 96.

19. Anselm, *Cur Deus*, 330–1.

20. Although Anselm begins with the premise of God's benevolence, still he offers a theory in which "the divine intention to save appears to be blocked by the divine justice that cannot simply overlook sin as damage to the honor of God, and so also as damage to the balance of justice" (Jennings, *Transforming Atonement*, 126).

21. Gorringe, *God's Just Vengeance*, 95. He adds that "this concern for justice is essentially a concern for the integrity of both the social order and the cosmic order which it mirrors."

22. See the entry on "satisfaction" in vol. 14.1 of *Dictionnaire de Theologie Catholique* (Paris: Letouzey et Ané, 1939), 1129–1210. For the discussion of the role of Roman law, see esp. 1135. The entry maintains that the Roman model does *not* demand complete or exact remuneration: "'*faire assez' pour que le créancer consentît à accorder remise de tout ou partie de la dette, pour qu'un offensé reconçat á tirer vengeance ou á poursuivre le châtiment de l'injure reçue*" (1135).

23. Anselm, *Cur Deus*, 348.

24. "Since theology is concerned with the relations between God and man, it must always be making assertions about the nature of man," Mary Douglas, *Purity and Danger: An Analysis of Concepts of Pollution and Taboo* (London: Routledge & Kegan Paul, 1966), 11.

25. And vice versa; as Pelikan points out, "[T]he metaphor of satisfaction by Christ was derived, at least in part, from the disciplinary satisfaction of the church" (*Reformation*, 250).

26. John T. McNeill and Helena M. Gamer, introduction to *Medieval Handbooks of Penance*, ed. and trans. John T. McNeill and Helena M. Gamer (New York: Octagon

Books, 1965), 6. See also McNeill, *A History of the Cure of Souls* (New York: Harper-Collins, 1977), 88–111.

27. McNeill, *Cure of Souls*, 97.

28. Tertullian, *Treatises on Penance*, ed. and trans. William P. Le Saint (Westminster, MD: Newman Press, 1959), 31, italics mine.

29. Ibid., 97.

30. Allen Frantzen, *The Literature of Penance in Anglo-Saxon England* (New Brunswick, NJ: Rutgers University Press, 1983), 7. For the commitment "*de proportionner exactement la peine à la gravité de la faute*" see *Dictionnaire*, 14.1:1175. See also James A. Brundage, *Medieval Canon Law* (London: Longman, 1995), 24–6.

31. *Medieval Handbooks*, 113.

32. Bossy, *History*, 49; Frantzen, *Literature of Penance*, 30. Consider also McNeill and Gamer: "While in general the [penitential handbooks] have the appearance of exact schedules of equivalents between crime and punishment, frequently the confessor is reminded that penalties are to be not so much equated with offenses as adjusted to personalities" (*Medieval Handbooks of Penance*, 46).

33. As Frantzen writes, "the difference between these penitential systems is of the utmost importance for history and literature, for they made different demands on the clergy and created different experiences for the laity" (*Literature of Penance*, 6).

34. Thomas Tentler, *Sin and Confession on the Eve of the Reformation* (Princeton, NJ: Princeton University Press, 1977), 12.

35. Isidore of Seville, *The Etymologies of Isidore of Seville*, ed. and trans. Stephen A. Barney (Cambridge: Cambridge University Press, 2006), 150.

36. *Culpa* was the debt of sin of which only Christ or the priest, as Christ's vicar, could absolve the penitent; *poena* was the temporal or purgatorial punishment owed by the sinner toward God's justice; it was for *poena* that the individual had the agency to satisfy.

37. Delumeau, *Sin and Fear*, 195–7. Tentler ascribes the shift to the ninth century (*Sin and Confession*, 16). For the construction of sorrow through penitential liturgies, see Karen Wagner, "*Cum Aliquis Venerit ad Sacerdotem*: Penitential Experience in the Central Middle Ages," *A New History of Penance*, 208–16.

38. For penance as a sacrament, see Aquinas: "Now it is manifest that in Penance the ceremony is done so that something holy is signified, both on the part of the penitent sinner as well as on the part of the priest who absolves. For what the penitent sinner does and says signifies that his heart has turned away from sin; likewise the priest, through what he does and says with regard to the penitent, signifies the work of God forgiving sin. Thus it is manifest that Penance which is performed in the Church is a sacrament" (*Summa Theologiae: Latin Text and English Translation*, ed. and trans. Thomas Gilby, O. P. and T. C. O'Brien (New York: McGraw Hill, 1964), 60:5. Aquinas defines the parts of penance: "Hence on the part of a penitent there is required first, the intention of making amends, which is taken care of by contrition; secondly, that he submit himself to the judgment of the priest representing God, which is accomplished by confession; thirdly, that he make recompense according to the judgment of God's minister, which is done through satisfaction. Therefore contrition, confession, and satisfaction are designated the parts of Penance" (60:167).

39. Jacques Le Goff, *Your Money or Your Life: Economy and Religion in the Middle Ages* (Cambridge, MA: Zone Books, 1988), 11–2.

40. Ibid., 12.

41. Delumeau, *Sin and Fear*, 197; Katherine Little, *Confession and Resistance: Defining the Self in Late Medieval England* (South Bend, IN: University of Notre Dame Press, 2006), 1; Tentler, *Sin and Confession*, 16.

42. Tentler, *Sin and Confession*, 16, 18.

43. Peter Lombard, *Sentences, Book 4* in Elizabeth Frances Rogers, *Peter Lombard and the Sacramental System* (Merrick, NY: Richwood Publishing Co., 1976), 170.

44. David Aers, "A Whisper in the Ear of Early Modernists; or Reflections on Literary Critics Writing the 'History of the Subject,'" *Culture and History, 1350–1600: Essays on English Communities, Identities, and Writing*, ed. David Aers (Detroit: Wayne State University Press, 1992): 177–202.

45. Joseph Goering, "The Scholastic Turn: Penitential Theology and Law in the Schools," *A New History of Penance*, 226.

46. Certainly the priest's role in designing penances remained: see Pierre Michaud-Quantin, *Sommes de Casuistique et Manuels de Confession au Moyen Âge* (Louvain: Editions Nauwelaerts, 1962), 8–9.

47. Mary C. Mansfield, *The Humiliation of Sinners: Public Penance in Thirteenth-Century France* (Ithaca, NY: Cornell University Press, 1995), 49.

48. Lee W. Patterson, "Chaucerian Confession: Penitential Literature and the Pardoner," *Medievalia et Humanistica* (Cambridge: Cambridge University Press, 1976), 7:173, fn. 65.

49. Lombard, *Sentences*, 171, italics mine. See also Goering: "for Lombard, although sins are forgiven by God as soon as one is truly sorry for them [*contritio*], nevertheless confession to a priest [*confessio*] and exterior penance [*satisfactio*] is in some way also necessary" ("Scholastic Turn," 230–1).

50. Mary Braswell, *The Medieval Sinner: Characterization and Confession in the Literature of the English Middle Ages* (Rutherford, NJ: Fairleigh Dickinson University Press, 1983), 15.

51. Siegfried Wenzel, *Fasciculus Morum: A Fourteenth-Century Preacher's Handbook* (University Park: Pennsylvania State University Press, 1989), 507, italics mine.

52. *Of Schrifte and Penance: The Middle English Prose Translation of Le Manuel des Péchés*, ed. Klaus Bitterling (Heidelberg: Universitatsverlag, 1998), 117, italics mine.

53. Anne Thayer, *Penitence, Preaching and the Coming of the Reformation* (Aldershot, UK: Ashgate, 2002), 103, italics mine.

54. *Dictionnaire*, 14.1:1176.

55. *Speculum Sacerdotale*, ed. Edward H Weatherly, Early English Text Society Original Series (hereafter cited as EETS O.S. 200 (London: Oxford University Press, 1936), 200:66.

56. John Mirk, *Instructions for Parish Priests*, ed. Edward Peacock, EETS O.S. 31 (Suffolk, UK: Boydell & Brewer, 2000), ll. 1511–8..

57. Delumeau, *Sin and Fear*, 203.

58. Thomas of Chobham, *Summa Confessorum*, ed. F. Broomfield (Louvain: Editions Nauwelaerts, 1968), 321.

59. For a discussion of these terms, see Gordon J. Spykman, *Attrition and Contrition at the Council of Trent* (Kampen, Netherlands: J. H. Kok, 1955, *passion*).

60. Ashley Null, *Thomas Cranmer's Doctrine of Repentance: Renewing the Power to Love* (Oxford: Oxford University Press, 2000), 39.

61. Ibid., 22.

62. Heiko Obermann, *The Harvest of Medieval Theology: Gabriel Biel and Late Medieval Nominalism* (Cambridge, MA: Harvard University Press, 1963), 160. Consider also Alister McGrath: "The soteriology of the *via moderna* . . . is based upon the presuppostion that God's promises of grace are *conditional*: God has promised to bestow grace upon man upon condition that he does *quod in se est*" (*Luther's Theology of the Cross*, 107).

63. *Cajetan Responds: A Reader in Reformation Controversy*, ed. Jared Wicks (Washington, DC: Catholic University Press, 1978), 214.

64. For the theology of *facere quod in se est* as a source of the covenantal and personalist inclinations of Lutheran theology, see Alister McGrath, *Intellectual Origins of the European Reformation* (Oxford: Basil Blackwell, 1987), 80–6. But Luther and other Reformers rejected *facere quod in se est* as it reduced the role of Christ in human atonement: there was an "evident Christological lacuna in the soteriology of the *via moderna*, in that the salvation of mankind may be discussed without reference to the incarnation and death of Christ" (82). For similarities between Biel's and Luther's contritionism, see Spykman, *Attrition and Contrition*, 88.

65. McGrath, *Origins*, 117.

66. *Jacob's Well*, ed. Arthur Brandeis, EETS O.S. 115 (Rochester, NY, 1998), 65.

67. John Fisher, *Treatyse Concernynge . . . the Seven Penytencyall Psalms*, in *The English Works of John Fisher*, ed. J. E. B. Mayor, EETS E.S. 27 (London: N. Trübner & Co., 1876), 24.

68. "It is well known that Luther found the burden of his sins intolerable and experienced increased anxiety, rather than consolation, as he went through the penitential process" (Thayer, 5). See also Rittgers, *Reformation of the Keys*, 112. For a critique of the supposition that medieval confession placed an "intolerable and unassuageable burden of guilt . . . on men's consciences," see Lawrence Duggan, "Fear and Confession on the Eve of the Reformation," *Archiv für Reformationgeschichte* 75 (1984): 153–75. I discuss this at greater length in chapter 3.

69. *Apology of the Augsburg Confession*, in *The Book of Concord: The Confessions of the Evangelical Church*, ed. Theodore G. Tappert (Philadelphia: Muhlenberg Press, 1959), 190.

70. Thomas Scott, *A Godlie Sermon of Repentaunce and Amendment of Life* (London, 1585), A8r. Whitehead sums this up effectively: "The shift is, effectively, from penance to repentance. Not that sacramental penance excluded a repentant attitude: the shift is rather based on Luther's assertion of its primacy, and his rejection of more active and institutional ways to forgiveness" ("Poena et Culpa," 292).

71. For the importance of the shift, consider Diarmid MacCulloch: "Most notorious was Erasmus's retranslation of Gospel passages (especially Matthew 3:2) where John the Baptist is presented in the Greek as crying out to his listeners in the wilderness: *metanoeite*. Jerome had translated this as *poenitentiam agite*, 'do penance,' and the

medieval Church had pointed to the Baptist's cry as biblical support for its theology of the sacrament of penance. Erasmus said that what John had told his listeners to do was to come to their senses, or repent, and he translated the command into Latin as *resipiscite*. Much turned on one word" (*The Reformation: A History* [New York: Viking Press, 2003], 96). See also James Simpson, *Burning to Read: English Fundamentalism and Its Reformation Opponents* (Cambridge, MA: Belknap Press, 2007), 73–5; C. John Sommerville, *The Secularization of Early Modern England* (New York: Oxford University Press, 1992), 46.

72. For this process of "contest and negotiation, adjustment and accommodation, as diverse constituencies struggled to work out the consequences of religious change for social, political, and cultural life," see David Cressy and Lori Anne Ferrell, introduction to *Religion and Society in Early Modern England: A Sourcebook*, ed. David Cressy and Lori Anne Ferrell (London: Routledge, 1996), 1.

73. Martin Luther, "The Sacrament of Penance, 1519," trans. E. Theodore Bachman, in vol. 35 of *Luther's Works*, ed. E. Theodore Bachman (Philadelphia, Muhlenberg Press, 1960), 12; "The Babylonian Captivity of the Church, 1520" trans. A. T. W. Steinhäuser, in vol. 36 of *Luther's Works*, ed. Abdel Ross Wentz (Philadelphia, Muhlenberg Press, 1955), 89.

74. "What Luther thus saw was a church enmeshed in a type of activism that tortured rather than comforted the sensitive and distressed conscience and that found it more profitable to encourage endless doing rather than confident being. In actual practice this meant that the church was fostering salvation by works instead of just by faith" (E. Theodore Bachman, Introduction to "The Sacrament of Penance," in *Luther's Works* 35:6).

75. In *The Oxford Encyclopedia of the Reformation*, ed. Hans J. Hillerbrand (New York: Oxford University Press, 1996), 1:314.

76. Bossy, *Christianity*, 93. Aulen believes that Luther, harkening back to early Greek interpretations of Christ's triumphal resurrection after the Passion, subscribed to a less juridical theory of Christ's Passion than the other Reformers. Pelikan explains that Reformers taught that Christ's obedient suffering "not only rendered passive satisfaction to the punitive justice of God (as Anselm had taught), but active satisfaction to the demands of the law for a perfectly righteous life," (*Reformation* 4:152).

77. Bossy, *Christianity*, 94. For a similar reading in terms of Luther's understanding of *iustitia*, see Brian Cummings, *The Literary Culture of the Reformation: Grammar and Grace* (Oxford: Oxford University Press, 2002), esp. 59–99.

78. Debora Shuger, "The Reformation of Penance," *Huntington Library Quarterly* 71.4 (2008): 562.

79. *Apology of the Augsburg Confession*, 182, 184.

80. Jean Calvin, *The Institution of the Christian Religion* (London, 1561), T2r, italics mine. See also Calvin, *Institutes of the Christian Religion*, ed. John T. McNeill and trans. Ford Lewis Battles, 2 vols. (Philadelphia: Westminster Press, 1960), 1:592–701.

81. Calvin, *Institution*, T2r–3v. Consider also Calvin's successor in Geneva, Theodore Beza: "If the death and passion of Jesus Christe bee sufficient to salvation and if he be the true Jesus, that is to saye, true and onelye saviour, howe then shall that be true which they saye, that there is but the faulte or offence pardoned? and concerninge the payne, that it is onelye chaunged from eternall into temporall, in suche sorte that we

must paye it in this worlde, or in another. But if this bee false, as it is most false, what grounde have they [Catholics] then to buylde theyr meryte and satisfaction towardes God, their Purgatorie and indulgences and such lyke?" (*A Briefe and Pithie Summe of the Christian Faith*, trans. R. F. [London, 1565], S5v).

82. Heinrich Bullinger, *Fiftie Godlie and Learned Sermons Diuided into Five Decades* (London, 1577), 583.

83. Though see Sarah Beckwith for the connection between penance and the Eucharist (*Shakespeare and the Grammar of Forgiveness* [Ithaca, NY: Cornell University Press, 2011], 35).

84. Though see James Simpson for the belief that the articles, while maintaining penance, were already "destroying" and "diminishing" its sacramental status (*The Oxford English Literary History: Reform and Cultural Revolution* [Oxford: Oxford University Press, 2004], 324, 325).

85. William Tyndale, *The Obedience of a Christian Man*, ed. David Daniell (London: Penguin Books, 2000), 85.

86. Null, *Doctrine of Repentance*, 122.

87. Ibid., 156, italics mine.

88. John Bradford, *A Sermon of Repentaunce* (London, 1553), B7r.

89. Christopher Haigh, *English Reformations: Religion, Politics, and Society under the Tudors* (Oxford: Clarendon Press, 1993), 202. For the entrenchment of Calvinism in the English polity, despite significant ecclesiological and liturgical disagreements among the population, see Nicholas Tyacke, *Anti-Calvinists: The Rise of English Arminianism, c. 1590–1640* (Oxford: Clarendon Press, 1987).

90. Patrick Collinson, *The Religion of Protestants: The Church in English Society 1559–1625* (Oxford: Clarendon Press, 1982), 38.

91. "Homilie of Repentance," in *Certaine Sermons or Homilies* (Gainesville, FL: Scholars' Facsimiles and Reprints, 1968), 259. The homily does preserve a qualified use of the word satisfaction for restitution to other people: "We do learne, what is the satisfaction, that God doth require of us, which is, that we ceasse from evyll, and do good, and if we have done any man wrong, to endevour our selves to make hym true amendes, to the uttermoste of our power" (269).

92. For the "tenacious and widespread . . . survival of the old religion during and after Elizabeth's reign," see J. J. Scarisbrick, *The Reformation and the English People* (Oxford: Basil Blackwell, 1984), 136–61. For an overview of the polemical controversy in late sixteenth-century print, see R. W. Southern, *Elizabethan Recusant Prose* (London: Sands, 1950), esp. 30–43.

93. Myers, *Poor Sinning Folk*, 8.

94. *The Canons and Decrees of the Sacred and Oecumenical Council of Trent*, ed. and trans. J. Waterworth (London: Dolman, 1848), 14th sess., chaps. 12, 13, and 14. This position had already been articulated in a catholic response to the *Augsburg Confession* (1530): "When they [the Reformers] ascribe only two parts to penitence, they come into conflict with the whole church, which from the time of the apostles has held and believed that there are three parts in penitence: contrition, confession, and satisfaction" (*The Book of Concord: The Confessions of the Evangelical Lutheran Church*, trans. and ed. Theodore G. Tappert [Philadelphia: Muhlenberg Press, 1959], 182, fn. 7).

95. See John Bossy, *The English Catholic Community, 1570–1850* (London: Darton, Longman and Todd, 1975); Arthur F. Marotti, *Religious Ideology and Cultural Fantasy: Catholic and Anti-Catholic Discourses in Early Modern England* (Notre Dame, IN: University of Notre Dame Press, 2005); Alison Shell, *Catholicism, Controversy and the English Literary Imagination* (Cambridge: Cambridge University Press, 1999).

96. Robert Parsons, *A Christian Directorie* (Rouen, 1585), 829–30. For a full discussion of the Parsons and Bunny texts and they ways in which they "show dissimilar doctrinal positions on issues that divided Catholics and Protestants, and shared aspects of a rigorous religious mentality of the late sixteenth-century," see Brad Gregory, "The 'True and Zealous Seruice of God': Robert Parsons, Edmund Bunny, and *The First Booke of the Christian Exercise*," *Journal of Ecclesiastical History* 45 (1994): 242.

97. Parsons, *Christian Directorie*, 830.

98. For contemporary observations on the attractiveness and advance of Catholicism both in England and abroad, consider Sir Edwin Sandys (son of the archbishop), who remarked first in 1605 that "in the choyse of them [friars] whom they send out to preach, in the diligence and paines which they take in theyr sermons, in the ornaments of eloquence, and grace of action, in their shew of pietie and reverence towards God, of zeale towards his truth, of love towards his people . . . they match their adversaries [Protestants] in theyr best, and in the rest doe farre exceed them" (quoted from Sir Edwin Sandys, *Europae Speculum or, A View or Survey of the State of Religion in the Westerne Parts of the World* [The Hague, 1629], 78).

99. John Merbecke, *A Booke of Notes and Common Places* (London, 1581), 803–4.

100. Daniel Dyke, *Two Treatises, The one, of Repentance, the Other, of Christ's Temptations* (London, 1616), A3v, italics mine.

101. Henry Holland, *Davids Faith and Repentance* (London, 1589), *3v.

102. Bishop Edwin Sandys, *Sermons* (London, 1585), 11–2, italics mine.

103. William Perkins, *An Exposition of the Symbole or Creed of the Apostles* (London, 1595), 176.

104. Katherine Jackson Lualdi and Anne T. Thayer, introduction to *Penitence in the Age of Reformations* (Aldershot, UK: Ashgate, 2000), 1.

105. Alexandra Walsham, *Providence in Early Modern England* (Oxford: Oxford University Press, 1999), 148.

106. As Pelikan suggests, followers of Luther and Calvin, although disagreeing on various points, "recognized that all of them agreed on this doctrine [justification by faith] as the foundation of the entire Reformation, in fact, the chief doctrine of Christianity and the chief point of difference separating Protestantism from Roman Catholicism" (*Reformation* 4:138–9).

107. William Tyndale, "Preface to the New Testament," in *Documents of the English Reformation 1526–1701*, ed. Gerald Bray (Cambridge: James Clarke, 2004), 25.

108. Arthur Dent, *The Hand-maid of Repentance* (London, 1614), C2r. For the rise of experimental predestination, see R. T. Kendall, *Calvin and English Calvinism to 1649* (New York: Oxford University Press, 1979).

109. Dyke, *Two Treatises*, 6.

110. Ibid., 25.

111. Shuger, "Reformation of Penance," passim. Hannibal Hamlin also suggests that "in this debate, Protestants and Catholics shared more than they admitted" ("Sobs for Sorrowful Souls: Versions of the Penitential Psalms for Lay Devotion," *Private and Domestic Devotion in Early Modern Britain*, ed. Jessica Martin and Alec Ryrie [Aldershot, UK: Ashgate, 2012], 211).

112. Alec Ryrie, *Being Protestant in Early Modern England* (Oxford: Oxford University Press, 2013), 54.

113. Perkins, *A Reformed Catholike* (London, 1598), H3v–4r, italics mine.

114. Diarmid MacCulloch offers a pithy summation of the way in which Protestant cause and effect could come to resemble a works-based theology: "Experimental Calvinism unwittingly led those who embraced it back towards a doctrine of works, because it constantly focused the attention on the search for visible proofs of election" (*The Later Reformation in England* [New York: Palgrave, 2001], 75).

115. Perkins, *Reformed Catholike*, I2r, italics mine.

116. *A Path-way to Penitence* (London, 1591), A5r.

117. Andrew Willet, *Synopsis Papismi* (London, 1592), 505, 515, italics mine.

118. Francis Marbury, *Notes of the Doctrine of Repentance* (London, 1602), B4v.

119. Thomas Scott, *A Godlie Sermon of Repentaunce and Amendment of Life* (London, 1585), D7v–D8r.

120. Richard Stock, *The Doctrine and Use of Repentance* (London, 1608), B7, D7, D8.

121. Arthur Dent, *The Plaine Mans Path-way to Heaven* (London, 1601), U4r–U4v, italics mine.

122. George Gifford, *A Briefe Discourse of Certaine Points of the Religion . . . which may bee termed the Countrie Divinitie* (London, 1582), *3v–4r.

123. Ibid., 33v, 68r–70r, italics mine.

124. *Path-way*, A5r.

125. Gregory Kneidel, "Herbert and Exactness," *English Literary Renaissance* 36.2 (2006): 278–303.

126. Gifford, *Briefe Discourse*, 68r.

127. Gary Kuchar, *The Poetry of Religious Sorrow in Early Modern England* (Cambridge: Cambridge University Press, 2008), 10, 11.

128. See Ronald K. Rittgers on Luther's understanding of the way assurance allows for joy in tribulation ("Embracing the 'true relic' of Christ: Suffering, Penance, and Private Confession in the Thought of Martin Luther," in *A New History of Penance*, ed. Abigail Firey [Leiden, Netherlands: Brill, 2008], 382).

129. Dyke, *Two Treatises*, 30–1.

130. Ibid., 48. Dyke goes on to argue that this sorrow must nevertheless be moderated or "proportioned to our sinnes": "for though we cannot exceed in the displeasure of our willes against sinne, yet we may in the testification of this displeasure in weeping, fasting, pining, and macerating the body" (48–50).

131. Consider Dent: "The perswasion of God's love toward us, is the roote of all our love and chearfull obedience towards him. For therefore we love him and obey him, because we know he hath loved us first, and written our names in the booke of life. But on the contrary, the doctrine of the Papists, which would have men alwayes doubt and

feare in a servile sort, is most hellish and uncomfortable" (*Plaine Mans Path-way*, S4v–S5r).

132. Samuel Hieron, *Davids Penitentiall Psalme Opened* (Cambridge, 1617), 55. Hieron is careful, however, to return to the orthodox position: "What good can I doe, which I am not absolutely and peremptorily bound to do, and if it be my duty, how shall that be of force to satisfie the justice of God for the things wherein I have miscarried?" (55).

133. Richard Hooker, *Of the Laws of Ecclesiastical Polity*, in *The Folger Library Edition of the Works of Richard Hooker*, ed. W. Speed Hill et al., 7 vols. (Cambridge, MA: Belknap Press, 1977–98), 3:54.

134. Peter Lake, *Anglicans and Puritans? Presbyterianism and English Conformist Thought from Whitgift to Hooker* (London: Allen and Unwin, 1988), 148.

135. Hooker, *Laws*, 53, 54.

136. Ibid, 54, italics mine.

137. Ibid., 55.

138. Cajetan, *Cajetan Responds*, 83.

139. Hooker, 67.

140. Hooker, 54, italics mine.

141. Other books have looked at the place of repentance on stage but not in terms of its Reformation rescripting. See Herbert Jack Heller, *Penitent Brothellers: Grace, Sexuality, and Genre in Thomas Middleton's City Comedies* (Newark: University of Delaware Press, 2000); and Robert Grams Hunter, *Shakespeare and the Comedy of Forgiveness* (New York: Columbia University Press, 1965).

Chapter 2

1. For seminal discussions of *Doctor Faustus* as a morality, see David Bevington, *From* Mankind *to Marlowe: Growth of Structure in the Popular Drama of Tudor England* (Cambridge, MA: Harvard University Press, 1962), 245–65; and Robert Potter, *The English Morality Play: Origins, History, and Influence of a Dramatic Tradition* (London: Routledge & Kegan Paul, 1975), 125–9. For *Faustus* as a "Calvinist deformation of the morality tradition" that "embeds the old morality conventions . . . in ironic contexts," see John Stachniewski, *The Persecutory Imagination: English Puritanism and the Literature of Religious Despair* (Oxford: Clarendon Press, 1991), 300, 302.

2. Christopher Marlowe, *Doctor Faustus*, ed. David Scott Kastan (New York: Norton, 2005), Prol. 8. All subsequent citations from this edition of the A-text unless otherwise indicated.

3. Cited from Thomas Rogers, *English Creede, Consenting with the True Auncient Catholique and Apostolique Church* (London, 1585), A5v.

4. Peter Marshall, *Beliefs and the Dead in Reformation England* (Oxford: Oxford University Press, 2002), 111.

5. Ibid., 118.

6. Marlowe, *Doctor Faustus*, 1.3.92.

7. Clifford Davidson, *From Creation to Doom* (New York: AMS Press, 1984), 135–51.

8. For a comprehensive discussion of the publication history of both the German and English editions of the book, including the suggestion of a lost *EFB* published as early as 1588, see John Henry Jones, introduction to *The English Faust Book: A Critical Edition* (Cambridge: Cambridge University Press, 1994), 1–54.

9. *EFB*, 104.

10. Ibid., 104.

11. Ibid., 109–10.

12. Richard Waswo explains the way in which Protestantism, against its medieval forebears, came "to envision hell less as a place than as a state of mind" ("Damnation, Protestant Style: *Macbeth, Faustus*, and Christian Tragedy," *Journal of Medieval and Renaissance Studies* [1974]: 71). His citation from Henry Smith's *Sermons* (1593) is useful: " 'If there be any hell in this world, they which feele the worm of conscience gnawing upon their hearts, may truly say, that they have felt the torments of hell' " (77).

13. Gertrude Himmelfarb, *Tours of Hell: An Apocalyptic Form in Jewish and Christian Literature* (Philadelphia: University of Pennsylvania Press, 1984), 75–105.

14. As Georges Minois suggests, from the earliest instances Christian discussions of hell have always overflowed their basis in the New Testament; they are *"debordements imaginatifs"* meant for believers as well as non-believers: *"Les maigres allusions bibliques ne satisfont pas la curiosité des fidèles, qui veut des details, du pittoresque: on va donc les inventer. Le success de ces legends leur conferera un tel prestige qu'elles seront incorporées dans le corps de doctrine official"* (*Histoire des Enfers* [Paris: Fayard, 1991], 79). For his discussion of punishments matching the crime in the earliest centuries of Christianity and then in the High Middle Ages, see esp. 111, 188.

15. Barbara Palmer, "The Inhabitants of Hell: Devils," *The Iconography of Hell* (Kalamazoo: Medieval Institute Publications, 1992), 20. For the "banalization" of hell during these centuries, see Minois, 210–37.

16. For a discussion of these contexts see Palmer, "Inhabitants," *passim*.

17. Thomas Scott, *A Godlie Sermon of Repentaunce and Amendment of Life* (London, 1585), E8.

18. See Pamela Sheingorn, " 'Who can open the doors of his face?' The Iconography of Hell Mouth," in *The Iconography of Hell*, 1–19. *Henslowe's Diary* includes "j Hell mought" in a 1598 inventory for the Admiral's men (*Henslowe's Diary*, ed. R. A. Foakes, 2nd ed. [Cambridge: Cambridge University Press, 2002], 319).

19. *EFB*, 109.

20. Ibid., 175.

21. *Breefe Treatise Exhorting Sinners to Repentance, Commonly Called, The Conversion of a Sinner* (London, 1580), C6r–D2v; George Meriton, *A Sermon of Repentance* (London, 1607), E4.

22. Richard Greenham, *Seven Godly and Fruitfull Sermons*, in *The Works of the Reverend and Faithfull Servant of Jesus Christ, M. Richard Greenham* (London, 1599), M7v.

23. Introduction to *EFB*, 9.

24. *EFB*, 108.

25. Ibid., 108.

26. According to a strict Calvinist reading, Faustus's fixation on the underworld, as both an object of interest and as the internal experience of despair, identifies the subject

as already damned. John Stachniewski offers the most thorough reading of *Faustus* as "accurately dramatized Calvinist dogma" (292). In a useful corrective, Peter Iver Kaufman suggests that Faustus's misery could "be a little hell for which he should be grateful, as a summons to repentance and sign of election; for some pietists believed it was good to feel inexcusably wicked and wretched" (*Prayer, Despair, and Drama: Elizabethan Introspection* [Urbana: University of Illinois Press, 1996], 85). Other positions on the issue of predestination are addressed below.

27. John Parker, *The Aesthetics of Anti-Christ: From Christian Drama to Christopher Marlowe* (Ithaca, NY: Cornell University Press, 2007); and Adrian Streete, *Protestantism and Drama in Early Modern England* (Cambridge: Cambridge University Press, 2008). I discuss specific aspects of their arguments below. For the persistence of the *imitatio Christi* tradition, see Elizabeth K. Hudson, "English Protestants and the *imitatio Christi*, 1580–1620," *Sixteenth-Century Journal* (1988): 541–58.

28. For the harrowing of hell as the subject of the "earliest of all liturgical plays," see Richard Axton, *European Drama of the Early Middle Ages* (Pittsburgh, PA: University of Pittsburgh Press, 1975), 61.

29. J. A. MacCulloch, *Harrowing of Hell: A Comparative Study of an Early Christian Doctrine* (Edinburgh, 1930), 71.

30. Zbigniew Izydorczyk, introduction to *The Medieval Gospel of Nicodemus: Texts, Intertexts, and Contexts in Western Europe*, ed. Zbigniew Izydorczyk (Tempe, AZ: MRTS, 1997), 1.

31. Ibid., 3.

32. Quotation from Parker, *Aesthetics of Antichrist*, 130. For the place of cycle drama, see William Henry Hulme, introduction to *The Middle English Harrowing of Hell and Gospel of Nicodemus*, ed. William Henry Hulme EETS O.S. 94, 98–100 (London: Kegan Paul, 1907), lx–lxx; C. W. Marx, "Gospel of Nicodemus in Old English and Middle English," in *The Medieval Gospel of Nicodemus*, ed. Zbigniew Izydorczyk (Tempe, AZ: MRTS, 1997), 210–59; C. W. Marx, *The Devil's Rights and the Redemption in the Literature of Medieval England* (Cambridge: D.S. Brewer, 1995), 80–99; Karl Tamburr, *The Harrowing of Hell in Medieval England* (Cambridge: D.S. Brewer, 2007).

33. *A Late Middle English Version of the Gospel of Nicodemus*, ed. Bengt Lindström (Uppsala, Sweden: Almquist & Wiksell, 1974), 99.

34. Ibid., 111–2.

35. Ibid., 113, 117.

36. Tamburr, *Harrowing of Hell*, 46.

37. The trickster is thus tricked: "The devil was outwitted, not knowing Who the ransom was. Christ escaped from his clutches, spoiling the spoiler of his prey," (MacCulloch, *Harrowing of Hell*, 200).

38. "It was fitting that Christ descend into hell. First, he came to bear our punishment and to free us from it . . . . Man had merited by his sins not only the death of his body but also his own descent into hell. If then Christ died in order to free us from death, it was fitting that he descend into hell in order to deliver us also from going down into hell" (St. Thomas Aquinas, *Summa Theologiae*, 54:155).

39. Marx, *The Devil's Rights*, 26. For Thomistic orthodoxy, see Tamburr, *Harrowing of Hell*, 32.

40. Christopher Bond, "Medieval Harrowings of Hell and Spenser's House of Mammon," *English Literary Renaissance* 37.2 (2007): 190.

41. Tamburr, *Harrowing of Hell*, 127. A scene from the *Privity of the Passion* is exemplary: "Behold here now the great mercy and the goodness of our Lord, who would descend down to hell . . . . He might have sent one of his angels to have visited his servants and taken them out of hell and presented them to him wherever he had desired. But his great charity and his meekness would only allow that he should die; therefore he came in his own person, lord of all things, and visited them not as his servants, but as his friends, and was there with them until Sunday morning," in *Cultures of Piety: Medieval English Devotional Literature in Translation*, ed. Anne Clark Bartlett and Thomas H. Bestul (Ithaca, NY: Cornell University Press, 1999), 101.

42. Tamburr, *Harrowing of Hell*, 114, 127.

43. "The Harrowing of Hell" in *The York Plays: A Critical Edition of the York Corpus Christi Play as Recorded in British Library Additional MS 35290*, ed. Richard Beadle, EETS s.s. 23 (Oxford: Oxford University Press, 2009), l. 4. For the complicated relation of York and Towneley, with an understanding that the Towneley "Harrowing" "follows the York version very closely for the most part," see Peter Happé, *The Towneley Cycle: Unity and Diversity* (Cardiff: University of Wales Press, 2007), 27.

44. "Harrowing," ll. 155–6.

45. For the harrowing of hell as a "new episode in the old combat myth" see Neil Forsyth, *The Old Enemy: Satan and the Combat Myth* (Princeton, NJ: Princeton University Press, 1987), 45.

46. Based on this passage Christopher Marx argues that both York and Towneley reject Devil's Rights theory ("The Problem of the Doctrine of the Redemption," 26–9). For a more complicated approach that sees the preservation of the model of the "trickster tricked," see John Parker: "Such talionic reciprocity spoke to the ultimate justice of Christ's triumph, in that a triumph without trickery, over a trickster, would have been *less* fair" (*Aesthetics of Antichrist*, 174).

47. "Harrowing," ll. 271–2.

48. Ibid., ll. 328, 348.

49. Rosemary Woolf, *The English Mystery Plays* (Berkeley: University of California Press, 1972), 271–2.

50. "Christ's Passion is as it were the universal cause of salvation for both the living and the dead. But a universal cause is applied to particular effects through something special. As therefore the power of Christ's Passion is applied to the living by the sacraments which configure us to his Passion, that power was also applied to the dead through his descent into hell" (St. Thomas Aquinas, *Summa Theologiae*, 54:155). Clifford Davidson insists that the cycle plays represent not Christ's victory but its aftermath: "All that remains in the harrowing episode is a mock battle and a ceremonious rescue of souls," (*From Creation to Doom*, 137).

51. Lawrence Clopper, who emphasizes the *persistence* of biblical drama into the later sixteenth century against earlier governmental "suppression" theories, explains the decline and eventual demise of the cycle plays as the result of "the economics of the venture [that] helped create the conditions for the intervention of ecclesiastical and royal authorities" (*Drama, Play, and Game: English Festive Culture in the Medieval and*

Early Modern Period [Chicago: University of Chicago Press, 2001], 286). For the classic statement of the suppression theory, see Harold Gardiner, *Mysteries End* (New Haven, CT: Yale University Press, 1946, reprinted 1967). For an important early correction to this model and its echoes in other studies, see Bing D. Bills, "'The Suppression Theory' and the English Corpus Christi Play: A Re-Examination," *Theatre Journal* (1980): 157–68. For incarnational aesthetics see Michael O'Connell, *The Idolatrous Eye: Iconoclasm and Theater in Early Modern England* (New York: Oxford University Press, 2000).

52. Alexander Hume, *A Rejoynder to Doctor Hil Concerning the Descense of Christ into Hell* (Edinburgh, 1594), B8v.

53. Adam Hill, *The Defence of the Article: Christ Descended into Hell* (London, 1592), A3r.

54. Dewey Wallace, "Puritan and Anglican: The Interpretation of Christ's Descent into Hell in Elizabethan Theology," *Archiv fur Reformationgeschichte* 69 (1978): 248–87, quote on 248.

55. Ibid., 253.

56. Martin Luther, *A Treatise, Touching the Libertie of a Christian*, trans. James Bell (London, 1579), D4r.

57. Wallace, "Interpretation of Christ's Descent," 253.

58. *Formula of Concord* in *The Book of Concord: The Confessions of the Evangelical Lutheran Church*, trans. and ed. Theodore G. Tappert (Philadelphia: Muhlenberg Press, 1959), 492.

59. Ibid., 492.

60. Ibid., 492.

61. Heinrich Bullinger, *Fiftie Godlie and Learned Sermons Divided in Five Decades* (London, 1577), 65–6.

62. Jacques LeGoff, *Birth of Purgatory* (Chicago: University of Chicago Press, 1984), 45.

63. See, for instance, Stephen Greenblatt, *Hamlet in Purgatory* (Princeton, NJ: Princeton University Press, 2001).

64. Consider Ann Faulkner's discussion of a performance at Barking Abbey of the Harrowing of Hell: "Although contemporary theologians may have argued that Christ entered hell in the spirit as Anima Christi, the Barking playwright clearly envisioned an embodied Christus and a staging informed by physicality" ("The Harrowing of Hell at Barking Abbey and in Modern Production," in *The Iconography of Hell*, 153).

65. John Calvin, *Institutes of the Christian Religion*, ed. John T. McNeill and trans. Ford Lewis Battles, 2 vols. (Philadelphia: Westminster Press, 1960), 1: 515–6.

66. Ibid., 517–8.

67. Wallace, "Interpretation of Christ's Descent," 253.

68. John Strype, *Annals of the Reformation,* 2 vols. (London, 1735), 1: 348. Wallace quotes this document (260) but does not include the final lines about fears of "Tragedies and Dissensions." As Wallace explains, "The drafters of the article, however, did not heed the Bishop's appeal for clarity; instead they heeded what he said about the variety of interpretations then current and chose a bare affirmation of the descent without explanation" (260).

69. Elizabeth I herself remarked on the controversy and its threat as a source of dissension in an address to her bishops in 1585, when she complained of ministers: "so curious in searching matters above their capacity as they preach they wot not what—that there is no Hell but a torment of conscience" (cited in Vivian Commensoli, *"Household Business": Domestic Plays of Early Modern England* [Toronto: University of Toronto Press, 1997], 10).

70. Dewey Wallace remarks the important place of the doctrine in the Protestant experience of assurance: "The practical writers of the period tended to meditate very personally and affectionately on Christ's sufferings and to heighten the extent of those sufferings. Toward the end of the Elizabethan period, our writers argued not just that Christ died on behalf of the elect, but that he underwent the very same pains due to the elect and suffered, on the cross, the weight of the full wrath of God against sinners" (*Protestants and Predestination*, 48).

71. From *The Institution of a Christian Man*, in *Formularies of Faith Put Forth by Authority during the Reign of Henry VIII*, ed. Charles Lloyd (Oxford: Oxford University Press, 1866), 41.

72. John Carlisle, *A Discourse Concerning Two Divine Positions* (London, 1582), O7r–O7v. Carlisle's positions were not published until 1582, when they appeared as a rebuttal to a treatise printed in 1562 at Louvain by the Catholic and former Oxford scholar Richard Smith. A comment on the earlier controversy was made by Martin Micronius in a letter to Heinrich Bullinger (see Wallace, "Interpretation of Christ's Descent," 256).

73. Ibid., N5v–N6r.

74. John Northbrooke, *Spiritus Est Vicarius Christi in Terra* (London, 1571), B4v, A3r.

75. Ibid., B4v.

76. Alexander Nowell, *Catechisme, or First Instruction and Learning* (London, 1570), K2v, italics mine.

77. Ibid., K4r.

78. Wallace, "Interpretation of Christ's Descent," 284.

79. Rogers, *English Creede*, B1v.

80. John Baker, *Lectures of J.B. Upon the XII Articles* (London, 1581), F8v–G1v.

81. Andrew Willet, *Synopsis Papismi* (London, 1592), A3r, 2R4v.

82. Ibid., 2R5r, 2R6v. Like Northbrooke and Baker, Willet insisted that a real descent made superfluous demands on Christ's atonement, which ended on the Cross: "Christ suffered fully in body and soule upon the crosse, when he cried, consummatum est, it is finished: that is, he had fully appeased the wrath of god by his sufferings," (2R7r).

83. See Wallace, "Interpretation of Christ's Descent," 269.

84. Hill, *Defence of the Article*, B4v.

85. Ibid., B2r, italics mine.

86. John Higgins, *An Answere to Master William Perkins, Concerning Christs Descension into Hell* (Oxford, 1602), 44.

87. Bishop Thomas Bilson, *The Effect of Certaine Sermons Touching the Full Redemption of Mankind by the Death and Bloud of Christ Jesus* (London, 1599), B1r.

88. Ibid., H1v. In a later publication of 1604 Bilson emphasized that the Calvinist position threatened to fictionalize hell altogether: "To bring Christs soule within the

compasse of hell paines, you flash out the fire of hell as a fable and turne out of service the rest of the torments there," *The Survey of Christes Sufferings for Mans Redemption and of His Descent to Hades or Hel for Our Deliverance* (London, 1604), D3r.

89. Henry Jacob, *A Treatise of the Sufferings and Victory of Christ, in the Work of Our Redemption* (Middleburg, 1598), A8r, B4r.

90. Ibid., C1r. Consider also the Scottish Presbyterian Alexander Hume, who says that a real or local descent operated "contrary to the sufficiency of Christs sacrifice," which "paid a full ransome for our sinnes before, and left nothing behinde to be done in Hell," (*A Rejoynder*, B8v).

91. Richard Parkes, *A Briefe Answere unto Certaine Objections and Reasons against the Descension of Christ into Hell* (London, 1604), A2r.

92. Ibid., H3v, G4v.

93. For the creation of, and differences between, distinct Reformed Christologies see Horton Davies, *Worship and Theology in England, 1558–1603* (Princeton, NJ: Princeton University Press, 1975), 67–69.

94. John Bossy, "Practices of Satisfaction, 1215–1700," in *Retribution, Repentance, and Reconciliation: Papers Read at the 2002 Summer Meeting and 2003 Winter Meeting of the Ecclesiastical History Society* (Suffolk, UK: Boydell & Brewer, 2004), 109.

95. Harry Levin, *The Overreacher, A Study of Christopher Marlowe* (Boston: Beacon Press, 1964), 111.

96. Edward Snow, "Marlowe's *Doctor Faustus* and the Ends of Desire," in *Two Renaissance Mythmakers, Christopher Marlowe and Ben Jonson*, ed. Alvin B. Kernan (Baltimore, MD: Johns Hopkins University Press, 1977), 70, 71. I would like to thank Graham Hammill for calling this essay to my attention.

97. C. L. Barber, "The Form of Faustus' Fortunes Good or Bad," *Tulane Drama Review* 8 (1964): 95.

98. For an important account of the distinction between the more radical A-text's "Württemberg" and the more "Anglican" B-text's "Wittenberg," see Leah Marcus, *Unediting the Renaissance: Shakespeare, Marlowe, Milton* (New York: Routledge, 1996), 41–67. Although it might be possible to distinguish discrete approaches to the Descent by the A and B texts, I do not do so here.

99. Jonathan Dollimore, *Radical Tragedy: Religion, Ideology, and Power in the Drama of Shakespeare and His Contemporaries* (Chicago: University of Chicago Press, 1984), 112. For a related description of Faustus's speech as a performance that "go[es] through the motions of choice" in order to counter his lack of volition, see Stachniewski, *Persecutory Imagination*, 294.

100. As Richard Waswo says, this "hint that Faustus wants to exercise the powers of Christ is confirmed in the conclusion of the speech, the fervid and explicit declaration of Faustus's wish to be God" ("Damnation, Protestant Style," 80).

101. Adrian Streete, " 'Consummatum Est': Calvinist Exegesis, Mimesis, and *Doctor Faustus*," *Literature & Theology* 15.2 (2001): 148. See also the comments of R. M. Cornelius: "Faustus not only aspires to have Christ-like attributes but also quotes or paraphrases some of the statements said by or about Christ" (*Christopher Marlowe's Use of the Bible* [New York: Peter Lang, 1984], 97).

102. The Norton glosses the line: "makes no distinction between the Christian hell and the classical Elysium" (16). For Nashe's jibe, see his letter to the "gentlemen students of both universities," prefaced to Robert Greene's *Menaphon* (London, 1589),**3r.

103. John Stachniewski, *Persecutory Imagination*, 330.

104. *The Towneley Plays*, ed. Martin Stevens and A. C. Cawley, EETS s.s. 13 (Oxford: Oxford University Press, 1994), l. 213.

105. Patrick Cheney, *Marlowe's Counterfeit Profession: Ovid, Spenser, Counter-Nationhood* (Toronto: University of Toronto Press, 1997), 206.

106. The appearance to the protagonist of devils not summoned by him is the introduction to one of Marlowe's putative sources, Nathaniel Woodes *The Conflict of Conscience*, a dramatization of the life of Francis Spira. For the relation between the plays, see Lily B. Campbell, "*Doctor Faustus*: A Case of Conscience," *PMLA* 67.2 (1952): 219–39.

107. *EFB*, 120, 121.

108. Robert Greene, *Friar Bacon and Friar Bungay*, ed. J.A. Lavin (London: Benn, 1969), 11.7–10.

109. Robert Greene, *Greene's Newes Both from Heaven and Hell* (London, 1593), G4r. For early modern journeys to the underworld, see Benjamin Boyce, "News from Hell: Satiric Communications with the Netherworld in English Writing of the Seventeenth and Eighteenth Centuries," *PMLA* 58.2 (1943): 402–37; Anne Lake Prescott, "Intertextual Topology: English Writers and Pantagruel's Hell," *English Literary Renaissance* 23.2 (1993): 244–66. For the medieval tradition, excluding Dante, see Eileen Gardiner, *Medieval Visions of Heaven and Hell: A Sourcebook* (New York: Garland, 1993).

110. For a full discussion of the theatricality of the descent into hell, see Parker, *Aesthetics of Antichrist*, 162–79.

111. John Cox, *The Devil and the Sacred in English Drama, 1350–1642* (Cambridge: Cambridge University Press, 2000), 117.

112. William Perkins, *An Exposition of the Symbole or Creed of the Apostles* (Cambridge, 1595), 247.

113. Andrew Willet, *Limbo-mastix* (London, 1604), H2r.

114. See Adrian Streete, "Calvinist Conceptions of Hell in Marlowe's *Doctor Faustus*," *Notes & Queries* 47.4 (2000), 430–2.

115. Patricia Cahill, "Killing by Computation: Military Mathematics, the Social Body, and Marlowe's *Tamburlaine*," in *The Arts of Calculation*, ed. David Glimp and Michelle Warren (London: Palgrave, 2004), 168.

116. Todd H.J. Pettigrew, "'Faustus . . . for Ever': Marlowe, Bruno, and Infinity," *Comparative Critical Studies* 2.2 (2005): 262.

117. Such an argument may be said to be the other side of the coin to Pettigrew's suggestion that the contract represents Faustus's "refusal to rationally engage the infinite" (264). For the existential appeal of the contract during plague-time, see Christopher Ricks, "Faustus and Hell on Earth," *Essays in Criticism* 35 (1985): 101–20.

118. Nowell, *Catechism*, N3v.

119. See Stachniewski, *Persecutory Imagination*, and McAlindon, "*Doctor Faustus*: The Predestination Theory," *English Studies* 76.3 (1995): 215–20.

120. Charles Clay Doyle, "One Drop of Christ's Streaming Blood: A Gloss on *Doctor Faustus*," *Cahiers Elisabethains* 17 (1980): 85–7.

121. From the famous "Baines Note," reprinted in Constance Kuriyama, *Christopher Marlowe: A Renaissance Life* (Ithaca, NY: Cornell University Press, 2002), 221.

122. Pompa Banerjee, "I, Mephastophilis: Self, Other, and Demonic Parody in Marlowe's *Doctor Faustus*," *Christianity and Literature* 42.2 (1993): 225.

123. Neil Forsyth, "Heavenly Helen," *Etudes de Lettres* 4 (1987): 19.

124. Cecile Williamson Cary, "'It circumscribes us here': Hell on the Renaissance Stage," in *The Iconography of Hell*, 189–90.

Chapter 3

1. *A Brief Fourme of Confession* (Antwerp, 1576), B5r.

2. Daniel Dyke, *Two Treatises. The One, of Repentance, the Other, of Christs Temptations* (London, 1616), 23.

3. Adrian Streete, *Protestantism and Drama in Early Modern England* (Cambridge: Cambridge University Press, 2008), 209.

4. In this way I follow work on the relation between early modern revenge tragedy and contemporary religious upheaval by scholars such as Huston Diehl, who explores revenge drama as a rehearsal of a "new mode of seeing" attendant on Protestant eucharistic theology (*Staging Reform, Reforming the Stage: Protestantism and Popular Theater in Early Modern England* (Ithaca, NY: Cornell University Press, 1997); and Michael Neill, who sees the genre as a secular substitute for "the wholesale displacement of the dead from their familiar place in the order of things by the Protestant abolition of purgatory and ritual intercession" in *Issues of Death: Mortality and Identity in English Renaissance Tragedy* (Oxford: Clarendon Press, 1997), 46. For related arguments, see Thomas P. Anderson, *Performing Early Modern Trauma from Shakespeare to Milton* (Aldershot, VT: Ashgate, 2006); and Thomas Rist, *Revenge Tragedy and the Drama of Commemoration in Reforming England* (Aldershot, VT: Ashgate, 2008).

5. William Ian Miller, *Eye for an Eye* (Cambridge: Cambridge University Press, 2006), 68.

6. Miller, *Eye for an Eye*, 140. For moral objections to the satisfaction theory of revenge, which condones revenge as long as it is seen to inhere in a response to the nature of crime itself, rather than the needs of the victim, see Peter French, *The Virtues of Vengeance* (Lawrence: University of Kansas Press, 2001), 222.

7. Folger Shakespeare Library, V.A.134, p. 35.

8. Edward Muir is particularly helpful: "Vendetta embodied a principle of compensation, 'eye for eye, tooth for tooth,' for a debt created by an insult or injury . . . . people have long conceived of revenge as an exchange that followed the general economic rule that the transfer of any value should be returned in kind and with an increment if possible" (*Mad Blood Stirring: Vendetta & Factions in Friuli during the Renaissance* [Baltimore: Johns Hopkins University Press, 1993], 68).

9. Miller, *Eye for an Eye*, 65.

10. "Revenge is a self-engaged and retrospective action taken privately against an equal who has injured one's honor. Its purpose is not to get rid of someone who is in the

way, or to harm someone who succeeds where the avenger has failed, for it is not a mode of advancement or even of self-defense. Its intention is rather to restore the broken outline of self suffered in an unprovoked attack from a member of one's own class or group" (Anne Pippin Burnett, *Revenge in Attic and Later Tragedy* [Berkeley: University of California Press, 1998], 2).

11. French, *Virtues of Vengeance*, 30. Implying a "yes" answer, Miller asks, "Are there as many types of satisfaction as there are individuals to be satisfied?" (*Eye for an Eye*, 144).

12. Linda Woodbridge, *English Revenge Drama: Money, Resistance, Equality* (Cambridge: Cambridge University Press, 2010), 15, 40. Woodbridge goes on to acknowledge that "revengers co-opt a religious vocabulary made familiar by controversy," but— given the interests of her argument—she does not pursue how the controversy itself affected revenge drama, which is one of the goals of this chapter (40). For another useful discussion of such "problems of commensurability," see Carla Mazzio, "The Three-Dimensional Self: Geometry, Melancholy, Drama" in *The Arts of Calculation: Numerical Thought in Early Modern Europe*, ed. David Glimp and Michelle R. Warren (New York: Palgrave Macmillan, 2004), 39–66, esp. 56.

13. Mary C. Mansfield, *The Humiliation of Sinners: Public Penance in Thirteenth-Century France* (Ithaca, NY: Cornell University Press, 1995), 12.

14. Consider 2 Corinthians 7:11: "For godly grief produces a repentance that leads to salvation and brings no regret, but worldly grief produces death. For see what earnestness this godly grief has produced in you, what eagerness to clear yourselves, what indignation, what alarm, what longing, what zeal, what punishment!" (Here I use the Interpreter's Bible, based on the Revised Standard Version. I discuss alternative early modern translations in the text.)

15. For the permeable boundaries between punishment and restitution, see Woodbridge, *English Revenge Drama*, 84.

16. Peter Lombard, *Sentences, Book 4* in Elizabeth Frances Rogers, *Peter Lombard and the Sacramental System* (Merrick, NY: Richwood Publishing Co., 1976), 155.

17. Thomas of Chobham, *Summa Confessorum*, ed. F. Broomfield (Louvain: Editions Nauwelaerts, 1968), 5.

18. Cited in Ashley Null, *Thomas Cranmer's Doctrine of Repentance: Renewing the Power to Love* (Oxford: Oxford University Press, 2000), 34, fn. 22.

19. Cited in Richard Strier, "Herbert and Tears," *ELH* 46 (1979): 227; Peter Canisius, *An Introduction to the Catholick Faith* (Rouen: 1633), E5r.

20. C. W., *Summarie of Controversies: Wherein the Chiefest Points of the Holy Catholike Romane Faith, are . . . Proved, against the Sectaries of this Age* (London, 1616), 207–8.

21. Alexandra Walsham, *Providence in Early Modern England* (Oxford: Oxford University Press, 1999), 90.

22. *Liturgical Services: Liturgies and Occasional Forms of Prayer Set Forth in the Reign of Queen Elizabeth* (Cambridge: Cambridge University Press, 1847), 491.

23. Ibid., 479.

24. Peter Lake with Michael Questier, *The Anti-Christ's Lewd Hat: Protestants, Papists and Players in Post-Reformation England* (New Haven, CT: Yale University Press, 2002), 623.

25. Marinus van Beek, *An Enquiry into Puritan Vocabulary* (Groningen, Netherlands: Wolters-Noordhoff, 1969), 68, italics in the original.

26. Jean Calvin, *The Institution of the Christian Religion,* trans. Thomas Thymme (London, 1561), R4r.

27. Arthur Dent, *A Sermon of Repentance* (London, 1587), B8r, italics mine.

28. Stephen Egerton, *A Lecture Preached by Maister Egerton* (London, 1603), C4v, italics in the original, C5r, italics mine.

29. Francis Marbury, *Notes of the Doctrine of Repentance* (London, 1602), B4r.

30. George Meriton, *A Sermon of Repentance* (London, 1607), B3r–3v.

31. The scriptural distinctions are consistent with a classical model according to which "punishment, *kolasis,* is a reasonable response to an act of wrongdoing, because it concentrates on the recipient, looks to the future, and tries to teach virtue, whereas vengeance, which attempts to satisfy him who inflicts it, is senseless and bestial because it looks backward to strike at a past deed" (Burnett, *Revenge,* 7). Consider the Geneva Bible translation: "For beholde, this thing that ye have bene goldy sorie, what great care it hath wroght in you: yea, what clearing of your selves, yea (what) indignacion: yea, (what) feare: yea (how) great disire, yea, (what) a zeale: yea, (what) *punishment*." The King James Version of 1611 renders *vindictam* as "revenge": "For godly sorrow worketh repentance to salvation not to be repented of: but the sorrow of the world worketh death. For behold this selfsame thing, that ye sorrowed after a godly sort, what carefulness it wrought in you, yea, *what* clearing of yourselves, yea, *what* indignation, yea, *what* fear, yea, *what* vehement desire, yea, *what* zeal, yea, *what* revenge!" For the bulk of theologians and dramatists discussed in the chapter, however, revenge and punishment were usually used interchangeably.

32. Null, *Cranmer's Doctrine of Repentance,* 113.

33. *Apology of the Augsburg Confession,* in *The Book of Concord: The Confessions of the Evangelical Lutheran Church,* trans and ed. Theodore G. Tappert (Philadelphia: Muhlenberg Press, 1959), 205. Consider also Calvin: "We must not hereof gather that men in punishing them selves, doe countervayle, and make satisfaction for the punishment which they have deserved at the handes of God, thereby to deliver them selves from the hande of God" (*A Commentarie upon S. Pauls Epistles to the Corinthians,* trans. Thomas Thymme [London,1577], 262v).

34. William Perkins, *A Reformed Catholike* (London, 1598), I2r.

35. Ibid., I2v. Perkins goes on to say that "these kinde of actions"—subduing corruption, bridling affection, mortifying sin—"are *restrainments* properly, and no punishments." His concern here about using the term punishment, even as he continues to insist on penitential *revenge* (an insistence that reverses the trend of the early Reformed biblical translations) is an instructive reminder of how charged as well as slippery the language around penitence could be.

36. Dyke, *Two Treatises,* 139, 142, 145.

37. *The New Testament of Jesus Christ* (Rheims, 1582), 483, italics mine.

38. Though see Martha Tuck Rozett, who notes the connection in her discussion of the rhetoric of election: "Even more extreme . . . is the self-punishment inflicted by the true believer referred to as 'revenge,' frequently described in Puritan tracts as the last of the seven stages of repentance. . . . Revenge of this kind was a legitimate action which

could be performed in the service of God, one to which the ordinary believer might have the occasion to resort" (*The Doctrine of Election and the Emergence of Elizabethan Tragedy* [Princeton, NJ: Princeton University Press, 1984], 70).

39. Eleanor Prosser, *Hamlet and Revenge* (Stanford, CA: Stanford University Press, 1971); Thomas Rist, *Revenge Tragedy and the Drama of Commemoration in Reforming England* (Burlington, VT: Ashgate, 2008); Fredson Bowers, *Elizabethan Revenge Tragedy, 1587–1642* (Princeton, NJ: Princeton University Press, 1940); Ronald Broude, "Revenge and Revenge Tragedy in Renaissance England," *Renaissance Quarterly* 28.1 (1975): 38–58; Catherine Belsey, *The Subject of Tragedy* (London: Methuen, 1985). For the argument that revenge tragedy is an "extension of the drama of retribution" which stands in contrast to the early modern pulpit's "lesson of salvation, of repentance, mercy, and grace," see James A. Reynolds, *Repentance and Retribution in Early English Drama* (Salzburg, Austria: Salzburg Studies in English Literature, 1982), 24, 25.

40. Francis Bacon, *The Essays*, ed. John Pitcher (London: Penguin Books, 1985), 72.

41. "The passion of revenge, then, is such that, once the mind is freed from the restraints that normally control that passion, a fatal chain of events is set in progress. Transformations take place within the avenger, who, though requiring a certain period of time, alters his perception of the world to an extent that will enable him to perform heinous deeds and make his own death in atonement for these deeds inevitable" (Charles and Elaine Hallett, *The Revenger's Madness: A Study of Revenge Tragedy Motifs* [Lincoln: University of Nebraska Press, 1980], 12). The sense of "atonement" here is clearly nontheological in any real sense.

42. Pierre de La Primaudaye, *The French Academie* (London, 1586), 382; Anthony Copley, *A Fig for Fortune* (London, 1596), E4r.

43. The revenger's so-called delay, his postponement of reprisal in order to establish the grounds and strategies for his actions, is a crystalline example of revenge's tendency to provoke repentance and thus "self-revenge." The delay was understood in the period as a kind of double crime: either the most devious form of revenge ("punish[ing] more with not punishing then the hastiest Executioner") or a failure or betrayal of the victim (William Cornwallis, *Essayes* (London, 1600–1601), C8v). It thus served as a reminder of an abiding and ineradicable transgression in the revenger himself. At the same time it also provides the space for the revenger to acknowledge and castigate himself.)

For a full discussion of the generic basis of the delay and the way it "cover[s] the temporal gap between the advent of the desire to revenge and the violent act precipitated by it," see Hallett and Hallett, *The Revenger's Madness*, 84–9. Lorna Hutson has recently contextualized the genre's famous instances of hesitation in terms of changing procedures in Elizabethan jurisprudence; they represent, she says, "the deferral of discovery—the protracted processes of detection, pre-trial examination, trial, and evidence evaluation" (*The Invention of Suspicion: Law and Mimesis in Shakespeare and Renaissance Drama* [Oxford: Oxford University Press], 2008], 9).

44. Terry Eagleton, *Sweet Violence: The Idea of the Tragic* (Malden, MA: Blackwell, 2003), 151.

45. For universal corruption, see Peter Mercer, *Hamlet and the Acting of Revenge* (London: Macmillan, 1987), 45. William Shakespeare, *Hamlet*, in *The Riverside Shakespeare*, ed. G. B. Evans (New York: Houghton Mifflin, 1974), 1.2.135–6. For the

"trauma" of original sin, see my "Hamlet's 'first corse': Repetition, Trauma, and the Displacement of Redemptive Typology," *Shakespeare Quarterly* 54.4 (2003): 424–8.

46. Margreta de Grazia, Hamlet *without Hamlet* (Cambridge: Cambridge University Press, 2007).

47. Saint Augustine, *Answer to the Pelagians*, trans. Roland J. Teske, vol. 23 in *The Works of Saint Augustine*, ed. John E. Rotelle, O.S.A. (Hyde Park, NY: New City Press, 1997), 403–63, esp. 446–54.

48. Paula Fredriksen, *Sin: The Early History of an Idea* (Princeton, NJ: Princeton University Press, 2012), 125.

49. See Alister McGrath, *Luther's Theology of the Cross: Martin Luther's Theological Breakthrough* (Oxford: Blackwell, 1985), esp. 99–148.

50. David Cressy summarizes the Protestant position(s) on baptism: "The mainstream position of the Church of England was that baptism had limited efficacy, and did not wash away all sin. Anyone who suggested that the ceremony itself, or any of its particular elements, automatically secured forgiveness of sins would surely be condemned as superstitious" (*Birth, Marriage, and Death: Ritual, Religion, and the Life-Cycle in Tudor and Stuart England* [Oxford: Oxford University Press, 1997], 111). For the Fifth Session of the Council of Trent and its canons on the doctrine of original sin, see Hubert Jedin, *A History of the Council of Trent* (Edinburgh: Thomas Nelson and Sons, 1961), 125–65. (Authorized translation of Hubert Jedin, *Geschichte des Konzils von Trient*, 1957.)

51. Cited in Jean Delumeau, *Sin and Fear: The Emergence of a Western Guilt Culture, Thirteenth to Eighteenth Centuries*, trans. Eric Nicholson (New York: St. Martin's Press, 1990), 248.

52. William Perkins, *A Reformed Catholike* (London, 1598), B7v. Consider also Theodore Beza, who claimed claimed that the Roman church neither knew "howe deadly theyr sicknesse is" nor taught "that man is altogether dead by originall sinne, otherwyse called naturall corruption," but believed instead that "regeneration proceedeth not onely of grace, but there is a participation or concurrence betweene grace, & that which they call freewyll" (*A Briefe and Piththie Summe of the Christian Faith*, trans. R. F. [London, 1565], T2r).

53. Richard Sibbes, *The Complete Works of Richard Sibbes*, ed. Alexander Balloch Grosart, 7 vols. (Edinburgh: J. Nichol, 1862–64), 2:336.

54. John Donne, *The Sermons of John Donne*, ed. George Potter and Evelyn Simpson, 10 vols. (Berkeley: University of California Press, 1955), 2:101.

55. *The Benefite that Christians Receive by Jesus Christ Crucified* (London, 1573), B2r–B2v. For the composition of the book and the theological position of its Italian authors, see M. Anne Overell, *Italian Reform and English Reformations* (Aldershot, VT: Ashgate, 2008), 29–32.

56. David Scott Kastan, "'His Semblable Is His Mirror': Hamlet and the Imitation of Revenge," *Shakespeare Studies* 19 (1987), 112; Katherine Maus, introduction to *Four Revenge Tragedies* (Oxford: Oxford University Press, 1995), xi. This tendency of revenge led earlier critics to suggest that revenge plays meant to reinforce a Christian ethical system, grounded in Deuteronomy 32:35 and Romans 12:19, which insisted that vengeance should be left to God and that it perpetuates the sin which it tries to rectify. See

Prosser, *Hamlet and Revenge*; and Lily B. Campbell, "Theories of Revenge in Renaissance England," *Modern Philology* 28.3 (1931): 281–96. Insistence on the solely didactic nature of revenge plays has been corrected by numerous scholars, and most convincingly by Woodbridge, who argues for the appeal of the revenge play in confronting systemic unfairness: "Little angst about revenge is on display" in the drama, she says (*English Revenge Drama*, 24). But Campbell's sense that "there was a persistent condemnation of revenge in the *ethical teaching* of Shakespeare's England" remains accurate and useful (281, italics mine).

57. *Seneca His Tenne Tragedies, translated into Englysh* (London, 1581), D8v. Latin from the Loeb edition: *Seneca*, ed. John G. Fitch (2004), vol. 78, ll. 195–96. It is worth noting that the Tudor translator, Jasper Heywood, translates "*ulcisceris*" as "dost *enough* revenge" and not simply "dost revenge." Enough, here, is the translator's excess.

58. William Westerman, *Two Sermons of Assize* (London, 1600), B5v–B7r.

59. Robert Watson, "Tragedies of Revenge and Ambition," *The Cambridge Companion to Shakespearean Tragedy*, ed. Claire McEachern (Cambridge: Cambridge University Press, 2002), 172. Muir finds "little evidence that avengers took at all seriously the obligation not to increase excessively the level of insult; in fact, they typically thrilled in the large number and the gravity of the wounds delivered" (*Mad Blood Stirring*, 307, fn 27).

60. Gordon Braden, *Renaissance Tragedy and the Senecan Tradition: Anger's Privilege* (New Haven, CT: Yale University Press, 1985), 113. For a more recent assessment of the appeal of Seneca to Elizabethan authors in terms of traditions of advice to princes literature, see Jessica Winston, "Seneca in Early Elizabethan England," *Renaissance Quarterly* 59.1 (2006): 29–58.

61. For an earlier version of this reading of *The Spanish Tragedy*, see my " 'Conceived of young Horatio his son': *The Spanish Tragedy* and the Psychotheology of Revenge," in *A Companion to Tudor Literature*, ed. Kent Cartwright (Chichester, England: Wiley-Blackwell, 2010), 444–58.

62. Thomas Kyd, *The Spanish Tragedy*, ed. J. R. Mulryne (London: A&C Black, 1989), 2.5.9–10. All quotations from this edition.

63. Though see Lisa Hopkins on the way the Christian overtones are "rapidly superseded when the classical features" of the play's landscapes are made clear ("What's Hercules to Hamlet?" *Hamlet Studies* 1999: 117). I follow Lukas Erne, who declares *The Spanish Tragedy* "much more of a personal and, in particular, Christian tragedy than has hitherto been recognized, as much so, in some ways, as *Doctor Faustus*" ("Thomas Kyd's Christian Tragedy," *Renaissance Papers 2001*, 21)

64. Bowers, *Elizabethan Revenge Tragedy*, 71–2.

65. John Kerrigan, *Revenge Tragedy: Aeschylus to Armageddon* (Oxford: Oxford University Press, 1996), 173. In Crosbie's compelling formula, Hieronimo's revenge "becomes one of a number of expressions of household *oeconomia*, a form of propagation and extension of one's self by way of alternate means when lawful attempts to advance become retarded" ("Oeconomia and the Vegetative Soul: Rethinking Revenge in *The Spanish Tragedy*," *English Literary Renaissance* 38.1 (2008): 28.

66. Scott McMillin discusses Hieronimo's experience, both of the death of his son and his thwarted efforts at finding justice, as a "realization of self-loss" ("The Book of Seneca in *The Spanish Tragedy*," *SEL: Studies in English Literature, 1500–1700* 14 [1974]: 206).

67. Thomas Wright, *Passions of the Mind in General* (London, 1601), B1v–B2r.

68. "Outward mortifications" from Martin Luther, "Ninety-five Theses, 1517," trans. Harold J. Grimm, in vol. 31 of *Luther's Works*, ed. Harold J. Grimm (Philadelphia: Muhlenberg Press, 1957), 25. Rozett describes the pain, though not the guilt, of the revenging parent: "In an age which glorified martyrdom, to survive was in a very real sense more tragic than to perish, and the true victims are not the slaughtered children, but the parents who remain alive, tormented by the knowledge of their loss and unable to understand why God has permitted the death of innocents" (*Doctrine*, 181).

69. In his important article, Eugene D. Hill describes the way that the play's engagement with the underworld "take[s] the Senecan prologue and rewrite[s] it as an *inversion* of Book 6 of the *Aeneid*. In systematic fashion Kyd inverts the motifs of Vergil's marvelous katabasis," ("Senecan and Vergilian Perspectives in the *Spanish Tragedy*," *English Literary Renaissance* 15.2 [1985]: 150). For Kyd's appropriation of the pagan underworld for Christian purposes, see Erne, "Christian Tragedy," passim.

70. Greenham, *The Workes of the Reverend and Faithfull Servant of Jesus Christ M. Richard Greenham* (London, 1599), C5v.

71. For an extremely subtle account of Hieronimo's "revenge on language, on representation," see Carla Mazzio, "Staging the Vernacular: Language and Nation in Thomas Kyd's *The Spanish Tragedy*," *SEL: Studies in English Literature, 1500–1700* 38.2 (1998): 207–32.

72. *Benefit*, A6, A7v. My argument below emphasizes the connection Hamlet senses between his sinfulness and his father's, rather than, according to J. Dover Wilson, his mother's: "His blood is tainted, his very flesh corrupted, by what his mother has done, since he is bone of her bone and flesh of her flesh" (*What Happens in* Hamlet, 3rd ed. [Cambridge: Cambridge University Press, 1951], 42).

73. The psychoanalytic reading begins with Freud; according to him, Hamlet delays his revenge on Claudius because Claudius "shows Hamlet the repressed wishes of his own childhood realized. Thus the loathing which should drive him to revenge is replaced in him by self-reproaches, by scruples of conscience, which remind him that he himself is no better than the sinner whom he is to punish" (Sigmund Freud, *The Interpretation of Dreams*, in vol. 4 of *The Standard Edition*, ed. and trans. James Strachey [London: Hogarth Press, 1953], 264–6). For approaches to the Freudian insight informed by more recent developments in psychoanalytic theory, see Jacques Lacan, "Desire and the Interpretation of Desire in *Hamlet*," in *Literature and Psychoanalysis*, ed. Shoshana Felman (Baltimore: Johns Hopkins University Press, 1982), 11–52; Avi Ehrlich, *Hamlet's Absent Father* (Princeton, NJ: Princeton University Press, 1977); and especially Janet Adelman, *Suffocating Mothers: Fantasies of Maternal Origin in Shakespeare's Plays, Hamlet to the Tempest* (New York: Routledge, 1991), 11–37. For complaint satire, see Mercer, *Hamlet and the Acting of Revenge*.

74. William Shakespeare, *Hamlet*. In *The Riverside Shakespeare*, edited by G. Blakemore Evans, 2nd ed. (New York: Houghton Mifflin, 1997), 1.2.101–6. All quotations from this edition.

75. "[H]e is pervasively aware of human sin and shortcomings, particularly in himself," Roland Mushat Frye, *The Renaissance Hamlet: Issues and Responses in 1600* (Princeton, NJ: Princeton University Press, 1984), 177.

76. Stephen Greenblatt, *Hamlet in Purgatory* (Princeton, NJ: Princeton University Press, 2001), 214.

77. William Kerrigan provides a thorough overview of a tradition of *Hamlet* criticism shaped by the idea of the protagonist's inability to act; see *Hamlet's Perfection* (Baltimore: The Johns Hopkins University Press, 1994), 2–26.

78. De Grazia, Hamlet *without Hamlet*, 187.

79. See Ramie Targoff, "The Performance of Prayer," *Representations* 60 (1997): 49–69. Targoff is especially sensitive to the difficulties and nuances between true versus feigned contrition. Roland Mushat Frye considers the problem not in terms of real versus acted but rather the classic spiritual conundrum of attrition versus contrition: "[Claudius] is in a state which might be called attrition rather than contrition, or anguish rather than penitence" (*Renaissance Hamlet*, 136).

80. For the classic discussion of Hamlet as lacking an objective correlative, see T. S. Eliot, "Hamlet and His Problems," *The Sacred Wood* (London: Methuen, 1964), 95–103.

81. See for instance Steven Mullaney "Mourning and Misogyny: *Hamlet, The Revenger's Tragedy*, and the Final Progress of Elizabeth I, 1600–1607," *Shakespeare Quarterly* 45.2 (1994): 139–62.

82. I follow the established consensus since the 1980s that Middleton, rather than Cyril Tourneur, is the author of *The Revenger's Tragedy*. For a recent, focused summary of the authorship question, see Brian Corrigan, "Middleton, *The Revenger's Tragedy*, and Crisis Literature," *SEL: Studies in English Literature, 1500–1700* 38.2 (1998): 281–95. The play is anthologized in *Thomas Middleton: The Collected Works*, ed. Gary Taylor and John Lavagnino (Oxford: Clarendon Press, 2007), 543–93. My citations below are from this edition of the play, edited by MacDonald P. Jackson.

83. See, for instance, Peter Stallybrass, "Reading the Body and the Jacobean Theater of Consumption," *Renaissance Drama* 18 (1987): 121–48.

84. Peter Brooks argues that confessions may never be entirely voluntary insofar as they respond to a "need to stage a scene of exposure as the only propitiation of accusation, including self-accusation. Or . . . confession may be the product of the death-drive, the production of incriminating acts to assure punishment or even self-annihilation, and hence inherently suspect because in contradiction to the basic human instinct of self-preservation" (*Troubling Confessions: Speaking Guilt in Law and Literature* [Chicago: University of Chicago Press, 2000], 21).

85. "The institutions of forgiveness in Christian antiquity and the early middle ages relied principally on ascetic public acts to ensure obedience and offer consolation. Of course they demanded contrition and belief in divine mercy. Nevertheless they were systems of shame and . . . expiation. Private auricular confession, on the other hand, gradually turned the institutional energies of ecclesiastical penance inward. In the penitentials it still focused on expiatory, albeit private, acts of satisfaction for sin. But by the thirteenth century it had become primarily a private act, protected by the seal of the confessional, emphasizing the inner preparation and disposition of the penitent seeking help from a sacrament dispensed by a priest. It would be foolish to suppose that society itself, or even the church, renounced public shame and the mentality of expiation . . . . But sacramental confession, the principal means of forgiveness of sins, goes another route. The law is applied to the inner forum—the conscience of man—and forgiveness is offered only to

those who achieve that inner preparation. From a penance of shame and expiation, the church . . . had turned to a penance of guilt and remorse" (Thomas Tentler, *Sin and Confession on the Eve of the Reformation* [Princeton, NJ: Princeton University Press, 1977], 52).

86. Lombard, *Sentences*, 183–4.

87. *The Canons and Decrees of the Sacred and Oecumenical Council of Trent*, ed. and trans. J. Waterworth (London: Dolman, 1848), 14th sess., chap. 5.

88. *A Short and an Absolute Order of Confession* (1577), B5v–B6r.

89. For Counter-Reformation confession, see David Myers, *Poor Sinning Folk: Confession and Conscience in Counter-Reformation Germany* (Ithaca, NY: Cornell University Press, 1996), esp. 110–183.

90. Luther, "Sacrament of Penance, 1519," *Works* 35:20.

91. Lawrence Duggan, "Fear and Confession on the Eve of the Reformation," *Archiv für Reformationsgeschichte* 75 (1984): 153–75. For "butchery of conscience," see *The Oxford Encyclopedia of the Reformation*, ed. Hans J. Hillerbrand (New York: Oxford UP, 1996), 1:403. Consider also The *Apology of the Augsburg Confession*: "How much effort is devoted to the endless enumeration of sins, most of them against human traditions! And to torture godly minds still more, they imagine that this enumeration is a divine command . . . . They pretend that the sacrament grants grace *ex opere operato*, without a right attitude in the recipient, and they do not mention faith, which grasps the absolution and consoles the conscience . . . . What snares this requirement of complete confession has cast upon consciences! When will the conscience be sure that its confession is complete?" (*Apology*, 184, 198).

92. *Documents of the English Reformation 1526–1701*, ed. Gerald Bray (Cambridge: James Clarke, 2004), 22.

93. Thomas Becon, *Reliques of Rome* (London, 1563), 108r; Samuel Harsnett, *A Declaration of Egregious Popish Impostures* (London, 1603), A4r.

94. Richard Hooker, *Of the Laws of Ecclesiastical Polity*, in *The Folger Library Edition of the Works of Richard Hooker*, edited by W. Speed Hill et al., 7 vols. (Cambridge, MA: Belknap Press, 1977–98), 3:29.

95. See Ronald Rittgers, *The Reformation of the Keys: Confession, Conscience, and Authority in Sixteenth-Century Germany* (Cambridge, MA: Harvard University Press, 2004).

96. For the transformation, under Archbishop Thomas Cranmer's direction, of "the practice of pre-communion confession from a personal exchange between priest and penitent to a standardized utterance performed by the entire congregation," see Ramie Targoff, *Common Prayer: The Language of Public Devotion in Early Modern England* (Chicago: University of Chicago Press, 2001), 30; for the fostering by the Tudor and Stuart church of a "broad consensus in support of optional private confession," see Eric Josef Carlson, "Confession and Absolution in Caroline Cambridge: The 1637 Crisis in Context," in *Retribution, Repentance, and Reconciliation: Papers Read at the 2002 Summer Meeting and 2003 Winter Meeting of the Ecclesiastical History Society*, ed. Kate Cooper and Jeremy Gregory (Suffolk, UK: Boydell & Brewer, 2004), 187; and for the siphoning of confessional energies into catechistical literature that worked to "preserv[e] and enhance . . . the educational aspects of confession," see Christopher Marsh, *Popular Religion in Sixteenth-Century England: Holding Their Peace* (New York: St. Martin's Press, 1998), 82.

97. *A Path-way to Penitence* (London, 1592), C3v.

98. Christopher Haigh, *The Plain Man's Pathway to Heaven* (Oxford: Oxford University Press, 2007), 6. For a discussion of competing levels of shame and humiliation between penance in the church and penance in the marketplace, see Dave Postles, "Penance and the Market Place: a Reformation Dialogue with the Medieval Church (c. 1250–1600)," *Journal of Ecclesiastical History* 54 (2003): 441–69.

99. In F. G. Emmison, *Elizabethan Life: Morals & the Church Courts* (Chelmsford, Essex: Essex County Council, 1970), 281–90.

100. Henry Holland, *Davids Faith and Repentance* (London, 1589), C4r.

101. "Homilic of Repentance," in *Certaine Sermons or Homilies* (Gainesville, FL: Scholars' Focsimiles and Reprints, 1968), 266.

102. Thomas Wilson, *A Christian Dictionarie* (London, 1612), E7v–E8r.

103. Richard Pilkington, *Parallela: or the Grounds of the New Romane Catholike* (London, 1618), 278–9.

104. Patrick Collinson, "Shepherds, Sheepdogs, and Hirelings: The Pastoral Ministry in Post-Reformation England," *The Ministry: Clerical and Lay, Studies in Church History* 29 (1989): 219. For the argument that, in the absence of sacramental confession, the requirements of the ecclesiastical courts for public apology "assured that penance would also be automatically shameful and humiliating because the resort to public exposure was unmitigated and unmediated by any prior stages of private penance," see Sarah Beckwith, *Shakespeare and the Grammar of Forgiveness* (Ithaca, NY: Cornell University Press, 2011), 52. Beckwith does not acknowledge sufficiently the Reformed conventions that preserved private—though not auricular—confession.

105. Peter Stallybrass, "Reading the Body," 129.

106. See my "Confessing Mothers: The Maternal Penitent in Early Modern Revenge Tragedy," *The Impact of Feminism in English Renaissance Studies*, ed. Dympna Callaghan (Basingstoke, UK: Palgrave, 2007), 53–66.

107. Vindice's "mission," Stallybrass writes, "is justified by the virtuous enclosure of the woman's body while his function will be to display that body as both permeable and permeated. To put it another way, his own metamorphoses are produced by the uncertainty which he locates in woman's body" ("Reading the Body," 129–30); Karin Coddon, "For Show or Useless Property: Necrophilia and *The Revenger's Tragedy*," in *Revenge Tragedy: Contemporary Critical Essays*, ed. Stevie Simkin (New York: Palgrave, 2001), 121, 134. See also Michael Neill's discussion of the scene's "morbid eroticism" in "Death and *The Revenger's Tragedy*" in *Early Modern English Drama: A Critical Companion*, ed. Garrett A. Sullivan, Patrick Cheney, Andrew Hadfield (Oxford: Oxford University Press, 2006), 171.

108. Seneca, *Thyestes*, ll. 1102–4, 1037–8.

109. Tanya Pollard, *Drugs and Theater in Early Modern England* (Oxford: Oxford University Press, 2005), 114.

110. For Middleton's "moderate Puritan background," see Margot Heinemann, *Puritanism and Theatre: Thomas Middleton and Opposition Drama under the Early Stuarts* (Cambridge: Cambridge University Press, 1980), 51.

111. Kerrigan, *Hamlet's Perfection*, 151. Consider also Braden: "No other English avenger, indeed no other Shakespeare character, dies with such a sense of attained grace" (*Senecan Tradition*, 222).

112. Consider Steven Justice: "No one is satisfied, and nearly everyone is dead," ("Spain, Tragedy, and *The Spanish Tragedy*," *SEL: Studies in English Literature, 1500–1700* 25.2 [1985]: 287–8).

Chapter 4

1. Paul Whitfield White, *Theatre and Reformation: Protestantism, Patronage, and Playing in Tudor England* (New York: Cambridge University Press, 1993), 60. For the plays' role "as an instrument of Protestant educational reform," see David Bevington, "Staging the Reformation: Power and Theatricality in the Plays of William Wager," in *Interludes and Early Modern Society: Studies in Gender, Power and Theatricality*, ed. Peter Happé and Wim Hüsken (Amsterdam: Rodopi, 2007), 355.

2. For Shakespeare's debt to "proverbial plays," and thus to the Tudor moralities, as well as his ability to "take the 'proverb play' a step further by questioning the truth of the proverb which provides the play's theme," see Paula Neuss, "The Sixteenth-Century English 'Proverb' Play," *Comparative Drama* 18.1 (1984): 1–18, quotation on p. 17.

3. William Shakespeare, *The Merchant of Venice*, in *The Riverside Shakespeare*, ed. G. Blakemore Evans, 2nd ed. (New York: Houghton Mifflin, 1997), 2.2.150–1. All subsequent quotations of *Merchant* are from this edition. For the proverb "the grace of God is great (gear) enough," see M. P. Tilley, *Dictionary of the Proverbs in England in the Sixteenth and Seventeenth Centuries* (Ann Arbor: University of Michigan Press, 1950), G393.

4. For a strong reading of the role of Launcelot in the play, see Avraham Oz, "Dobbin on the Rialto: Venice and the Division of Identity," in *Shakespeare's Italy: Functions of Italian Locations in Renaissance Drama*, ed. Michele Marrapodi et al. (Manchester: Manchester University Press, 1993), 185–209.

5. "Overplus" is consistently used as a synonym for illicit or immoral financial gain, particularly in discussions of usury. See, for example, George Downame, *Lecture on the 15. Psalme* (London, 1604), 151.

6. For various accounts of this intersection, see James Aho, *Confession and Bookkeeping: The Religious, Moral, and Rhetorical Roots of Modern Accounting* (Albany: State University of New York Press, 2005), 1–7. See also Craig Muldrew, *The Economy of Obligation: The Culture of Credit and Social Relations in Early Modern England* (New York: St. Martin's Press, 1998), 132–46.

7. For "salvation market" see Odd Langholm, *Merchant in the Confessional: Trade and Price in the Pre-Reformation Penitential Handbooks* (Boston: Brill, 2003), 12. Specific aspects of "salvific economy" reinforce the overlap of the penitential and commercial: the notion of *foenus spirituale*, the gain or interest returned in heaven (or hell) for earthly deeds; and the notion of moral accounting, a penitential sensibility fostered by the conjunction of late medieval and Reformation confessional demands with the development of double-entry bookkeeping, with its scrupulous attention to spiritual debits and credits. For a bracing discussion of penitential exchange as an "anti-economy of deliverance," see John Parker, *The Aesthetics of Antichrist: From Christian Drama to Christopher Marlowe* (Ithaca, NY: Cornell University Press, 2007), 99.

8. Valerie Forman's focus on shared languages of redemption is an apt foil here; she observes that during the early modern period the "theorization of new economic practices . . . borrows from Christian models of redemption," and she studies the ways that "redemption is partially secularized then redeployed both in the economic realm and in dramatic form" (*Tragicomic Redemptions: Global Economics and the Early Modern English Stage* [Philadelphia: University of Pennsylvania Press, 2008], 14). I emphasize the shared model of satisfactory exchange undergirding both the economic and penitential realms and their intersection in the problem of financial sin. See also Patricia Parker's important discussion of Shakespeare's weaving of "commercial and biblical imagery of debt and redemption" in *The Comedy of Errors* (*Shakespeare from the Margins* [Chicago: University of Chicago Press, 1996], 75).

9. Langholm, *Merchant in the Confessional*, 4.

10. Helen White's summary remains useful: Protestant moral economists were "primarily concerned with . . . the calling of the sinner to repentance. The rebuking of sins, the enjoining of duty, the definition of ideals, the explication of ways and means, that is [their] business" (*Social Criticism in Popular Religious Literature of the Sixteenth Century* [New York: Macmillan Co., 1944], 192).

11. I thus qualify Jonathan Hall's useful summary of the general dynamic by which the Jew Shylock is made to bear the sins of global trade and law "in a *misrecognized and demonic* form. It is misrecognized in the form of Shylock's monstrous and archaic appetites" (*Anxious Pleasures: Shakespearean Comedy and the Nation State* [Madison, NJ: Fairleigh Dickinson University Press, 1995], 58). My point is that the Christians' anti-Judaic *ressentiment* is channeled through their perception of Shylock as, in Launcelot's terms, enough rather than as the figure of appetite.

12. For a description of these changes, as well as contemporaries' awareness of them, see Keith Wrightson, *Earthly Necessities: Economic Lives in Early Modern Britain* (New Haven, CT: Yale University Press, 2000). For the persistence of the notion of economics as "one department of moral conduct" well into the early modern period, see R. H. Tawney's introduction to Sir Thomas Wilson, *Discourse Upon Usury*, ed. R. H. Tawney (New York: Augustus M. Kelley, repr. 1965), 16.

13. Thomas Lupton, *A Dreame of the Devill and Dives* (London, 1584), B3v.

14. Thomas Lodge, *An Alarum against Usurers* (London, 1584), F3r.

15. White, *Social Criticism*, 198. For the development of legal as well as religious approaches to usury in the late sixteenth and seventeenth centuries so that "economic expediency was left as the only sure way for society to judge when usury occurred and whether it was bad," see Norman Jones, *God and the Moneylenders: Usury and the Law in Early Modern England* (Oxford: Blackwell, 1989), 5. For works that focus almost entirely on the doctrinal perspective, see Eric Kerridge, *Usury, Interest and the Reformation* (Aldershot, UK: Ashgate, 2002); David W. Jones, *Reforming the Morality of Usury: A Study of the Differences that Separated the Protestant Reformers* (New York: University Press of America, 2004).

16. The Scholastic argument, dating from at least the twelfth century, had endorsed a return above the principal in certain circumstances, including cases in which a creditor was damaged as a result of a default (*damnum emergens*) and cases in which a creditor had to forego, as a result of a loan, financial opportunities from which

he might otherwise have been able to profit (*lucrum cessans*). By the fifteenth century, as banking and monetized trade became more prevalent, these instruments were accepted as a condition of the loan, and not just as a remedy for its violation. See John T. Noonan, *The Scholastic Analysis of Usury* (Cambridge, MA: Harvard University Press, 1957). Consider also James Brundage: "By the end of the Middle Ages church authorities had begun to modify the canonical prohibition of all interest charges and to permit lenders to collect modest amounts of interest legally, while still condemning excessive interest as the social evil of usury" (*Medieval Canon Law* [London: Longman, 1995], 79).

17. Thomas Bell, *The Speculation of Usury* (London, 1596), D2v; David Hawkes, *The Culture of Usury in Early Modern England* (New York: Palgrave Macmillan, 2010), 16.

18. Roger Fenton, *A Treatise of Usurie* (London, 1611), E2v, italics mine.

19. Norman Jones, *God and the Moneylenders*, 24. In 1571, statute law (returning to a 1545 statute repealed under Edward VI in 1552) defined usury as taking more than ten percent interest. For the birth of the usury statute and its conservatism vis à vis the 1545 statute, see Jones, 48–65. Consider also Thomas Moisan's observation that "usury and trade existed in a relation that was far more ambiguous than anti-usury tracts might imply" ("'Which is the merchant here? And which the Jew?': Subversion and Recuperation in *The Merchant of Venice*," *Shakespeare Reproduced: The Text in History and Ideology*, ed. Jean E. Howard and Marion F. O'Connor [New York: Methuen, 1987], 196).

20. In *Tudor Economic Documents*, ed. R. H. Tawney and Eileen Power, 3 vols. (London: Longmans, 1924), 2:155. Consider also Tawney, who says that by the second half of the sixteenth century "the question was no longer whether interest was right or wrong, but whether the rate of interest legally sanctioned was at any given moment reasonable or excessive" ("Introduction," 133–4).

21. William Perkins, *Hepieikeia: or A Treatise of Christian Equitie* (Cambridge, 1604), B2v.

22. Henry Smith, *The Benefit of Contentation* (London, 1590), A4r.

23. For the doctrine of callings and its relation to contentation, see White, *Social Criticism*, 241–54.

24. John Carpenter, *Preparative to Contentation* (London, 1594), A2v–3r.

25. William Fulbecke, *Booke of Christian Ethicks or Moral Philosophie* (London, 1587), C3r, italics mine.

26. John Wheeler, *A Treatise of Commerce* (London, 1601), 54, 55.

27. Gerard Malynes, *St. George for England* (London, 1601), A6r, italics mine. For a recent discussion of Malynes's interest in "maintaining order within [the social] structure," see Andrea Finkelstein, *Harmony and the Balance: An Intellectual History of Seventeenth-Century Economic Thought* (Ann Arbor: University of Michigan Press, 2000), 40.

28. Philipp Caesar, *A General Discourse against the Damnable Sect of Usurers* (London, 1578), 22–3 italics mine.

29. For the role of the morality play "in relation to the interactions of economic, demographic, political and religious developments in late medieval society," see John Watkins, "The Allegorical Theatre: Moralities, Interludes and Protestant Drama," in

The Cambridge History of Medieval English Literature, ed. David Wallace (Cambridge: Cambridge University Press, 1999), 767.

30. Lawrence Clopper, *Drama, Play, and Game: English Festive Culture in the Medieval and Early Modern Period* (Chicago: University of Chicago Press, 2001), 285.

31. For the integration of repentance and city comedy, see Jean E. Howard, *Theater of a City: The Places of London Comedy, 1598–1642* (Philadelphia: University of Pennsylvania Press, 2006), esp. 70–105; and Herbert Jack Heller, *Penitent Brothellers: Grace, Sexuality, and Genre in Thomas Middleton's City Comedies* (Newark: University of Delaware Press, 2000).

32. Smith, *Benefit*, B7r.

33. *The Trial of Treasure*, in vol. 3 of *Dodsley's Old English Plays*, ed. W. Carew Hazlitt (London: Reeves and Turner, 1874), 284.

34. Ibid., 262, 267.

35. Ibid., 271.

36. Thomas Lupton, *A Moral and Pitieful Comedie, Intituled All for Money* (London, 1578), A2v.

37. For the thematic and moral significance of processional order in the Tudor interludes, see T. W. Craik, *The Tudor Interlude* (Leicester, UK: Leicester University Press, 1958), 97–9.

38. Lupton, *All for Money*, E2r, A2v.

39. *The Geneva Bible: A Facsimile of the 1560 Edition*, with an introduction by Lloyd E. Berry (Peabody, MA: Hendrickson Publishers, Inc., 2007).

40. William Wager, *Enough Is as Good as a Feast*, ed. R. Mark Benbow (Lincoln: University of Nebraska Press, 1967). All subsequent quotations are from this edition.

41. Neuss, "'Proverb' Play," 3.

42. Ineke Murakami, "Wager's Drama of Conscience, Convention, and State Constitution," *SEL: Studies in English Literature, 1500–1700* 47.2 (2007): 316. A revised version appears in her book *Moral Play and Counterpublic: Transformations in Moral Drama, 1465–1599* (New York: Routledge, 2011), 45–72.

43. For Wager's multiple rectorships during Elizabeth's reign, see Mark Eccles, "William Wager and His Plays," *English Language Notes* 18.4 (1981): 258–62.

44. Miles Mosse, *Arraignment and Conviction of Usurie* (London, 1595), D3r, italics mine.

45. Paul Whitfield White, "Interludes, Economics, and the Elizabethan Stage," in *The Oxford Handbook of Tudor Literature, 1485–1603*, ed. Mike Pincombe and Cathy Shrank (Oxford: Oxford University Press, 2009), 556. Bevington also acknowledges the play's "deep concern over economic and social issues such as rent gouging, the influx of immigrant labour, and economic hard times for the poor" ("Staging the Reformation," 375).

46. Eccles has documented Wager's role on a 1575 commission "to hear the petitions of poor prisoners in Ludgate and the two Counters in London . . . summon them and their creditors, and decide whether they could be freed on giving bond" ("William Wager," 259). As Eccles points out, Wager refers to these prisons in lines 360–2.

47. David Bevington, *From Mankind to Marlowe: Growth of Structure in the Popular Drama of Tudor England* (Cambridge, MA: Harvard University Press, 1962), 152–3. In

Enough Is as Good as a Feast, he explains, "instead of the alternating and progressive rise of the hero from fallen innocence to spiritual victory, we find . . . the progressive decline of the corrupted man to ultimate damnation" (162).

48. See Robert Potter, *English Morality Play* (London: Routledge & Kegan Paul, 1975), 7–10.

49. Bevington suggests that Worldly Man's desperate ending can be attributed to his "impenitence," which cancels out his earlier instincts towards worldly moderation and generosity (Mankind *to Marlowe*, 162).

50. Benbow cites Luke 12:46 and Matthew 25:30.

51. Craik, *Tudor Interlude*, 108.

52. Greg Walker, *The Politics of Performance in Early Renaissance Drama* (Cambridge: Cambridge University Press, 1998), 48–50.

53. David Coleman has explained this kind of subject position as a specialty of the Tudor homiletic drama, which "reveals how the disruption of Catholic sacramentality has also disrupted conventional means of dealing with sin" (*Drama and the Sacraments in Sixteenth-Century England: Indelible Characters* [Basingstoke, UK: Palgrave Macmillan, 2007], 10).

54. Peter Happé provides an important sense of the religious as well as intellectual background of the interlude audience: "If the performance context of many interludes was frequently in the hall in Tudor great houses, this must have meant the presence of powerful people was there to be exploited. This could happen both at the behest of such people through their patronage, or indeed there could be a critique directed at them." Introduction to *Interludes and Early Modern Society*, 9. Interludes performed by noble troupes were staged in public halls, churches, inns, and inn-yards as well.

55. Robert and Edward Skidelsky, *How Much Is Enough: Money and the Good Life* (New York: Other Press, 2012), 3.

56. Max Weber, *The Protestant Ethic and the Spirit of Capitalism*, ed. Richard Swedberg (New York: Norton, 2009), 90.

57. Howard, *Theater of a City*, 71.

58. Giovanni Botero, *Treatise Concerning the Causes of the Magnificencie of Certaine Cities*, trans. Robert Peterson (London, 1606), 64. For the light and dark sides of the myths of "Venice the rich," "Venice the wise," and "Venice the just," see James McPherson, *Shakespeare, Jonson, and the Myth of Venice* (Newark: University of Delaware Press, 1990). Carole Levin and John Watkins have recently pointed out that Venetian economic decline was matched by English success: "London was understood at the time to be growing at Venice's expense; at the same time they may have been happy to become the new Venice, they were nervous about this transformation on England's emerging national identity" (*Shakespeare's Foreign Worlds: National and Transnational Identities in the Elizabethan Age* [Ithaca, NY: Cornell University Press, 2009], 17). For "myths" of Venice as an exemplar of republican liberty and resistance to Rome, see Oliver Logan, *Culture and Society in Venice 1470–1790* (New York: Charles Scribner and Sons, 1972), 10–17; Edward Muir, *Civic Ritual in Venice* (Princeton, NJ: Princeton University Press, 1981), 14–33.

59. Lars Engle, " 'Thrift Is Blessing': Exchange and Explanation in *The Merchant of Venice*," *Shakespeare Quarterly* 37.1 (1986): 20.

60. Throughout this reading I emphasize Shylock's role as what Jeremy Cohen has called the "hermeneutic Jew": a figure created by the dominant Christian culture based on their particular theological needs (*Living Letters of the Law: Ideas of the Jew in Medieval Christianity* [Berkeley: University of California Press, 1999]). Certainly, there were topical or "real" Jews in Shakespeare's England—like the Spanish doctor Roderigo Lopez, whose notoriety informs the play (see David Katz, *The Jews in the History of England* [Oxford: Clarendon Press, 1994], 51–104). But I do not see any of Shylock's impulses or claims—even those that assert his humanity—as coming from a dramatic subjectivity than can ever be independent from his ideological function for the play's Venetian characters and English audience. Janet Adelman has offered a similar formulation for *Merchant*: "At the same time as the play encourages us to read Shylock realistically, as though a 'real' Jew . . . might become the monster of his legendary past, it also makes clear the extent to which he is merely a creature of the play, motivated by fantasies altogether outside his 'character' " (*Blood Relations: Christian and Jew in* The Merchant of Venice [Chicago: University of Chicago Press, 2008], 112).

61. See Harry Berger, *Making Trifles of Terrors: Redistributing Complicities in Shakespeare* (Stanford, CA: Stanford University Press, 1997), 8.

62. Christopher Marlowe, *The Jew of Malta*, in *The Complete Plays*, ed. Mark Thornton Burnett (London: Everyman, 1999).

63. Barbara Lewalski, "Biblical Allusion and Allegory in *The Merchant of Venice*," *Shakespeare Quarterly* 13.3 (1962): 327–43.

64. Both arguments are articulated in Adelman, *Blood Relation*; quotation on p. 112.

65. For discussions of Antonio's melancholy as a "socio-economically aroused affect" that registers both dismay and fear at the risks of the global market; as a symptom of Lutheran pessimism that the human will is "irrevocably irrational"; or as a mark of Venetian "loss of morale" at the close of the sixteenth century, see respectively Theodore Leinwand, *Theatre, Finance, and Society in Early Modern England* (Cambridge: Cambridge University Press, 1997), 1, 116; Lisa Freinkel, *Reading Shakespeare's Will: The Theology of Figure from Augustine to the Sonnets* (New York: Columbia University Press, 2002), 251; and J. R. Mulryne, "History and Myth in *The Merchant of Venice*," in *Shakespeare's Italy: Functions of Italian Locations in Renaissance Drama*, ed. Michele Marrapodi et al. (Manchester: Manchester University Press, 1993), 91. For recent readings of the political implications of his melancholy and masochism, see Henry S. Turner, "The Problem of the More-than-One: Friendship, Calculation, and Political Association in *The Merchant of Venice*," *Shakespeare Quarterly* 57.4 (2006): 413–42; and Drew Daniel, " 'Let me have judgment, and the Jew his will': Melancholy Epistemology and Masochistic Fantasy in *The Merchant of Venice*," *Shakespeare Quarterly* 61.2 (2010): 206–34.

66. Robert Burton, *The Anatomy of Melancholy* (New York: New York Review of Books, 2001), 319.

67. Ibid., 335.

68. Venice was widely acknowledged as a Catholic city-state, but its status as independent of Rome as well as a home for exiled or traveling Protestants was an early modern commonplace. Edwin Sandys, in his *Europae Speculum* (first printed 1605), comments that "all Italy hold[s] partly of the Pope & partly of the Empire, (save the Sign[ory] of Venice, which acknowledge no Lord," adding that Protestants are "scat-

tered" across the country and "especially in the State of Venice" ([London, 1629], 134, 157). For Elizabethan "optimists" who "continued to cherish the delusion that Venice might still become a protestant outpost in catholic Italy," see Anne Overell, *Italian Reform and English Reformations* (Aldershot, UK: Ashgate, 2008), 14.

69. For Antonio's melancholy, and the melancholic disposition of the play more generally, as a form of "impeded mourning" for Venice's "loss of trading power," see Levin and Watkins, *Shakespeare's Foreign Worlds*, 118–9, 140.

70. Aho suggests that fastidious double-entry bookkeeping grew out of an effort to ease the burden of the medieval and early modern merchant's "scrupulous preoccupation with sin" (*Confession and Bookkeeping*, xiv). See also Natasha Korda, "Dame Usury, Gender, Credit, and (Ac)counting in the Sonnets and *The Merchant of Venice*," *Shakespeare Quarterly* 60.2 (2009): 129–53.

71. For the connection to the Inquisition, see Adelman, *Blood Relations*, 123–4.

72. Julia Lupton, *Citizen-saints: Shakespeare and Political Theology* (Chicago: University of Chicago Press, 2005), 75.

73. Benjamin Nelson, *The Idea of Usury: From Tribal Brotherhood to Universal Otherhood*, 2nd ed. (Chicago: University of Chicago Press, 1963), passim.

74. William Thomas, *The History of Italy* (London, 1561), 77r, emphasis mine.

75. Thomas Coryate, *Coryats Crudities* (London, 1611), S4v, S5v, italics mine.

76. Robert C. Davis, introduction to *The Jews of Early Modern Venice*, ed. Robert C. Davis and Benjamin Ravid (Baltimore: Johns Hopkins University Press, 2001), xii. Donatella Calabi's essay in the same volume describes the ghetto, despite its "unheard of levels of misery" due to overcrowding, as a place of great "cultural and social vivacity [that] helped draw foreigners visiting Venice" into it ("The 'City of Jews,'" [39, 45]).

77. My interpretation here is not conventional. In his important reading of the play, Marc Shell describes Shylock's punning as the effect of a principle of increase and excess rather than containment or thrift: "As the Jew uses moneys . . . to supplement principals, so he uses puns to exceed the principal meanings of words" (*Money, Language and Thought: Literary and Philosophical Economies from the Medieval to the Early Modern Era* [Berkeley: University of California Press, 1982], 50). Korda reads "a good round sum" as a sign of Shylock's outdated, untrustworthy financial practices against Portia's more precise ones (Korda, "Dame Usury").

78. John Foxe, *Sermon Preached at the Christening a Certaine Jew* (London, 1578), C1v.

79. Sharon Achinstein, "John Foxe and the Jews," *Renaissance Quarterly* 54.1 (2001): 86. For an important reading of this kind of disdain as masking Christian envy of the "covenantal privileges and . . . distinctive laws which the Christian believer so much desired to inherit," see Harold Fisch, *The Dual Image: The Figure of the Jew in English and American Literature* (New York: Ktav, 1971), 17, 13.

80. Thus the persistent issue of whether the bond represents Shylock's financial modernity or his conservatism. For the former argument, see Richard Halpern, *Shakespeare among the Moderns* (Ithaca, NY: Cornell University Press, 1997), 162–4; for the latter, see Walter Cohen, "*The Merchant of Venice* and the Possibilities of Historical Criticism," *English Literary History* 49.4 (1982): 765–89.

81. Quotation from Miri Rubin, *Gentile Tales: The Narrative Assault on Late Medieval Jews* (New Haven, CT: Yale University Press, 1999), 5. James Shapiro enumerates

these beliefs in *Shakespeare and the Jews* (New York: Columbia University Press, 1996), 2–3, 43–111. R. Po-Hsia describes the gradual decline of ritual murder accusations and discourse as part of the "disenchantment" of the Reformation; nevertheless, as he explains, this shift did not represent the "winning [of] toleration for Judaism . . . but shifting the focus of Protestant anti-Judaism away from the late medieval obsession with Jewish magic and sacrifice to new forms of intolerance, which, however repressive, did not match the full fury of the ritual murder discourse they replaced" (*The Myth of Ritual Murder: Jews and Magic in Reformation Germany* [New Haven, CT: Yale University Press, 1988], 151).

82. Hsia calls attention to the function of ritual murder threats in producing "the powerful experience of sacrifice so central to the self-expression of late medieval piety in a century of the imitation of Christ and the many moving and gruesome depictions of the crucifixion" (*Myth of Ritual Murder*, 40–1).

83. For a rich alternative reading of Shylock as the "very figure . . . of the illimitable flesh" who "exceeds all fleshly determinant," see Freinkel, *Reading Shakespeare's Will*, 243.

84. Shapiro has made clear the role of the Jew in organizing Protestant and Catholic polemic; for both confessions, the adversary's objectionable characteristics are equated with Judaism (*Shakespeare and the Jews*, 8).

85. Eric Spencer, "Taking Excess, Exceeding Account: Aristotle Meets *The Merchant of Venice*," in *Money in the Age of Shakespeare: Essays in New Economic Criticism*, ed. Linda Woodbridge (New York: Palgrave Macmillan, 2003), 149. For Shylock's bond as "a grossly excessive penalty," see Kerridge, *Usury, Interest and the Reformation*, 8.

86. For a rich account of the multivalent relations—which could include identification as well as "othering"—between English Christians and real as well as biblical Jews, see Achsah Guibbory, *Christian Identity: Jews and Israel in Seventeenth-Century England* (Oxford: Oxford University Press, 2010).

87. For the generic tradition see Robert Weimann, *Shakespeare and the Popular Tradition in the Theater: Studies in the Social Dimension of the Dramatic Form and Function* (Baltimore: Johns Hopkins University Press, 1978), 149.

88. "It is characteristic of the Venetians that they look like the very picture of disinterestedness at the precise moment when their sly calculations cause the pot of gold to fall into their lap," (Rene Girard, " 'To entrap the wisest': A Reading of *The Merchant of Venice*," in *Literature and Society*, ed. Edward Said [Baltimore: Johns Hopkins University Press, 1980], 103).

89. See Matthew Biberman's compelling account of Shylock's movement from the stereotypical "Jew-Devil" to that of the "Jew-Sissy" in *Masculinity, Anti-Semitism and Early Modern English Literature: From the Satanic to the Effeminate Jew* (Burlington, VT: Ashgate, 2004), esp. 32–6.

90. See Fisch, *Dual Image*, 33.

91. For a comprehensive discussion of *The Merchant of Venice* and early modern racism, see M. Lindsay Kaplan, "Jessica's Mother: Medieval Constructions of Jewish Race and Gender in *The Merchant of Venice*," *Shakespeare Quarterly* 58.1 (2007): 1–30.

92. Girard sees the Christians becoming like the Jew: "Human flesh and money in Venice are constantly exchanged for one another" ("A Reading of *The Merchant of Venice*," 108).

93. Lawrence Danson offers the most comprehensive celebration of Portia as allowing "the law—while still remaining the law—[to be] made society's servant, not its master" (*The Harmonies of* The Merchant of Venice [New Haven, CT: Yale University Press, 1978], 120). More recent criticism has been rightfully suspicious of Portia's manipulations. See Coppelia Kahn, "The Cuckoo's Note: Male Friendship and Cuckoldry in *The Merchant of Venice*," in *Shakespeare's 'Rough Magic': Renaissance Essays in Honor of C.L. Barber*, ed. Peter Erickson and Coppelia Kahn (Newark: University of Delaware Press, 1985), 110.

94. Consider Engle's explanation of the play as defining "a system of exchange or conversion which works to the advantage of the 'blessed': those who, by religious or social situation, are placed to take advantage of exchange patterns" ("Exchange and Explanation," 21).

95. For the uncertain religious and social status of Jessica at the end of the play, see Mary Janell Metzger, " 'Now by My Hood, a Gentle and No Jew': Jessica, *The Merchant of Venice*, and the Discourse of Early Modern English Identity," *PMLA* 113.1 (1998): 52–63.

96. John Donne, *The Sermons of John Donne*, ed. George Potter and Evelyn Simpson, 10 vols. (Berkeley: University of California Press, 1955), 7:51, italics mine.

97. Henry Smith, *A Treatise of the Lords Supper* (London, 1591), C6v.

98. Andrew Willet, *Hexapla in Genesin and Exodum* (London, 1633), 197.

Chapter 5

1. Karen Newman, "Portia's Ring: Unruly Women and Structures of Exchange in *The Merchant of Venice*," *Shakespeare Quarterly* 38.1 (1987): 21. For the conventional terminology of the "marriage debt" as "a common synonym for coitus," see Margaret Sommerville, *Sex and Subjection: Attitudes to Women in Early-Modern Society* (New York: St. Martin's Press, 1995), 131.

2. Though for the fundamentally communal, public orientation of marriage at this time, particularly for Shakespeare, see Lisa Hopkins, *The Shakespearean Marriage: Merry Wives and Heavy Husbands* (New York: St. Martin's Press, 1998).

3. Martin Butler, *Theatre and Crisis, 1632–1642* (Cambridge: Cambridge University Press, 1984), 106.

4. For a definition of "sex tragedy" as a genre see Martin Wiggins, introduction to *Four Jacobean Sex Tragedies* (Oxford: Oxford University Press, 1998), vii; Butler, *Theatre and Crisis*, 216. For a comprehensive comparison of the two plays, with an emphasis on the ways in which Ford shifts the scene from the titanic heroism of *Othello* to the "confined world of little men" in *Love's Sacrifice*, see Dorothy Farr, *John Ford and the Caroline Theatre* (London: Macmillan, 1979), 60.

5. The "accounts" I discuss here include prescriptive and sermonic writings, biblical and legal commentary, and a range of popular literature on marriage. Laura Gowing, in her important account of the ways in which men's and women's "sexual acts had different contexts, meanings, and results," argues that such texts "made use of a common stock of ideas and images about marriage and the household to produce an ideal of social and familial order whose details were, for many households, largely irrelevant"

(*Domestic Dangers: Women, Words, and Sex in Early Modern London* [Oxford: Clarendon Press, 1996], 3, 27). And yet she later turns to drama and other forms of popular literature—a category from which prescriptive texts are not exempt—to explain the court testimonies that figure so centrally in her account: "Contemporary culture held a stock of stories in both oral and printed form whose contexts, events, and results could be rifled for the tales told in everyday life, in the moments of dispute, and at court" (58). I thus follow Lena Cowen Orlin here in the belief that "notional ideals for household relations [are] the precondition for an apprehension of real stresses on those relations" and thus most useful for a discussion of marriage in the history of satisfaction (*Private Matters and Public Culture in Post-Reformation England* [Ithaca, NY: Cornell University Press, 1994], 3). See also Christine Peters, who suggests that "despite the obvious divergence between prescriptive literature and practice, [prescriptive] texts show how the godly could rationalise the conflicting gender messages of Reformation religious culture, notions of patriarchal authority and lived experience" (*Patterns of Piety: Women, Gender and Religion in Late Medieval and Reformation England* [Cambridge: Cambridge University Press, 2003], 341).

6. "The language for the sexual act was of evacuation, expenditure, and the satisfaction of an itch," (Patricia Crawford, *Blood, Bodies and Families in Early Modern England* [Harlow, UK: Pearson Educational, 2004], 70).

7. 1 Cor. 7:9, KJV; Fran Dolan, *Marriage and Violence: The Early Modern Legacy* (Philadelphia: University of Pennsylvania Press, 2008), 47.

8. William Perkins, *Christian Oeconomie* (London, 1609), H8r, I1r. This was not, of course, a specifically Protestant premise; the Spanish humanist Juan Luis Vives, for instance, advises husbands that they "ought nat to gyve them selfe unto over moche pleasure, nor to delyte in any companye but theyr wyves . . . . it is nat convenient for them to be maisters of wantonnes and lechery unto theyr wyves. And let them ever remembre thys sayeng of Xystus the philosopher He is an adulterar with his wyfe, who so is over excedyng and over hote a lover" (*The Instruction of a Christen Woman*, ed. Virginia Beauchamp et al. [Urbana: University of Illinois Press, 2002], 119).

9. William Gouge, *Domesticall Duties* (London, 1622), 223.

10. Martin Ingram documents an anecdote in which a sixteenth-century father "gave approval to his daughter's choice of spouse to secure both 'the well bestowing of his daughter to live in the world as also the *satisfaction* of her own fantasy,'" (*Church Courts, Sex and Marriage in England, 1570–1640* [Cambridge: Cambridge University Press, 1987], 142, italics mine).

11. *Politeuphuia: Wits Common Wealth* (London, 1598), 188v.

12. Heinrich Bullinger, *The Christen State of Matrimony*, trans. Miles Coverdale (London, 1546), I6v, italics mine.

13. Ibid., I8v.

14. Ibid., K2v.

15. Gouge, *Domesticall Duties*, 45, second italics mine

16. John Witte, Jr., *From Sacrament to Contract: Marriage, Religion, and Law in the Western Tradition*, 2nd ed. (Louisville, KY: Westminster John Knox Press, 2012), 232.

17. Valerie Wayne, for instance, argues that the sexual dynamic preached by some homilists—that "his command becomes her wish"—suggests a "loss of volition [which]

accompanies the wife's total sexual submission" (introduction to Edmund Tilney, *The Flower of Friendship*, ed. Valerie Wayne [Ithaca, NY: Cornell University Press, 1992], 62). Peters warns against seeing these formulas as misogynistic, suggesting that they were "open to the idea that characteristics of behavior were not gendered," (*Patterns of Piety*, 332).

18. Dolan, *Marriage and Violence*, 3.

19. Gowing, *Domestic Dangers*, 78–9.

20. Mary Beth Rose, *The Expense of Spirit: Love and Sexuality in English Renaissance Drama* (Ithaca, NY: Cornell University Press, 1988), 142; Orlin, *Private Matters*, 195.

21. Richard Snawsel, *A Looking Glasse for Maried Folkes* (London, 1619), A4v–A5r, italics mine.

22. Ibid., F3r.

23. "By making [the husband and wife's] mutual repentance a precondition of marital unity, [snawsel] alters the Lutheran stress on hierarchy and the association of guilt with the wife alone; but he retains a strong biblical and doctrinal base" (Wayne, introduction, 32).

24. For an overview, see Witte, *Sacrament to Contract*, 79ff.

25. Ibid., 7.

26. Eric Josef Carlson, *Marriage and the English Reformation* (Cambridge: Blackwell Press, 1994), 8.

27. Ibid., 37.

28. *The Book of Common Prayer 1559: The Elizabethan Prayer Book*, ed. John E. Booty (Charlottesville: University of Virginia Press, 1976), 290.

29. Carlson, *Marriage and the English Reformation*, 49.

30. James Grantham Turner, *One Flesh: Paradisal Marriage and Sexual Relations in the Age of Milton* (Oxford: Clarendon Press, 1987), 79, 39.

31. Ercole Tasso, *Of Mariage and Wiving*, trans. R. T. (London, 1599), L2r.

32. Alexander Niccholes, *A Discourse of Marriage and Wiving* (London, 1615), B2v. Henry Smith's conventional account of the expulsion from Eden is also poised on this dialectic: "God so loved our Parentes," he writes, that even "when he punished them . . . he could scarce punish them for love, and therefore a comfort was folded in his judgement." That comfort was not only the promise of Christ but also the preservation of the "mutuall societie" of wedlock, whereby "God coupled two together, that the infinit troubles which lye upon us in this world, might be ended, with the comfort and helpe of one another" (*A Preparative to Mariage* [London, 1591]), B3v–B4; C2.

33. John Wing, *The Crowne Conjugall, or, the Spouse Royall* (London, 1632), 25, italics in text.

34. For the regulation of marital and sexual sins in the medieval confessionals, see Thomas Tentler, *Sin and Confession on the Eve of the Reformation* (Princeton, NJ: Princeton University Press, 1977), passim; Witte, *Sacrament to Contract*, 104; Pierre Michaud- Quantin, *Sommes de Casuistique et Manuels de Confession au Moyen Âge* (Louvain: Editions Nauwelaerts, 1962), 20. For the early modern period see Martin Ingram, *Church Courts*, passim; Gowing, *Domestic Dangers*, esp. 30–41; F. G. Emmison, *Morals & the Church Courts*, vol. 2 of *Elizabethan Life* (Chelmsford, UK: Essex County Council, 1973), 1–13.

35. Thomas Dekker, *Batchelars Banquet* (London, 1603), A2v, italics mine.

36. Kathleen M. Davies, "Continuity and Change in Literary Advice on Marriage," *Marriage and Society: Studies in the Social History of Marriage*, ed. R. B. Outhwaite (New York: St. Martin's Press, 1981), 65; R. H. Helmholz, *The Spirit of Classical Canon Law* (Athens: University of Georgia Press, 1996), 237–41.

37. Quote from Ingram, *Church Courts*, 135. For legal proceedings see also Ralph Houlbrooke, *Church Courts and the People during the English Reformation, 1520–1570* (Oxford: Oxford University Press, 1979), 55–63.

38. Witte, *Sacrament to Contract*, 139–45.

39. Bullinger, *Christen State*, C7v.

40. Ingram, *Church Courts*, 135.

41. Diana O'Hara, for instance, reminds us that it is "impossible to interpret behaviour [around courtship and marriage] without some sense of community, or indeed to regard it as unconstrained" (*Courtship and Constraint: Rethinking the Making of Marriage in Tudor England* [Manchester, UK: Manchester University Press, 2000], 42).

42. David Cressy, *Birth, Marriage, and Death: Ritual, Religion, and the Life-Cycle in Tudor and Stuart England* (Oxford: Oxford University Press, 1997), 255.

43. Edmund Tilney, *The Flower of Friendship: A Renaissance Dialogue Contesting Marriage*, ed. Valerie Wayne (Ithaca, NY: Cornell University Press, 1992), 110, italics mine.

44. Robert Cleaver, *Godly Forme of Household Government* (London, 1598), G3r, italics mine.

45. Smith, *Preparative*, C2v, italics mine.

46. Richard Bernard, *Ruths Recompence* (London, 1628), X3r, X3v.

47. *Politeuphuia*, 189, italics mine.

48. Bullinger, *Christen State*, B2r.

49. "Enforced marriage was probably the most significant debate about marriage in the period," Dympna Callaghan, introduction to *The Impact of Feminism in English Renaissance Studies*, ed. Dympna Callaghan (New York: Palgrave, 2007), 8.

50. Thomas Gataker, *A Good Wife Gods Gift and, a Wife Indeed. Two Mariage Sermons* (London, 1624), C1v.

51. Richard Heale, *An Apologie for Women* (Oxford, 1609), B4v.

52. Gouge, *Domesticall Duties,* cited in Dolan, 24. See also Peter Lake's discussion of the abused wife in "Deeds against Nature: Cheap Print, Protestantism and Murder in Early Seventeenth-Century England," in *Culture and Politics in Early Stuart England*, ed. Kevin Sharpe and Peter Lake (London: Macmillan, 1994), 267.

53. Gouge, 212–3.

54. William Shakespeare, *Much Ado about Nothing*, in *The Riverside Shakespeare*, ed. G. Blakemore Evans, 2nd ed. (New York: Houghton Mifflin, 1997), 2.1.72–80, italics mine.

55. For a reading of the play as presenting "marriage [as] virtue's repentance" for which women are responsible, see Harry Berger, "Against the Sink-a-Pace: Sexual and Family Politics in *Much Ado about Nothing*," *Shakespeare Quarterly* 33.3 (1982): 306.

56. *Tell-Trothes New-yeares Gift . . . With his Owne Invective against Jelosy* (London, 1593), F3.

57. Gataker, *Sermons*, F2r.

58. For a related reading of the inversion of marital ideals in the play's "carnivalesque derangement of marriage as a social institution," see Michael Bristol, "Charivari and the Comedy of Abjection in *Othello*," in *True Rites and Maimed Rites: Ritual and Anti-Ritual in Shakespeare and His Age*, ed. Linda Woodbridge and Edward Berry (Urbana: University of Illinois Press, 1992), 83.

59. Daniel Vitkus, "Turning Turk in *Othello*: Conversion and Damnation of the Moor," *Shakespeare Quarterly* 48.2 (1997): 154.

60. William Shakespeare, *Othello*, in *The Riverside Shakespeare*, ed. G. Blakemore Evans. 2nd ed. (New York: Houghton Mifflin, 1997), 1.3.144–57. All subsequent citations are to this edition.

61. I explain Othello's inability to make enough for his wife as the discursive effect of the revaluation of satisfaction in "Historicizing Satisfaction in Shakespeare's *Othello*," in *Rethinking Historicism from Shakespeare to Milton*, ed. Ann Baynes Coiro and Thomas Fulton (Cambridge: Cambridge University Press, 2012), 113–29.

62. Against readings that take this address as evidence of Othello's sexual embarrassment or panic, Natasha Korda suggests that Othello disavows not appropriate marital relations but rather his sole ownership of them: "Othello describe[s] his satisfaction as unbound by notions of property or possession," (*Shakespeare's Domestic Economies: Gender and Property in Early Modern England* [Philadelphia: University of Pennsylvania Press, 2002], 132).

63. William Whately, *A Bride-bush, or a Wedding Sermon* (London, 1617), B3r.

64. Bullinger, *Christen Marriage*, K4v.

65. Bristol, "Comedy of Abjection," 89.

66. Stephen Greenblatt, *Renaissance Self-Fashioning from More to Shakespeare* (Chicago: University of Chicago Press, 1980), 250.

67. Michael Neill, *Putting History to the Question: Power, Politics, and Society in English Renaissance Drama* (New York: Columbia University Press, 2000), 264.

68. Katherine Maus, *Inwardness and Theater in the English Renaissance* (Chicago: University of Chicago Press, 1995), 104–27; Stanley Cavell, *Disowning Knowledge in Six Plays of Shakespeare* (Cambridge: Cambridge University Press, 1987), 125–42.

69. Harry Berger, "Acts of Silence, Acts of Speech: How to Do Things with Othello and Desdemona," *Renaissance Drama* 33 (2004): 3–35.

70. Kenneth Burke's seminal "Othello: An Essay to Illustrate a Method," proposes that there is between Othello, Desdemona, and Iago "a tragic trinity of ownership in the profoundest sense of ownership, the property in human affections as fetishistically localized in the object of possession, while the possessor is himself possessed by his very engrossment" (*Hudson Review* 4 [1951]: 165–203, esp. 166–7).

71. Benedetto Varchi, *Blazon of Jealousie*, trans. R. F. (London, 1615), C3r.

72. Ibid., H3r; I2r–I2v.

73. See the definition of occupation, as the noun form of occupy, in Eric Partridge's *Shakespeare Bawdy*: "To copulate with (a woman), with an allusion to the two senses, 'take and retain possession of' . . . and 'to keep (a person) busy'" (London: Routledge Classics, 2001), 200.

74. Catherine Belsey, "Desire's Excess and the Renaissance Theatre: *Edward II, Troilus and Cressida, Othello*" in *Erotic Politics: Desire on the Renaissance Stage*, ed. Susan Zimmerman (London: Routledge, 1992), 96.

75. Edward Snow, "Sexual Anxiety and the Male Order of Things in *Othello*," *English Literary Renaissance* 10 (1980): 388. Greenblatt's seminal New Historicist reading understands Othello's guilt as *constituted* by the discourses and narratives of Christianity, which Iago manipulates; Snow, in an explicitly psychoanalytic reading, understands the guilt as *enhanced* or *exacerbated* by these discourses. He acknowledges that forms of Christianity can function "not to absolve guilt but to instill it" (390), but he warns that "it is important not to scapegoat Christianity . . . making it . . . the 'cause' of sexual disgust. The dialectic in Shakespeare between the psyche and the institutions it creates and is shaped by cannot be so easily resolved" (389). Arthur Kirsch's discussion in *Shakespeare and the Experience of Love* (Cambridge: Cambridge University Press, 1981) offers explicitly Freudian and Kleinian terms for Othello's sexual guilt and jealousy, which make his "rage against Cassio . . . a rage against himself that reaches back to the elemental and destructive triadic fantasies" of the infant (34).

76. Mark Breitenberg, *Anxious Masculinity in Early Modern England* (Cambridge: Cambridge University Press, 1996), 26.

77. Cavell, *Disowning Knowledge*, 35.

78. For a discussion of Desdemona's place as a "God" (or "god") for Othello in terms of the "very real concern of early Protestants that passionate love, even of one's spouse, may be idolatrous," see Huston Diehl, "Bewhored Images and Imagined Whores: Iconophobia and Gynophobia in Stuart Love Tragedies," *English Literary Renaissance* 26 (1992): 121.

79. Greenblatt, *Renaissance Self-Fashioning*, 246.

80. Richard Mallette sees Iago as a blasphemous preacher who bruises the ears of his listeners without soothing them with the promise of assurance ("Blasphemous Preacher: Iago and the Reformation," *Shakespeare and the Culture of Christianity in Early Modern England*, ed. Dennis Taylor and David N. Beauregard [New York: Fordham University Press, 2003], 382–414).

81. See Snow, "Sexual Anxiety," 384.

82. Emily Bartels, *Speaking of the Moor: from Alcazar to Othello* (Philadelphia: University of Pennsylvania Press, 2008), 5–6. Julia Lupton explains that Othello's appearance as a "black gentile of a universal church militant" is "continually shadowed by the more troubling possibility" that he has connections not to paganism but to Islam (*Citizen-saints: Shakespeare and Political Theology* [Chicago: University of Chicago Press, 2005], 105).

83. Vitkus, "Turks and Jews in *The Jew of Malta*," in *Early Modern English Drama: A Critical Companion*, ed. Patrick Cheney, Andrew Hadfield and Garrett Sullivan (New York: Oxford University Press, 2006), 65. For the way in which, in the wake of the Reformation, "Anglo-Protestant identity across Europe as well as in England was formed and expressed through recourse not to one dominant demonizing model, but to multiple and various models of the 'Turke' and Islam," see Matthew Dimmock, *New Turkes: Dramatizing Islam and the Ottomans in Early Modern England* (Burlington, VT: Ashgate Publishers, 2005), 4. For persistent stereotypes see Virginia Mason Vaughan, *Othello: A Contextual History* (Cambridge: Cambridge University Press, 1994), 14–34.

84. Andrew Willet, *A Treatise of Salomon's Marriage* (London, 1613), B3v.

85. Gail Paster, *Humoring the Body: Emotions and the Shakespearean Stage* (Chicago: University of Chicago Press, 2004), 75. For this internalization as a barometer of the

audience's "cultural need to create and destroy monsters: create them so that they may not create themselves, destroy them so that they may not procreate or multiply," see Arthur J. Little Jr., " 'An essence that's not seen': The Primal Scene of Racism in *Othello,*" *Shakespeare Quarterly* 44.3 (1993): 323.

86. Eric Griffin, *English Renaissance Drama and the Specter of Spain: Ethnopoetics and Empire* (Philadelphia: University of Pennsylvania Press, 2009), 183.

87. For suspicions and hostilities, see J. H. Elliott, *Spain, Europe and the Wider World, 1500–1700* (New Haven, CT: Yale University Press, 2009), 27–8.

88. Griffin, *Specter of Spain*, 193. This effect holds whether we consider Othello, whose baptism is made explicit in 2.3, "Catholic" or "Protestant." Such confessional pigeonholing is not necessary to observe the consequences for Othello of being introduced to the notion that he cannot make or be enough for his wife.

89. See Elliott, *Spain, Europe,* 29–30.

90. Ibid., 33. For a discussion of the literary exchange, see Dale B. J. Randall, *The Golden Tapestry; A Critical Survey of Non-Chivalric Spanish Fiction in English Translation: 1543–1657* (Durham, NC: Duke University Press, 1963).

91. L. A. Beaurline, introduction to Francis Beaumont and John Fletcher, *Love's Pilgrimage*, ed. L. A. Beaurline, vol. 2 in *The Dramatic Works in the Beaumont and Fletcher Canon*, ed. Fredson Bowers (Cambridge: Cambridge University Press, 1970), 569–72. Given the textual uncertainties, it is possible that the specific language of satisfaction is not Beaumont and Fletcher's but a reviser's, perhaps Philip Massinger. My arguments about the ironic and nostalgic uses of the term would apply to any of the three possible hands.

92. For a reading of these gender transgressions in the Cervantean source as a "romance critique of epic ambitions, exposing the internal anarchy—gendered and otherwise—of a masculinist imperial Spain," see Barbara Fuchs, "Empire Unmanned: Gender Trouble and Genoese Gold in Cervantes's 'The Two Damsels,'" *PMLA* 116.2 (2001): 285.

93. Francis Beaumont and John Fletcher, *Love's Pilgrimage*, ed. L. A. Beaurline, in vol. 2 of *The Dramatic Works in the Beaumont and Fletcher Canon*, ed. Fredson Bowers, 569–691 (Cambridge: Cambridge University Press, 1970), 4.1.139–42, italics mine. All subsequent citations are to this text.

94. Miguel Cervantes, *Exemplarie Novells in Sixe Books*, trans. James Mabbe (London, 1640), C1v–C2, italics mine.

95. For sexual intercourse as a means of binding a *de futuro* marital contract, see Houlbrooke, *Church Courts*, 60; Cressy, *Birth, Marriage,* 277.

96. Nancy Cotton Pearse, *John Fletcher's Chastity Plays: Mirrors of Modesty* (Lewisburg, PA: Bucknell University Press, 1973).

97. Herbert Blau, "The Absolved Riddle: Sovereign Pleasure and the Baroque Subject in the Tragicomedies of John Fletcher," *New Literary History* 17.3 (1986): 539–54.

98. For a discussion of how Fletcher's audience would have accepted his characters' conversions in ways a modern audience might distrust, see Robert Kean Turner, "Collaborators at Work: *The Queen of Corinth* and *The Knight of Malta,*" in *Shakespeare: Text, Language, Criticism: Essays in Honour of Marvin Spevack*, ed. Bernhard Fabian and Kurt Tetzeli von Rosador (Hildesheim: Olms, 1987), 315–33.

99. Barbara Fuchs, *Romance* (New York: Routledge, 2004), 64.

100. For Beaumont and Fletcher's interest in Spanish romance, see Gordon Mc-Mullan, *The Politics of Unease in the Plays of John Fletcher* (Amherst: University of Massachusetts Press, 1994), 25–62; Barbara Fuchs, "Beyond the Missing *Cardenio*: Anglo-Spanish Relations in Early Modern Drama," *Journal of Medieval and Early Modern Studies* 39.1 (2009): 143–59.

101. Trudi Darby and Alexander Samson, "'Last thought upon a windmill?': Cervantes and Fletcher," in *The Cervantean Heritage: Reception and Influence of Cervantes in Britain*, ed. J. A. G. Ardila (London: Legenda 2009), 207, 230, 211.

102. McMullan, *Politics of Unease*, 260.

103. For "ambivalent Hispanophilia," see Carmen Nocentelli, "Spice Race: *The Island Princess* and the Politics of Transnational Appropriation," *PMLA* 125.3 (2010): 572–88. John Stoye acknowledges the seventeenth-century paradox that "while popular opinion, in this matter well represented by the House of Commons, continued to express an Elizabethan antipathy towards Spain, the so-called 'Spanish faction' in the Stuart court and government was persistent and strong" (*English Travellers Abroad, 1604–1667* [New York: Octagon Books, 1968], 327).

104. Philip J. Finkelpearl, *Court and Country Politics in the Plays of Beaumont and Fletcher* (Princeton: Princeton University Press, 1990), 13–8.

105. John Stoye, *English Travellers*, 338.

Postscript

1. For the seminal distinction between representational and presentational modes in the drama, see Robert Weimann, *Shakespeare and the Popular Tradition in the Theater: Studies in the Social Dimension of the Dramatic Form and Function* (Baltimore: Johns Hopkins University Press, 1978).

2. Susan Cerasano, "Theater Entrepreneurs and Theatrical Economics," *The Oxford Handbook of Early Modern Theatre*, ed. Richard Dutton (Oxford: Oxford University Press, 2009), 385.

3. Jeremy Lopez, *Theatrical Convention and Audience Response in Early Modern Drama* (Cambridge: Cambridge University Press, 2003), 56.

4. Henry Crosse, *Virtues Commonwealth* (1603), in *Shakesperare's Theater: A Sourcebook*, ed. Tanya Pollard (Malden, MA: Blackwell Publishing, 2004), 193.

5. Ibid, 192.

6. Stephen Gosson, *The School of Abuse* (1579), in *Shakespeare's Theater*, 28.

7. *A Warning for Fair Women* (London, 1599), H2r.

8. Arthur Golding, *A Briefe Discourse of the Late Murther of Master George Sanders* (London, 1573), D1r.

9. For the persistence of public penance as well as the publicity of sacramental penance in the Middle Ages, see Mary C. Mansfield, *The Humiliation of Sinners: Public Penance in Thirteenth-Century France* (Ithaca, NY: Cornell University Press, 1995).

10. See Martin Ingram, *Church Courts, Sex and Marriage in England, 1570–1640* (Cambridge: Cambridge University Press, 1987), 54.

11. Peter Lake, "Deeds against Nature: Cheap Print, Protestantism and Murder in Early Seventeenth-Century England," in *Culture and Politics in Early Stuart England,* ed. Kevin Sharpe and Peter Lake (Basingstoke, UK: Macmillan, 1994), 271.

12. Ibid., 275.

13. See J. A. Sharpe and Thomas Lacqueur for the parameters of the debate. Sharpe argues for the role of "last dying speeches" in reinforcing state order; Lacqueur, citing the carnivalesque atmosphere of the execution, suggests they could undermine government control. J. A. Sharpe, "Last Dying Speeches: Religion, Ideology, and Public Execution in Seventeenth-Century England," *Past and Present* 107 (1985): 144–67; Thomas Laqueur, "Crowds, Carnival and the State in English Executions, 1604–1868," in *The First Modern Society: Essays in English History in Honour of Lawrence Stone,* ed. A. L. Beier, David Cannadine and James M. Rosenheim (Cambridge: Cambridge University Press, 1989), 305–55.

14. Lake, "Deeds against Nature," 275. See also David Postles, "Penance and the Marketplace: a Reformation Dialogue with the Medieval Church (c. 1250–1600)," *Journal of Ecclesiastical History* 54.3 (2003): 441–68.

15. Ramie Targoff, "The Performance of Prayer: Sincerity and Theatricality in Early Modern England," *Representations* 60 (1997): 50. See also Katherine Maus, *Inwardness and Theater in the English Renaissance* (Chicago: University of Chicago Press, 1995).

16. Ingram, *Church Courts,* 53.

17. Hubert Hall, "Some Penances Elizabethan Penances in the Diocese of Ely," *Transactions of the Royal Historical Society* 1 (1907): 276.

18. F. G. Emmison, *Morals & the Church Courts,* vol. 2 of *Elizabethan Life* (Chelmsford, UK: Essex County Council, 1973), 289.

19. *A Warning for Fair Women,* I3r–I3v, italics mine.

20. Ben Jonson, *Volpone,* in *The Complete Plays of Ben Jonson,* ed. G. A. Wilkes, vol. 3 (Oxford: Clarendon Press, 1982), Prol. 8.

21. Francis Beaumont, *The Knight of the Burning Pestle,* ed. Michael Hattaway (London: A&C Black, 1989), Prol. 7–9.

22. William Shakespeare, *Twelfth Night,* in *The Riverside Shakespeare,* ed. G. Blakemore Evans, 2nd ed. (New York: Houghton Mifflin, 1997), 5.1.408.

23. Richard Brome, *A Jovial Crew,* ed. Ann Haaker (London: Edward Arnold, 1968), Prol. 6, 21–2.

24. See Ronald Huebert, *The Performance of Pleasure in English Renaissance Drama* (Basingstoke, UK: Palgrave Macmillan, 2003), 4–5.

25. Crosse, *Virtues Commonwealth,* in *Shakespeare's Theater,* 193.

26. John Northbooke, *A Treatise against Dicing, Dancing, Plays, and Interludes, with Other Idle Pastimes* (1577), in *Shakespeare's Theater,* 9.

27. John Parker, *The Aesthetics of Anti-Christ: From Christian Drama to Christopher Marlowe* (Ithaca, NY: Cornell University Press, 2007), 160.

BIBLIOGRAPHY

Primary

Andrew, Malcolm, and Ronald Waldron, eds. "Pearl." In *The Poems of the Pearl Manuscript: Pearl, Cleanness, Patience, Sir Gawain and the Green Knight*, 4th ed. Exeter: University of Exeter Press, 2002.

Anon. *The Benefite that Christians Receive by Jesus Christ Crucified*. London, 1573. RSTC 19114.

———. *Breefe Treatise Exhorting Sinners to Repentance, Commonly Called, The Conversion of a Sinner*. London, 1580. RSTC 16899.

———. *A Brief Fourme of Confession*. Antwerp, 1576. RSTC 11181.

———. *A Path-way to Penitence*. London, 1591. RSTC 18328.5.

———. *A Short and an Absolute Order of Confession*. 1577. RSTC 18843.

———. *Tell-Trothes New-yeares Gift . . . With His Owne Invective against Jelosy*. London, 1593. RSTC 23867.5.

———. *A Warning for Fair Women*. London, 1599. RSTC 25089.

Anselm of Canterbury. *Why God Became Man [Cur Deus Homo]*. In *The Major Works*, edited by Brian Davies and G. R. Evans, 260–356. New York: Oxford University Press, 1998.

Apology of the Augsburg Confession. In *The Book of Concord: The Confessions of the Evangelical Lutheran Church*, translated and edited by Theodore G. Tappert, 97–285. Philadelphia: Muhlenberg Press, 1959.

Aquinas, St. Thomas. *Summa Theologiae. Latin Text and English Translation*. Translated and edited by Thomas Gilby, O.P., and T. C. O'Brien, O.P. 60 vols. New York: McGraw Hill Book Company, 1964.

Aristotle. *Nicomachean Ethics*. Edited by Hugh Treddenick. New York: Penguin, 2003.

Augsburg Confession. In *The Book of Concord: The Confessions of the Evangelical Lutheran Church*, translated and edited by Theodore G. Tappert, 23–96. Philadelphia: Muhlenberg Press, 1959.

Augustine, St. *Answer to the Pelagians*. Translated by Roland J. Teske. Vol. 23 of *The Works of Saint Augustine*, edited by John E. Rotelle, O.S.A. Hyde Park, NY: New City Press, 1997.

Bacon, Sir Francis. *The Essays*. Edited by John Pitcher. London: Penguin Books, 1985.

Baker, John. *Lectures of J. B. Upon the XII Articles*. London, 1581. RSTC 1219.

Bartlett, Anne Clark, and Thomas H. Bestul, eds. *Cultures of Piety: Medieval English Devotional Literature in Translation*. Ithaca, NY: Cornell University Press, 1999.

Beard, Thomas. *Theatre of Gods Judgements*. London, 1597. RSTC 1659.

Beaumont, Francis. *The Knight of the Burning Pestle*. Edited by Michael Hattaway. London: A&C Black, 1989.

Beaumont, Francis and John Fletcher. *Love's Pilgrimage*. Edited by L. A. Beaurline. Vol. 2 of *The Dramatic Works in the Beaumont and Fletcher Canon*, edited by Fredson Bowers, 569–691. Cambridge: Cambridge University Press, 1970.

Becon, Thomas. *The Reliques of Rome*. London, 1563. RSTC 1755.

Bernard, Richard. *Ruths Recompence*. London, 1628. RSTC 1962.

Bell, Thomas. *The Speculation of Usury*. London, 1596. RSTC 1828.

Beza, Theodore. *A Briefe and Piththie Summe of the Christian Faith*. Translated by R. F. London, 1565. RSTC 2007.

Bilson, Bishop Thomas. *The Effect of Certaine Sermons Touching the Full Redemption of Mankind by the Death and Bloud of Christ Jesus*. London, 1599. RSTC 3064.

———. *The Survey of Christes Sufferings for Mans Redemption and of His Descent to Hades or Hel for Our Deliuerance*. London, 1604. RSTC 3070.

Bitterling, Klaus, ed. *Of Schrifte and Penance: The Middle English Prose Translation of Le Manuel des Péchés*. Heidelberg: Universitatsverlag, 1998.

Blaxton, John. *The English Usurer*. London, 1634. RSTC 23129a.

Bodenham, John (attributed). *Politeuphuia: Wits Common wealth*. London, 1598. RSTC 15686.

The Book of Common Prayer 1559: The Elizabethan Prayer Book. Edited by John E. Booty. Charlottesville: University of Virginia Press, 1976.

Botero, Giovanni. *Treatise, Concerning the Causes of the Magnificencie and Greatnes of Cities*. Translated by Robert Peterson. London, 1606. RSTC 3405.

Bradford, John. *A Sermon of Repentaunce*. London, 1553. RSTC 3496.

Brandeis, Arthur, ed. *Jacob's Well*. EETS O.S. 115. Reprint. Rochester, NY: Boydell & Brewer, 1998.

Bray, Gerald, ed. *Documents of the English Reformation, 1526–1701*. Cambridge: James Clarke, 2004.

Brome, Richard. *A Jovial Crew*. Edited by Ann Haaker. London: Edward Arnold, 1968.

Bullinger, Heinrich. *The Christen State of Matrimony*. Translated by Miles Coverdale. London, 1546. RSTC 4048.

———. *Fiftie Godlie and Learned Sermons Divided into Five Decades*. Translated by H. I. London, 1577. RSTC 4056.

Burton, Robert. *The Anatomy of Melancholy*. New York: New York Review of Books, 2001.

Caesar, Philipp. *A General Discourse against the Damnable Sect of Usurers*. London, 1578. RSTC 4342.

Cajetan, Thomas. *Cajetan Responds: A Reader in Reformation Controversy*. Edited by Jared Wicks. Washington, DC: Catholic University Press, 1978.

Calvin, John M. *The Institution of the Christian Religion*. London, 1561. RSTC 4415.

———. *A Commentarie of John Calvine, upon the Firste Booke of Moses Called Genesis*. Translated by Thomas Thymme. London, 1578. RSTC 4393.

———. *A Commentarie upon S. Paules Epistles to the Corinthians*. Translated by Thomas Thymme. London, 1577. RSTC 4400.

———. *Institutes of the Christian Religion*. Edited by John T. McNeill, translated by Ford Lewis Battles. 2 vols. Philadelphia: Westminster Press, 1960.

Canisius, Peter. *An Introduction to the Catholick Faith*. Rouen, 1633. RSTC 14123.5.

The Canons and Decrees of the Sacred and Oecumenical Council of Trent. Edited and translated by J. Waterworth. London: Dolman, 1848.

Carlisle, John. *A Discourse Concerning Two Divine Positions*. London, 1582. RSTC 4654.

Cartwright, Francis. *The Life, Confession, and Heartie Repentance of Francis Cartwright, Gentleman*. London, 1621. RSTC 4704.

Cawdry, Robert. *A Table Alphabeticall*. London, 1604. RSTC 4884.

Cawley, A. C., ed. *Everyman*. In *Everyman and Medieval Miracle Plays*. London: Everyman's Library, 1974.

Cervantes, Miguel. *Exemplarie Novells in Sixe Books*. Translated by James Mabbe. London, 1640. RSTC 4914.

Cleaver, Robert. *Godly Forme of Household Government*. London, 1598. RSTC 5383.

Cooper, Thomas. *Thesaurus Linguae Romanae & Britannicae*. London, 1565. RSTC 5686.

Copley, Anthony. *A Fig for Fortune*. London, 1596. RSTC 5737.

Cornwallis, William. *Essayes*. London, 1600. RSTC 5775.

Coryate, Thomas. *Coryats Crudities*. London, 1611. RSTC 5808.

Dekker, Thomas. *Batchelars Banquet*. London, 1603. RSTC 6476.2.

Dent, Arthur. *A Sermon of Repentance*. London, 1587. RSTC 6655.5.

———. *Plaine Man's Path-way to Heaven*. London, 1601. RSTC 6626.5.

———. *The Hand-maid of Repentance*. London 1614. RSTC 6616.

Donne, John. *The Sermons of John Donne*. Edited by George Potter and Evelyn Simpson. 10 vols. Berkeley: University of California Press, 1955.

Downame, George. *Lecture on the 15. Psalme*. London, 1604. RSTC 7118.

Dyke, Daniel. *Two Treatises. The One, of Repentance, the Other, of Christs Temptations*. London, 1616. RSTC 7408.

Egerton, Stephen. *A Lecture Preached by Maister Egerton*. London, 1603. RSTC 7539.

Fenton, Roger. *A Treatise of Usurie*. London, 1611. RSTC 10806.

Fish, Simon. *A Supplication of the Poore Commons.* London, 1546. RSTC 10884.

Fisher, Bishop John. *Treatyse Concernynge . . . the Seven Penytencyall Psalms.* In *The English Works of John Fisher.* Edited by J. E. B. Mayor, 1–267. EETS O.S. 27. London: N. Trübner & Co., 1876.

Foakes, R. A., ed. *Henslowe's Diary.* 2nd ed. Cambridge: Cambridge University Press, 2002.

Folger Shakespeare Library, V.A.134.

Formula of Concord. In *The Book of Concord: The Confessions of the Evangelical Lutheran Church,* translated and edited by Theodore G. Tappert, 463–636. (Philadelphia: Muhlenberg Press, 1959).

Foxe, John. *A Sermon Preached at the Christening a Certaine Jew.* London, 1578. RSTC 11248.

———. *Actes and Monuments of Matters Most Special and Memorable, Happening in the Church.* London, 1583. RSTC 11225.

Fulbecke, William. *Booke of Christian Ethicks or Moral Philosophie.* London, 1587. RSTC 11409.

A Garden of Spirituall Flowers. London, 1620. RSTC 21213.6.

Gataker, Thomas. *A Good Wife Gods Gift and, a Wife Indeed. Two Mariage Sermons.* London, 1624. RSTC 11660.

Gifford, George. *A Briefe Discourse of Certaine Points of the Religion . . . which may bee termed the Countrie Divinitie.* London, 1582. RSTC 11846.

Golding, Arthur. *A Briefe Discourse of the Late Murther of Master George Sanders.* London, 1573. RSTC 111985.

Gouge, William. *Of Domesticall Duties.* London, 1622. RSTC 12119.

Greene, Robert. *Greene's Newes Both from Heaven and Hell.* London, 1593. RSTC 12259.

———. *Friar Bacon and Friar Bungay.* Edited by J. A. Lavin. London: Benn, 1969.

Greenham, Richard. *The Works of the Reverend and Faithfull Servant of Jesus Christ, M. Richard Greenham.* London, 1599. RSTC 12313.5.

Grotius, Hugo. *A Defence of the Catholick Faith Concerning the Satisfaction of Christ.* Translated by W. H. London, 1692. Wing G2107.

Hakewill, George. *An Answere to a Treatise Written by Dr. Carier.* London, 1616. RSTC 12610.

Harsnett, Samuel. *A Declaration of Egregious Popish Impostures.* London, 1603. RSTC 12880.

Heale, William. *An Apologie for Women.* Oxford, 1609. RSTC 13104.

Hieron, Samuel. *Davids Penitentiall Psalme Opened.* Cambridge, 1617. RSTC 13394a.

Higgins, John. *An Answere to Master William Perkins, Concerning Christs Descension into Hell.* Oxford, 1602. RSTC 13442.

Hill, Adam. *The Defence of the Article: Christ Descended into Hell.* London, 1592. RSTC 13466.

Holland, Henry. *Davids Faith and Repentance.* London, 1589. RSTC 13586.5.

"An Homilie of Repentance." In *Certaine Sermons or Homilies.* Gainesville, FL: Scholars' Facsimiles and Reprints, 1968. Facsimile of 1623 edition.

Hooker, Richard. *Of the Laws of Ecclesiastical Polity.* In *The Folger Library Edition of the Works of Richard Hooker.* Edited by W. Speed Hill et al. 7 vols. Cambridge, MA: Belknap Press, 1977–98.

Hulme, William Henry, ed. *The Middle English Harrowing of Hell and Gospel of Nico-demus.* EETS O.S. 94, 98–100. London: Kegan Paul, 1907.

Hume, Alexander. *A Rejoynder to Doctor Hil Concerning the Descense of Christ into Hell.* Edinburgh, 1594. RSTC 13948.

Isidore of Seville. *The Etymologies of Isidore of Seville.* Edited and translated by Stephen A. Barney. Cambridge: Cambridge University Press, 2006.

Jacob, Henry. *A Treatise of the Sufferings and Victory of Christ, in the Work of Our Redemption.* Middleburg, 1598. RSTC 14340.

Jones, John Henry, ed. *The English Faust Book: A Critical Edition.* Cambridge: Cambridge University Press, 1994.

Jonson, Ben. *Volpone.* Vol. 3 of *The Complete Plays of Ben Jonson.* Edited by G. A. Wilkes. Oxford: Clarendon Press, 1982.

Kyd, Thomas. *The Spanish Tragedy.* Edited by J. R. Mulryne, 2nd ed. London: A&C Black, 1989.

Lever, Christopher. *A Crucifixe.* London, 1607. RSTC 15536.

Lindström, Bengt, ed. *A Late Middle English Version of the Gospel of Nicodemus.* Uppsala, Stockholm: Almquist & Wiksell, 1974.

Liturgical Services: Liturgies and Occasional Forms of Prayer Set Forth in the Reign of Queen Elizabeth. Cambridge: Cambridge University Press, 1847.

Lloyd, Charles, ed. *Formularies of Faith Put Forth by Authority during the Reign of Henry VIII.* Oxford: Oxford University Press, 1866.

Lodge, Thomas. *An Alarum against Usurers.* London, 1584. RSTC 16653.

Lombard, Peter. *Sentences, Book 4.* In Elizabeth Frances Rogers, *Peter Lombard and the Sacramental System.* Merrick, NY: Richwood Publishing Co., 1976.

Lupton, Thomas. *A Moral and Pitieful Comedie Intituled, All for Money.* London, 1578. RSTC 16949.

———. *A Dreame of the Devill and Dives.* London, 1584. RSTC 16947.3.

Luther, Martin. *A Treatise, Touching the Libertie of a Christian.* Translated by James Bell. London, 1579. RSTC 16996.

———. *Lectures on Genesis, Chapters 1–5,.* Translated by George Schick. Vol. 1 of *Luther's Works,* edited by Jaroslav Pelikan. St. Louis, MO: Concordia Publishing, 1958.

———. "Ninety-five Theses, 1517." Translated by Harold J. Grimm. Vol. 31 of *Luther's Works,* edited by Harold J. Grimm, 17–33. Philadelphia: Muhlenberg Press, 1957.

———. "The Sacrament of Penance, 1519." Translated by E. Theodore Bachman. Vol. 35 of *Luther's Works,* edited by E. Theodore Bachman, 3–22. Philadelphia: Muhlen-berg Press, 1960.

———. "The Babylonian Captivity of the Church, 1520." Translated by A. T. W. Stein-häuser. Vol. 36 of *Luther's Works,* edited by Abdel Ross Wentz, 3–126. Philadelphia, Muhlenberg Press, 1955.

———. *Basic Theological Writings.* Edited by Timothy Lull. Minneapolis, MN: Fortress Press, 1989.

Marbury, Francis. *Notes of the Doctrine of Repentance.* London, 1602. RSTC 17305.

Marlowe, Christopher. *Doctor Faustus.* Edited by David Scott Kastan. New York: Norton, 2005.

————. *The Jew of Malta*. In *The Complete Plays*, edited by Mark Thornton Burnett, 458–536. London: Everyman, 1999.

McNeill, John T., and Helena M. Gamer, ed. and trans. *Medieval Handbooks of Penance*. New York: Octagon Books, 1965.

Merbecke, John. *A Booke of Notes and Common Places*. London, 1581. RSTC 17299.

Meriton, George. *A Sermon of Repentance*. London, 1607. RSTC 17839.

Middleton, Thomas. *The Revenger's Tragedy*. In *Thomas Middleton: The Collected Works*, edited by Gary Taylor and John Lavagnino, 543–93. Oxford: Clarendon Press, 2007.

Mirk, John. *Instructions for Parish Priests*. Edited by Edward Peacock. EETS O.S. 31. Reprint. Suffolk, UK: Boydell & Brewer, 2000.

Mosse, Miles. *Arraignment and Conviction of Usurie*. London, 1595. RSTC 18207.

R. N. *The Christians Manna*. St. Omer, 1613. RSTC 18334.

Nashe, Thomas. "Letter." In *Menaphon*, by Robert Greene. London, 1589. RSTC 12272.

The New Testament of Jesus Christ. Rheims, 1582.

Niccholes, Alexander. *A Discourse of Marriage and Wiving*. London, 1615. RSTC 18514.

Northbrooke, John. *Spiritus Est Vicarius Christi in Terra*. London, 1571. RSTC 18663.

Nowell, Alexander. *A Catechism, or First Instruction and Learning*. London, 1570. RSTC 18708.

Parkes, Richard. *A Briefe Answere unto Certaine Objections and Reasons against the Descension of Christ into Hell*. London, 1604. RSTC 19296.

Parsons, Robert. *A Christian Directorie*. Rouen, 1585. RSTC 19354.1.

Perkins, William. *Two Treatises. I. Of the Nature and Practise of Repentance*. London, 1595. RSTC 19760.5.

————. *An Exposition of the Symbole or Creed of the Apostles*. London, 1595. RSTC 19703.

————. *A Reformed Catholike*. London, 1598. RSTC 19736.

————. *Hepieikeia: or A Treatise of Christian Equitie*. Cambridge, 1604. RSTC 19699.

————. *Christian Oeconomie*. London, 1609. RSTC 19677.

Pilkington, Richard. *Parallela: or the Grounds of the New Romane Catholike*. London, 1618. RSTC 19933.

Pollard, Tanya, ed. *Shakespeare's Theater: A Sourcebook*. Malden, MA: Blackwell Publishing, 2004.

De la Primaudaye, Pierre. *The French Academie*. London, 1586. RSTC 15233.

Rogers, Thomas. *The English Creede, Consenting with the True Auncient Catholique and Apostolique Church*. London, 1585. RSTC 21226.5.

Sandys, Archbishop Edwin. *Sermons*. London, 1585. RSTC 21713.

Sandys, Edwin. *Europae Speculum or, A View or Survey of the State of Religion in the Westerne Parts of the World*. The Hague, 1629. RSTC 21718.

Scott, Thomas. *A Godlie Sermon of Repentaunce and Amendment of Life*. London, 1585. RSTC 22108.

Segar, William. *Booke of Armes and Honor*. London, 1590. RSTC 22163.

Seneca. *His Tenne Tragedies, translated into Englysh*. London, 1581. RSTC 22221.

Seneca. *Thyestes*. In *Seneca*, vol. 78, edited by John G. Fitch. Cambridge: Loeb Editions, 2004.

Shakespeare, William. *Hamlet*. In *The Riverside Shakespeare*, edited by G. Blakemore Evans. 2nd ed. New York: Houghton Mifflin, 1997.

————. *The Merchant of Venice*. In *The Riverside Shakespeare*, edited by G. Blakemore Evans. 2nd ed. New York: Houghton Mifflin, 1997.

————. *Much Ado about Nothing*. In *The Riverside Shakespeare*, edited by G. Blakemore Evans. 2nd ed. New York: Houghton Mifflin, 1997.

————. *Othello*. In *The Riverside Shakespeare*, edited by G. Blakemore Evans. 2nd ed. New York: Houghton Mifflin, 1997.

————. *Twelfth Night*. In *The Riverside Shakespeare*, edited by G. Blakemore Evans, 2nd ed. New York: Houghton Mifflin, 1997.

Sibbes, Richard. *The Complete Works of Richard Sibbes*. Edited by Alexander Balloch Grosart. 7 vols. Edinburgh: J. Nichol, 1862–4.

Smith, Henry. *The Benefit of Contentation*. London, 1590. RSTC 2298694.

————. *A Treatise of the Lord's Supper*. London, 1591. RSTC 22705.

————. *A Preparative to Mariage*. London, 1591. RSTC 22686.

Snawsel, Richard. *A Looking Glasse for Maried Folkes*. London, 1610. RSTC 22886.5.

Stevens, Martin, and A. C. Cawley, eds. *The Towneley Plays*. Vol. 1. EETS S.S. 13. Oxford: Oxford University Press, 1994.

Stock, Richard. *The Doctrine and Use of Repentance*. London, 1608. RSTC 23274.5.

Tasso, Ercole. *Of Mariage and Wiving*. Translated by R. T. London, 1599. RSTC 23690.

Tawney, R. H. and Eileen Power, eds. *Tudor Economic Documents*. 3 vols. London: Longmans, 1924.

Tertullian. *Treatises on Penance*. Edited and translated by William P. Le Saint. Westminster, MD: Newman Press, 1959.

Thomas of Chobham. *Summa Confessorum*. Edited by F. Broomfield. Louvain: Editions Nauwelaerts, 1968.

Thomas, William. *The History of Italy*. London, 1561. RSTC 24019.

Tilney, Edmund. *The Flower of Friendship: A Renaissance Dialogue Contesting Marriage*. Edited by Valerie Wayne. Ithaca, NY: Cornell University Press, 1992.

The Trial of Treasure. Vol. 3 of *Dodsley's Old English Plays*. Edited by W. Carew Hazlitt, 257–301. London, 1874.

Tyndale, William. *The Obedience of a Christian Man*. Edited by David Daniell. London: Penguin Books, 2000.

————. "Preface to the New Testament." In *Documents of the English Reformation 1526–1701*, edited by Gerald Bray, 17–31. Cambridge: James Clarke, 2004.

Varchi, Benedetto. *Blazon of Jealousie*. Translated by R. F. London, 1615. RSTC 25593.

Vaux, Laurence. *A Catechism*. Louvain, 1568. RSTC 24625.

Vives, Juan Luis. *The Instruction of a Christen Woman*. Edited by Virginia Beauchamp et al. Urbana: University of Illinois Press, 2002.

W., C. *Summarie of Controversies: Wherein the Chiefest Points of the Holy Catholike Romane Faith, are . . . Proved, against the Sectaries of This Age*. London, 1616. RSTC 26047.

Wadsworth, James. *The Contrition of a Protestant Preacher, Converted To Be a Catholique Scholler*. St. Omer, 1615. RSTC 24924.5.

Wager, William. *Enough Is as Good as a Feast*. Edited by R. Mark Benbow. Lincoln: University of Nebraska Press, 1967.

Weatherly, Edward H., ed. *Speculum Sacerdotale.* EETS O.S. 200. London: Oxford University Press, 1936.

Wenzel, Siegfried ed. *Fasciculus Morum: A Fourteenth-Century Preacher's Handbook.* University Park: Pennsylvania State University Press, 1989.

Westerman, William. *Two Sermons of Assize.* London, 1600. RSTC 25282.

Whately, William. *A Bride-bush, or a Wedding Sermon.* London, 1617. RSTC 25296.

Wheeler, John. *A Treatise of Commerce.* London, 1601. RSTC 25331.

Willet, Andrew. *Synopsis Papismi.* London, 1592. RSTC 25696.

———. *Limbo-mastix.* London, 1604. RSTC 25692.

———. *A Treatise of Salomon's Marriage.* London, 1613. RSTC 25705.

———. *Hexapla in Genesin and Exodum.* London, 1633. RSTC 25685.

Willis, R. *Mount Tabor. Or Private Exercises of a Penitent Sinner.* London, 1639. RSTC 25752.

Wilson, Thomas. *A Discourse upon Usury.* Edited by R. H. Tawney. New York: Augustus M. Kelley, repr. 1965.

Wilson, Thomas. *A Christian Dictionarie.* London, 1612. RSTC 25786.

Wilson, Bishop Thomas. *The Effect of Certaine Sermons Touching the Full Redemption of Mankind by the Death and Bloud of Christ Jesus.* London, 1599. RSTC 3064.

Wing, John. *The Crowne Conjugall, or, the Spouse Royall.* London, 1632. RSTC 25845.

Wright, Thomas. *Passions of the Mind in General.* London, 1601. RSTC 26039.

The York Plays: A Critical Edition of the York Corpus Christi Play as Recorded in British Library Additional MS 35290. Edited by Richard Beadle, EETS S.S. 23. Oxford: Oxford University Press, 2009.

Secondary

Achinstein, Sharon. "John Foxe and the Jews." *Renaissance Quarterly* 54.1 (2001): 86–120.

Adelman, Janet. *Suffocating Mothers: Fantasies of Maternal Origin in Shakespeare's Plays, Hamlet to the Tempest.* New York: Routledge, 1991.

———. *Blood Relations: Christian and Jew in The Merchant of Venice.* Chicago: University of Chicago Press, 2008.

Aers, David. "A Whisper in the Ear of Early Modernists; or Reflections on Literary Critics Writing the 'History of the Subject.'" In *Culture and History, 1350–1600: Essays on English Communities, Identities, and Writing,* edited by David Aers, 177–202. Detroit: Wayne State University Press, 1992.

Aho, James. *Confession and Bookkeeping: The Religious, Moral, and Rhetorical Roots of Modern Accounting.* Albany: State University of New York Press, 2005.

Anderson, Judith. *Translating Investments: Metaphor and the Dynamic of Cultural Change in Tudor-Stuart England.* New York: Fordham University Press, 2005.

Anderson, Thomas P. *Performing Early Modern Trauma from Shakespeare to Milton.* Burlington, VT: Ashgate, 2006.

Annas, Julia. *The Morality of Happiness.* New York: Oxford University Press, 1993.

Appleby, Joyce. *Economic Thought and Ideology in Seventeenth-Century England.* Princeton, NJ: Princeton University Press, 1978.

Aulen, Gustaf. *Christus Victor; An Historical Study of the Three Main Types of the Idea of the Atonement.* Translated by A. G. Herbert. New York: Macmillan, 1951.

Axton, Richard. *European Drama of the Middle Ages.* Pittsburgh, PA: University of Pittsburgh Press, 1975.

Bannerjee, Pompa. "I, Mephastophilis: Self, Other, and Demonic Parody in Marlowe's *Doctor Faustus." Christianity and Literature* 42.2 (1993): 221–41.

Barber, C. L. "The Form of Faustus' Fortunes Good or Bad." *Tulane Drama Review* 8.4 (1964): 92–119.

Bartels, Emily. *Speaking of the Moor: From Alcazar to Othello.* Philadelphia: University of Pennsylvania Press, 2008.

Beaureguard, David. *Catholic Theology in Shakespeare's Plays.* Newark: University of Delaware Press, 2008.

Beaurline, L. A. Textual introduction to *Love's Pilgrimage,* edited by L. A. Beaurline. Vol. 2 of *The Dramatic Works in the Beaumont and Fletcher Canon,* edited by Fredson Bowers, 569–73. Cambridge: Cambridge University Press, 1970.

Beckwith, Sarah. *Shakespeare and the Grammar of Forgiveness.* Ithaca, NY: Cornell University Press, 2011.

Belsey, Catherine. *The Subject of Tragedy.* London: Methuen, 1985.

———. "Desire's Excess and the Renaissance Theatre: *Edward II, Troilus and Cressida, Othello."* In *Erotic Politics: Desire on the Renaissance Stage,* edited by Susan Zimmerman, 84–102. London: Routledge, 1992.

———. *Desire: Love Stories in Western Culture.* London: Blackwell, 1994.

Berger, Adolf. *Encyclopedic Dictionary of Roman Law.* Philadelphia: American Philosophical Society, repr. 1991.

Berger, Harry. "Against the Sink-a-Pace: Sexual and Family Politics in *Much Ado about Nothing." Shakespeare Quarterly* 33.3 (1982): 302–13.

———. *Making Trifles of Terrors: Redistributing Complicities in Shakespeare.* Stanford, CA: Stanford University Press, 1997.

———. "Acts of Silence, Acts of Speech: How to Do Things with Othello and Desdemona." *Renaissance Drama* 33 (2004): 3–35.

Bevington, David. *From Mankind to Marlowe: Growth of Structure in the Popular Drama of Tudor England.* Cambridge, MA: Harvard University Press, 1962.

———. "Staging the Reformation: Power and Theatricality in the Plays of William Wager." In *Interludes and Early Modern Society: Studies in Gender, Power and Theatricality,* edited by Peter Happé and Wim Hüsken. Amsterdam: Rodopi, 2007.

Biberman, Matthew. *Masculinity, Anti-Semitism and Early Modern English Literature: From the Satanic to the Effeminate Jew.* Burlington, VT: Ashgate, 2004.

Bills, Bing D. "'The Suppression Theory' and the English Corpus Christi Play: A Re-Examination." *Theatre Journal* 32 (1980): 157–68.

Birch, David. *Early Reformation English Polemics.* Salzburg, Austria: Institut für Anglistik und Amerikanistik, 1983.

Blau, Herbert. "The Absolved Riddle: Sovereign Pleasure and the Baroque Subject in the Tragicomedies of John Fletcher." *New Literary History* 17.3 (1986): 539–54.

Bond, Christopher. "Medieval Harrowings of Hell and Spenser's House of Mammon." *English Literary Renaissance* 37.2 (2007): 175–92.

Boose, Lynda. "Othello's Handkerchief: 'The Recognizance and Pledge of Love.'" In *Othello: A Norton Critical Edition*, edited by Edward Pechter, 262–75. New York: Norton, 2004.

Bossy, John. *The English Catholic Community, 1570–1850*. London: Darton, Longman and Todd, 1975.

———. *History of Christianity in the West, 1475–1700*. Oxford: Oxford University Press, 1985.

———. "Practices of Satisfaction, 1215–1700." In *Retribution, Repentance, and Reconciliation: Papers Read at the 2002 Summer Meeting and 2003 Winter Meeting of the Ecclesiastical History Society*, edited by Kate Cooper and Jeremy Gregory, 106–18. Suffolk, UK: Boydell & Brewer, 2004.

Bowers, Fredson. *Elizabethan Revenge Tragedy, 1587–1642*. Princeton, NJ: Princeton University Press, 1940.

Boyce, Benjamin. "News from Hell: Satiric Communications with the Netherworld in English Writing of the Seventeenth and Eighteenth Centuries." *PMLA* 58.2 (1943): 402–37.

Braden, Gordon. *Renaissance Tragedy and the Senecan Tradition: Anger's Privilege*. New Haven, CT: Yale University Press, 1985.

Braswell, Mary. *The Medieval Sinner: Characterization and Confession in the Literature of the English Middle Ages*. Rutherford, NJ: Fairleigh Dickinson University Press, 1983.

Breitenberg, Mark. *Anxious Masculinity in Early Modern England*. Cambridge: Cambridge University Press, 1996.

Bristol, Michael. "Charivari and the Comedy of Abjection in *Othello*." In *True Rites and Maimed Rites: Ritual and Anti-Ritual in Shakespeare and His Age*, edited by Linda Woodbridge and Edward Berry, 75–97. Urbana: University of Illinois Press, 1992.

Brooks, Peter. *Troubling Confessions: Speaking Guilt in Law and Literature*. Chicago: University of Chicago Press, 2000.

Broude, Ronald. "Revenge and Revenge Tragedy in Renaissance England." *Renaissance Quarterly* 28.1 (1975): 38–58.

Brundage, James A. *Medieval Canon Law*. London: Longman, 1995.

Burke, Kenneth. "Othello: An Essay to Illustrate a Method." *Hudson Review* 4 (1951): 165–203.

Burnett, Anne Pippin. *Revenge in Attic and Later Tragedy*. Berkeley: University of California Press, 1998.

Butler, Martin. *Theatre and Crisis, 1632–1642*. Cambridge: Cambridge University Press, 1984.

Cahill, Patricia. "Killing by Computation: Military Mathematics, the Social Body, and Marlowe's *Tamburlaine*." In *The Arts of Calculation: Numerical Thought in Early Modern Europe*, edited by David Glimp and Michelle Warren, 165–86. London: Palgrave, 2004.

Calabi, Donatella. "The 'City of the Jews.'" In *The Jews of Early Modern Venice*, edited by Robert C. Davis and Benjamin Ravid, 31–49. Baltimore, MD: Johns Hopkins University Press, 2001.

Callaghan, Dympna. Introduction to *The Impact of Feminisim in English Renaissance Studies*, edited by Dympna Callaghan, 1–29. New York: Palgrave, 2007.

Campbell, Lily B. "Theories of Revenge in Renaissance England." *Modern Philology* 28.3 (1931): 281–96.

———. "*Doctor Faustus*: A Case of Conscience." *PMLA* 67.2 (1952): 219–39.

Carlson, Eric Josef. *Marriage and the English Reformation.* Oxford: Blackwell, 1994.

———. "Cassandra Banished? New Research on Religion in Tudor and Early Stuart England." In *Religion and the English People, 1500–1640: New Voices, New Perspectives,* edited by Eric Josef Carlson. Kirksville, MO: Truman State University Press, 1998.

———. "Confession and Absolution in Caroline Cambridge: The 1637 Crisis in Context." In *Retribution, Repentance, and Reconciliation: Papers Read at the 2002 Summer Meeting and 2003 Winter Meeting of the Ecclesiastical History Society,* edited by Kate Cooper and Jeremy Gregory, 180–93. Suffolk, UK: Boydell & Brewer, 2004.

Cary, Cecile Williamson. " 'It circumscribes us here': Hell on the Renaissance Stage." In *The Iconography of Hell,* edited by Clifford Davidson and Thomas H. Seiler, 187–207. Kalamazoo, MI: Medieval Institute Publications, 1992.

Cavell, Stanley. *Disowning Knowledge in Six Plays of Shakespeare.* Cambridge: Cambridge University Press, 1987.

Cerasano, Susan. "Theater Entrepreneurs and Theatrical Economics." In *The Oxford Handbook of Early Modern Theatre,* edited by Richard Dutton, 380–95. Oxford: Oxford University Press, 2009.

Cheney, Patrick. *Marlowe's Counterfeit Profession: Ovid, Spenser, Counter-Nationhood.* Toronto: University of Toronto Press, 1997.

Clopper, Lawrence M. "English Drama: From Ungodly *Ludi* to Sacred Play." *The Cambridge History of Medieval English Literature,* edited by David Wallace, 739–66. Cambridge: Cambridge University Press, 1999.

———. *Drama, Play, and Game: English Festive Culture in the Medieval and Early Modern Period.* Chicago: University of Chicago Press, 2001.

Coddon, Karin S. " 'For Show or Useless Property': Necrophilia and *The Revenger's Tragedy.*" In *Revenge Tragedy: Contemporary Critical Essays,* edited by Stevie Simkin, 121–41. New York: Palgrave, 2001.

Cohen, Charles Lloyd. *God's Caress: The Psychology of Puritan Religious Experience.* Oxford: Clarendon Press, 1986.

Cohen, Jeremy. *Living Letters of the Law: Ideas of the Jew in Medieval Christianity.* Berkeley: University of California Press, 1999.

Cohen, Walter. "*The Merchant of Venice* and the Possibilities of Historical Criticism," *English Literary History* 49.4 (1982): 765–89.

Coleman, David. *Drama and the Sacraments in Sixteenth-Century England: Indelible Characters.* Basingstoke, UK: Palgrave Macmillan, 2007.

Collinson, Patrick. *The Religion of Protestants: The Church in English Society 1559–1625.* Oxford: Clarendon Press, 1982.

———. "Shepherds, Sheepdogs, and Hirelings: The Pastoral Ministry in Post-Reformation England." *The Ministry: Clerical and Lay, Studies in Church History* 29 (1989): 185–220.

———. "England." In *The Reformation in National Context,* edited by Robert W. Scribner, Roy Porter, and Mikúlaš Teich, 80–94. Cambridge: Cambridge University Press, 1994.

Commensoli, Vivian. *'Household Business': Domestic Plays of Early Modern England.* Toronto: University of Toronto Press, 1997.

Cornelius, R. M. *Christopher Marlowe's Use of the Bible.* New York: Peter Lang, 1984.

Corrigan, Brian. "Middleton, *The Revenger's Tragedy*, and Crisis Literature." *SEL* 38.2 (1998): 281–95.

Cox, John. *The Devil and the Sacred in English Drama, 1350–1642.* Cambridge: Cambridge University Press, 2000.

Crawford, Patricia. *Blood, Bodies and Families in Early Modern England.* Harlow, UK: Pearson Educational, 2004.

Cressy, David. *Birth, Marriage, and Death: Ritual, Religion, and the Life-Cycle in Tudor and Stuart England.* Oxford: Oxford University Press, 1997.

Cressy, David, and Lori Anne Ferrell. Introduction to *Religion and Society in Early Modern England: A Sourcebook*, edited David Cressy and Lori Anne Ferrell, 1–11. London: Routledge, 1996.

Crockett, Bryan. *The Play of Paradox: Stage and Sermon in Renaissance England.* Philadelphia: University of Pennsylvania Press, 1995.

Crosbie, Christopher. "Oeconomia and the Vegetative Soul: Rethinking Revenge in *The Spanish Tragedy.*" *English Literary Renaissance* 38.1 (2008): 3–33.

Cummings, Brian. *The Literary Culture of the Reformation: Grammar and Grace.* Oxford: Oxford University Press, 2002.

Daniel, Drew. "'Let me have judgment, and the Jew his will': Melancholy Epistemology and Masochistic Fantasy in *The Merchant of Venice.*" *Shakespeare Quarterly* 61.2 (2010): 206–34.

Danson, Lawrence. *The Harmonies of* The Merchant of Venice. New Haven, CT: Yale University Press, 1978.

Darby, Trudi, and Alexander Samson. "'Last thought upon a windmill?' Cervantes and Fletcher." In *The Cervantean Heritage: Reception and Influence of Cervantes in Britain*, edited by J. A. G. Ardila, 223–33. London: Legenda, 2009.

Davidson, Clifford. *From Creation to Doom.* New York: AMS Press, 1984.

Davies, Horton. *Worship and Theology in England, 1558–1603.* Princeton, NJ: Princeton University Press, 1975.

Davies, Kathleen M. "Continuity and Change in Literary Advice on Marriage." In *Marriage and Society: Studies in the Social History of Marriage*, edited by R. B. Outhwaite, 58–80. New York: St. Martin's Press, 1981.

Davis, Robert C. Introduction to *The Jews of Early Modern Venice*, edited by Robert C. Davis and Benjamin Ravid, vii–xix. Baltimore, MD: Johns Hopkins University Press, 2001.

Dawson, Anthony. "Shakespeare and Secular Performance." In *Shakespeare and the Cultures of Performance*, edited by Paul Edward Yachnin and Patricia Badir, 83–97. Burlington, VT: Ashgate, 2008.

Degenhardt, Jane Hwang, and Elizabeth Williamson. Introduction to *Religion and Drama in Early Modern England: The Performance of Religion on the Renaissance Stage*, edited by Jane Hwang Degenhardt and Elizabeth Williamson, 1–18. Burlington, VT: Ashgate, 2011.

De Boer, Wietse. "At Heresy's Door: Borromeo, Penance, and Confessional Boundaries in Early Modern Europe." In *A New History of Penance*, edited by Abigail Firey, 343–76. Leiden, Netherlands: Brill, 2008.

De Grazia, Margreta. *Hamlet without Hamlet.* Cambridge: Cambridge University Press, 2007.

De Grazia, Margreta, Maureen Quilligan, and Peter Stallybrass. Introduction to *Subject and Object in Renaissance Culture*, edited by Margreta de Grazia, Maureen Quilligan, and Peter Stallybrass, 1–16. Cambridge: Cambridge University Press, 1996.

Delumeau, Jean. *Sin and Fear: The Emergence of a Western Guilt Culture, 13th–18th Centuries.* New York: Palgrave Macmillian, 1990.

Diaz, Joanne. "Grief as Medicine for Grief: Complaint Poetry in Early Modern England, 1559–1609." PhD., dissertation, Northwestern University, 2008.

Dictionnaire de Théologie Catholique. Vol. 14.1. Paris: Librarie Letouzey et Ané, 1939.

Diehl, Huston. "Bewhored Images and Imagined Whores: Iconophobia and Gynophobia in Stuart Love Tragedies." *English Literary Renaissance* (1996): 111–37.

———. *Staging Reform, Reforming the Stage: Protestantism and Popular Theater in Early Modern England.* Ithaca, NY: Cornell University Press, 1997.

Dimmock, Matthew. *New Turkes: Dramatizing Islam and the Ottomans in Early Modern England.* Burlington, VT: Ashgate, 2005.

Dolan, Fran. *Marriage and Violence: The Early Modern Legacy.* Philadelphia: University of Pennsylvania Press, 2008.

Dollimore, Jonathan. *Radical Tragedy: Religion, Ideology, and Power in the Drama of Shakespeare and His Contemporaries.* Chicago: University of Chicago Press, 1984.

Douglas, Mary. *Purity and Danger: An Analysis of Concepts of Pollution and Taboo.* London: Routledge & Kegan Paul, 1966.

Doyle, Charles Clay. "One Drop of Christ's Streaming Blood: A Gloss on *Doctor Faustus.*" *Cahiers Elisabethains* 17 (1980): 85–7.

Duffy, Eamon. *Stripping of the Altars: Traditional Religion in England 1400–1580.* New Haven, CT: Yale University Press, 1992.

Duggan, Lawrence. "Fear and Confession on the Eve of the Reformation." *Archiv für Reformationgeschichte* 75 (1984): 153–75.

Eagleton, Terry. *Sweet Violence: The Idea of the Tragic.* Malden, MA: Blackwell, 2003.

———. "Tragedy and Revolution." In *Theology and the Political: The New Debate*, edited by Creston Davis, John Milbank, and Slavoj Zizek 7–21. Durham, NC: Duke University Press, 2005.

Eccles, Mark. "William Wager and His Plays." *English Language Notes* 18.4 (1981): 258–62.

Ehrlich, Avi. *Hamlet's Absent Father.* Princeton, NJ: Princeton University Press, 1977.

Elias, Norbert. *Power and Civility.* Vol. 2 of *The Civilizing Process.* Translated by Edmund Jephcott. New York: Pantheon Books, 1982.

Eliot, T. S. *Essays on Elizabethan Dramatists.* New York: Harcourt Brace, 1960.

———. *The Sacred Wood: Essays on Poetry and Criticism.* London: Methuen, 1964.

Elliott, J. H. *Spain, Europe and the Wider World, 1500–1700.* New Haven, CT: Yale University Press, 2009.

Emmison, F. G. *Morals & the Church Courts*. Vol. 2 of *Elizabethan Life*. Chelmsford, UK: Essex County Council, 1973.

Engle, Lars. "'Thrift Is Blessing': Exchange and Explanation in *The Merchant of Venice*." *Shakespeare Quarterly* 37.1 (1986): 20–37.

Erne, Lukas. "Thomas Kyd's Christian Tragedy." *Renaissance Papers 2001*. 17–34.

Farr, Dorothy. *John Ford and the Caroline Theatre*. London: Macmillan, 1979.

Faulkner, Anne. "The Harrowing of Hell at Barking Abbey and in Modern Production." In *The Iconography of Hell*, edited by Clifford Davidson and Thomas H. Seiler, 141–57. Kalamazoo, MI: Medieval Institute Publications, 1992.

Fincham, Kenneth. Introduction to *The Early Stuart Church, 1603–1642*, edited by Kenneth Fincham, 1–22. Hampshire, UK: Macmillan, 1993.

Finkelpearl, Philip J. *Court and Country Politics in the Plays of Beaumont and Fletcher*. Princeton, NJ: Princeton University Press, 1990.

Finkelstein, Andrea. *Harmony and the Balance: An Intellectual History of Seventeenth-Century Economic Thought*. Ann Arbor: University of Michigan Press, 2000.

Finlan, Stephen. *Problems with Atonement*. Collegeville, MN: Liturgical Press, 2005.

Firey, Abigail. Introduction to *A New History of Penance*, edited by Abigail Firey, 1–18. Leiden, Netherlands: Brill, 2008.

———, ed. *A New History of Penance*. Leiden, Netherlands: Brill, 2008.

Fisch, Harold. *The Dual Image: The Figure of the Jew in English and American Literature*. New York: Ktav, 1971.

Forman, Valerie. *Tragicomic Redemptions: Global Economics and the Early Modern English Stage*. Philadelphia: University of Pennsylvania Press, 2008.

Forsyth, Neil. "Heavenly Helen." *Etudes de Lettres* 4 (1987): 11–21.

———. *The Old Enemy: Satan and the Combat Myth*. Princeton, NJ: Princeton University Press, 1987.

Foucault, Michel. *The History of Sexuality, Volume I: An Introduction*. New York: Vintage, 1980.

Frantzen, Allen. *The Literature of Penance in Anglo-Saxon England*. New Brunswick, NJ: Rutgers University Press, 1983.

Fredriksen, Paula. *Sin: The Early History of an Idea*. Princeton, NJ: Princeton University Press, 2012.

Freinkel, Lisa. *Reading Shakespeare's Will: The Theology of Figure from Augustine to the Sonnets*. New York: Columbia University Press, 2002.

French, Peter. *The Virtues of Vengeance*. Lawrence: University of Kansas Press, 2001.

Freud, Sigmund. *The Interpretation of Dreams*. Vol. 4 of *The Standard Edition*, edited and translated by James Strachey. London: Hogarth Press, 1953.

Frye, Roland Mushat. *Shakespeare and Christian Doctrine*. Princeton, NJ: Princeton University Press, 1963.

———. *The Renaissance Hamlet: Issues and Responses in 1600*. Princeton, NJ: Princeton University Press, 1984.

Fuchs, Barbara. "Empire Unmanned: Gender Trouble and Genoese Gold in Cervantes's 'The Two Damsels.'" *PMLA* 116.2 (2001): 285–99.

———. *Romance*. New York: Routledge, 2004.

———. "Beyond the Missing *Cardenio*: Anglo-Spanish Relations in Early Modern Drama." *Journal of Medieval and Early Modern Studies* 39.1 (2009): 143–59.

Gardiner, Eileen. *Medieval Visions of Heaven and Hell: A Sourcebook.* New York: Garland, 1993.

Gardiner, Harold. *Mysteries End.* New Haven, CT: Yale University Press, 1946, reprinted 1967.

Garner, Bryan A., ed. *Black's Law Dictionary.* 9th ed. St. Paul, MN: West, 2009.

George, Charles and Katherine George. *The Protestant Mind of the English Reformation: 1570–1640.* Princeton, NJ: Princeton University Press, 1961.

Girard, René. "'To entrap the wisest': A Reading of *The Merchant of Venice.*" In *Literature and Society*, edited by Edward Said, 100–119. Baltimore, MD: Johns Hopkins University Press, 1980.

———. *Things Hidden Since the Foundation of the World.* Stanford, CA: Stanford University Press, 1987.

Goering, Joseph. "The Scholastic Turn: Penitential Theology and Law in the Schools." In *A New History of Penance*, edited by Abigail Firey, 219–38. Leiden, Netherlands: Brill, 2008.

Gorringe, Timothy. *God's Just Vengeance: Crime, Violence and the Rhetoric of Salvation.* Cambridge: Cambridge University Press, 1996.

Goux, Jean-Joseph. *Symbolic Economies: After Marx and Freud.* Ithaca, NY: Cornell University Press, 1990.

Gowing, Laura. *Domestic Dangers: Women, Words, and Sex in Early Modern London.* Oxford: Clarendon Press, 1996.

Green, Ian. *The Christian's ABC: Catechisms and Catechizing in England, c. 1530–1740.* Oxford: Clarendon Press, 1996.

Greenblatt, Stephen. *Renaissance Self-Fashioning from More to Shakespeare.* Chicago: University of Chicago Press, 1980.

———. *Hamlet in Purgatory.* Princeton, NJ: Princeton University Press, 2001.

Gregory, Brad. "The 'True and Zealous Seruice of God': Robert Parsons, Edmund Bunny, and *The First Booke of the Christian Exercise.*" *Journal of Ecclesiastical History* 45.2 (1994): 238–69.

———. *The Unintended Reformation.* Cambridge, MA: Harvard University Press, 2012.

Griffin, Eric. *English Renaissance Drama and the Specter of Spain: Ethnopoetics and Empire.* Philadelphia: University of Pennsylvania Press, 2009

Gross, Kenneth. *Shakespeare's Noise.* Chicago: University of Chicago Press, 2001.

———. *Shylock Is Shakespeare.* Chicago: University of Chicago Press, 2006.

Guibbory, Acshah. *Christian Identiy, Jews, and Israel in Seventeenth-Century England.* Oxford: Oxford University Press, 2010.

Haigh, Christopher. *English Reformations: Religion, Politics, and Society under the Tudors.* Oxford: Clarendon Press, 1993.

———. *The Plain Man's Pathway to Heaven.* Oxford: Oxford University Press, 2007.

Hall, Hubert. "Some Elizabethan Penances in the Diocese of Ely." *Transactions of the Royal Historical Society* 1 (1907): 263–77.

Hall, Jonathan. *Anxious Pleasures: Shakespearean Comedy and the Nation State.* Madison, NJ: Fairleigh Dickinson University Press, 1995.

Hallett, Charles and Elaine Hallett. *The Revenger's Madness: A Study of Revenge Tragedy Motifs.* Lincoln: University of Nebraska Press, 1980.

Halpern, Richard. *Shakespeare among the Moderns.* Ithaca, NY: Cornell University Press, 1997.

Hamlin, Hannibal. "Sobs for Sorrowful Souls: Versions of the Penitential Psalms for Lay Devotion." In *Private and Domestic Devotion in Early Modern Britain,* edited by Jessica Martin and Alec Ryrie, 211–35. Aldershot, UK: Ashgate, 2012.

Hamm, Berndt. *The Reformation of Faith in the Context of Late Medieval Theology and Piety: Essays.* Edited and translated by Robert J. Bast. Boston: Brill, 2004.

Happé, Peter. Introduction to *Interludes and Early Modern Society: Studies in Gender, Power and Theatricality,* edited by Peter Happé and Wim Hüsken. Amsterdam: Rodopi, 2007.

———. *The Towneley Cycle: Unity and Diversity.* Cardiff: University of Wales Press, 2007.

Harris, Jonathan Gil. *Sick Economies: Drama, Mercantilism, and Disease in Shakespeare's England.* Philadelphia: University of Pennsylvania Press, 2004.

Hawkes, David. *The Culture of Usury in Renaissance England.* New York: Palgrave Macmillan, 2010.

Heinemann, Margot. *Puritanism and Theatre: Thomas Middleton and Opposition Drama under the Early Stuarts.* Cambridge: Cambridge University Press, 1980.

Heller, Herbert Jack. *Penitent Brothellers: Grace, Sexuality, and Genre in Thomas Middleton's City Comedies.* Newark: University of Delaware Press, 2000.

Helmholz, R. H. *The Spirit of Classical Canon Law.* Athens: University of Georgia Press, 1996.

Hill, Eugene D. "Senecan and Vergilian Perspectives in *The Spanish Tragedy.*" *English Literary Renaissance* 15.2 (1985): 143–65.

Hillerbrand, Hans J., ed. *The Oxford Encyclopedia of the Reformation.* 4 vols. New York: Oxford University Press, 1996.

Himmelfarb, Gertrude. *Tours of Hell: An Apocalyptic Form in Jewish and Christian Literature.* Philadelphia: University of Pennsylvania Press, 1984.

Hirschfeld, Heather. "Hamlet's 'first corse': Repetition, Trauma, and the Displacement of Redemptive Typology." *Shakespeare Quarterly* 54.4 (2003): 424–48.

———. "Confessing Mothers: The Maternal Penitent in Early Modern Revenge Tragedy." *The Impact of Feminism in English Renaissance Studies,* edited by Dympna Callaghan, 53–66. Basingstoke, UK: Palgrave, 2007.

———. "'Conceived of young Horatio his son': *The Spanish Tragedy* and the Psychotheology of Revenge." *A Companion to Tudor Literature,* edited by Kent Cartwright, 444–58. Chichester, England: Wiley-Blackwell, 2010.

———. "Historicizing Satisfaction in Shakespeare's *Othello.*" *Rethinking Historicism from Shakespeare to Milton,* edited by Ann Baynes Coiro and Thomas Fulton, 113–29. Cambridge: Cambridge University Press, 2012.

Hopkins, Lisa. *The Shakespearean Marriage: Merry Wives and Heavy Husbands.* New York: St. Martin's Press, 1998.

———. "What's Hercules to Hamlet?" *Hamlet Studies* 21.1–2 (1999): 114–43.

Houlbrooke, Ralph. *Church Courts and the People during the English Reformation, 1520–1570.* Oxford: Oxford University Press, 1979.

Howard, Jean F. *Theater of a City: The Places of London Comedy, 1598–1642.* Philadelphia: University of Pennsylvania Press, 2006.

Hudson, Deal W. *Happiness and the Limits of Satisfaction.* Lanham, MD: Rowman and Littlefield, 1996.

Hudson, Elizabeth K. "English Protestants and the *Imitatio Christi*, 1580–1620." *Sixteenth-Century Journal* 19.4 (1988): 541–58.

Huebert, Ronald. *The Performance of Pleasure in English Renaissance Drama.* Basingstoke, UK: Palgrave Macmillan, 2003.

Hunter, Robert Grams. *Shakespeare and the Comedy of Forgiveness.* New York: Columbia University Press, 1965.

Hutson, Lorna. *The Invention of Suspicion: Law and Mimesis in Shakespeare and Renaissance Drama.* Oxford: Oxford University Press, 2008.

Ingram, Martin. *Church Courts, Sex and Marriage in England, 1570–1640.* Cambridge: Cambridge University Press, 1987.

Izydorczyk, Zbigniew. Introduction to *The Medieval Gospel of Nicodemus: Texts, Intertexts, and Contexts in Western Europe*, edited by Zbigniew Izydorczyk. Tempe, AZ: MRTS, 1997.

Jackson, Ken, and Arthur F. Marotti. "The Turn to Religion in Early Modern English Studies." *Criticism* 46.1 (2004): 167–90.

Jedin, Hubert. *A History of the Council of Trent.* Edinburgh: Thomas Nelson and Sons, 1961. (Authorized translation of Hubert Jedin, *Geschichte des Konzils von Trient*, 1957.)

Jennings, Theodore. *Transforming Atonement.* Minneapolis, MN: Fortress Press, 2009.

Jones, David T. *Reforming the Morality of Usury: A Study of the Differences that Separated the Protestant Reformers.* New York: University Press of America, 2004.

Jones, Howard Mumford. *The Pursuit of Happiness.* Ithaca, NY: Cornell University Press, 1953.

Jones, Norman. *God and the Moneylenders: Usury and the law in Early Modern England.* Oxford: Basil Blackwell, 1989.

Justice, Stephen. "Spain, Tragedy, and *The Spanish Tragedy*." *SEL: Studies in English Literature, 1500–1700* 25.2 (1985): 271–88.

Kahn, Coppelia. "The Cuckoo's Note: Male Friendship and Cuckoldry in *The Merchant of Venice*." In *Shakespeare's 'Rough Magic': Renaissance Essays in Honor of C. L. Barber*, edited by Peter Erickson and Coppelia Kahn, 104–12. Newark: University of Delaware Press, 1985.

Kaplan, Lindsay. "Jessica's Mother: Medieval Constructions of Jewish Race and Gender in *The Merchant of Venice*." *Shakespeare Quarterly* 58.1 (2007): 1–30.

Kastan, David Scott. "'His Semblable Is His Mirror': Hamlet and the Imitation of Revenge." *Shakespeare Studies* 19 (1987): 111–124.

Katz, David. *The Jews in the History of England.* Oxford: Clarendon Press, 1994.

Kaufman, Peter Iver. *Prayer, Despair, and Drama: Elizabethan Introspection.* Urbana: University of Illinois Press, 1996.

Kendall, R. T. *Calvin and English Calvinism to 1649.* New York: Oxford University Press, 1979.

Kerridge, Eric. *Usury, Interest and the Reformation*. Aldershot, UK: Ashgate, 2002.

Kerrigan, John. *Revenge Tragedy: Aeschylus to Armageddon*. Oxford: Oxford University Press, 1996.

Kerrigan, William. *Hamlet's Perfection*. Baltimore, MD: Johns Hopkins University Press, 1994.

———. "*Macbeth* and the History of Ambition." In *Freud and the Passions*, edited by John O'Neill, 13–24. University Park: Pennsylvania State University Press, 1996.

Kirsch, Arthur. *Shakespeare and the Experience of Love*. Cambridge: Cambridge University Press, 1981.

Knapp, Jeffrey. *Shakespeare's Tribe: Church, Nation, and Theater in Renaissance England*. Chicago: University of Chicago Press, 2002.

Kneidel, Gregory. "Herbert and Exactness." *English Literary Renaissance* 36.2 (2006): 278–303.

Kolve, V. A. "Everyman and the Parable of the Talents." In *Medieval English Drama: Essays Critical and Contextual*, edited by Jerome Taylor and Alan H. Nelson, 316–40. Chicago: University of Chicago Press, 1972.

Korda, Natasha. *Shakespeare's Domestic Economies: Gender and Property in Early Modern England*. Philadelphia: University of Pennsylvania Press, 2002.

———. "Dame Usury, Gender, Credit, and (Ac)counting in the Sonnets and *The Merchant of Venice*." *Shakespeare Quarterly* 60.2 (2009): 129–53.

Kuchar, Gary. *The Poetry of Religious Sorrow in Early Modern England*. Cambridge: Cambridge University Press, 2008

Kuriyama, Constance. *Christopher Marlowe: A Renaissance Life*. Ithaca, NY: Cornell University Press, 2002.

Lacan, Jacques. "Desire and the Interpretation of Desire in *Hamlet*." In *Literature and Psychoanalysis*, edited by Shoshana Felman, 11–52. Baltimore, MD: Johns Hopkins University Press, 1982.

———. *The Other Side of Psychoanalysis: The Seminar of Jacques Lacan Book XVII*. Translated by Russell Grigg. New York: W. W. Norton & Co., 2007.

Lake, Peter. "Calvinism and the English Church, 1570–1635." *Past and Present* 114 (1987): 32–76.

———. *Anglicans and Puritans? Presbyterianism and English Conformist Thought from Whitgift to Hooker*. London: Allen & Unwin, 1988.

———. "Deeds against Nature: Cheap Print, Protestantism and Murder in Early Seventeenth-Century England." In *Culture and Politics in Early Stuart England*, edited by Kevin Sharpe and Peter Lake, 257–83. Basingstoke, UK: Macmillan, 1994.

——— with Michael Questier. *The Anti-Christ's Lewd Hat: Protestants, Papists and Players in post-Reformation England*. New Haven, CT: Yale University Press, 2002.

Lander, Jesse K. *Inventing Polemic: Religion, Print, and Literary Culture in Early Modern England*. Cambridge: Cambridge University Press, 2006.

Langholm, Odd. *Merchant in the Confessional: Trade and Price in the Pre-Reformation Penitential Handbooks*. Boston: Brill, 2003.

Laqueur, Thomas. "Crowds, Carnival and the State in English Executions, 1604–1868." In *The First Modern Society: Essays in English History in Honour of Lawrence Stone*, edited by A. L. Beier, David Cannadine, and James M. Rosenheim, 305–55. Cambridge: Cambridge University Press, 1989.

Le Goff, Jacques. *The Birth of Purgatory.* Chicago: University of Chicago Press, 1984.

———. *Your Money or Your Life: Economy and Religion in the Middle Ages.* Cambridge, MA: Zone Books, 1988.

Leinwand, Theodore. *Theatre, Finance, and Society in Early Modern England.* Cambridge: Cambridge University Press, 1997.

Levin, Carole, and John Watkins. *Shakespeare's Foreign Worlds: National and Transnational Identities in the Elizabethan Age.* Ithaca, NY: Cornell University Press, 2009.

Levin, Harry. *The Overreacher: A Study of Christopher Marlowe.* Boston: Beacon Press, 1964.

Lewalski, Barbara. "Biblical Allusion and Allegory in *The Merchant of Venice.*" *Shakespeare Quarterly* 13.3 (1962): 327–43.

Lewis, C. S. *Studies in Words.* Cambridge: Cambridge University Press, 1960.

Little, Arthur J. "'An Essence that's not seen': The Primal Scene of Racism in *Othello.*" *Shakespeare Quarterly* 44.3 (1993): 304–24

Little, Katherine. *Confession and Resistance: Defining the Self in Late Medieval England.* South Bend, IN: University of Notre Dame Press, 2006.

Logan, Oliver. *Culture and Society in Venice 1470–1790.* New York: Charles Scribner's and Sons, 1972.

Lopez, Jeremy. *Theatrical Convention and Audience Response in Early Modern Drama.* Cambridge: Cambridge University Press, 2003.

Lualdi, Katherine Jackson, and Anne T. Thayer. Introduction to *Penitence in the Age of Reformations,* edited by Katharine Jackson Lualdi and Anne T. Thayer, 1–9. Aldershot, UK: Ashgate, 2000.

Lupton, Julia Reinhart. *After-Lives of the Saints: Hagiography, Typology and Renaissance Literature.* Stanford, CA: Stanford University Press, 1996.

———. *Citizen-saints: Shakespeare and Political Theology.* Chicago: University of Chicago Press, 2005.

MacClure, Millar. *The Paul's Cross Sermons.* Toronto, University of Toronto Press, 1958.

MacCulloch, Diarmid. *The Later Reformation in England.* New York: Palgrave, 2001.

———. *The Reformation: A History.* New York: Viking Press, 2003.

MacCulloch, J. A. *Harrowing of Hell: A Comparative Study of an Early Christian Doctrine.* Edinburgh: T. & T. Clark, 1930.

Mallette, Richard. "Blasphemous Preacher: Iago and the Reformation." In *Shakespeare and the Culture of Christianity in Early Modern England,* edited by Dennis Taylor and David N. Beauregard, 382–414. New York: Fordham University Press, 2003.

Manley, Lawrence. "Proverbs, Epigrams, and Urbanity in Renaissance London." *English Literary Renaissance* (1985): 247–76.

Mann, Jill. "Satisfaction and Payment in Middle English Literature." *Studies in the Age of Chaucer* 5 (1983): 17–48.

Mansfield, Mary C. *The Humiliation of Sinners: Public Penance in Thirteenth-Century France.* Ithaca, NY: Cornell University Press, 1995.

Marcus, Leah. *Unediting the Renaissance: Shakespeare, Marlowe, Milton.* New York: Routledge, 1996.

Marotti, Arthur F. *Religious Ideology and Cultural Fantasy: Catholic and Anti-Catholic Discourses in Early Modern England.* Notre Dame, IN: University of Notre Dame Press, 2005.

Marsh, Christopher. *Popular Religion in Sixteenth-Century England: Holding Their Peace.* New York: St. Martin's Press, 1998.

Marshall, Peter. *Beliefs and the Dead in Reformation England.* Oxford: Oxford University Press, 2002.

———. *Reformation England, 1480–1643.* New York: Oxford University Press, 2003.

Marx, C. W. "The Problem of the Doctrine of the Redemption in the Middle English Mystery Plays and the *Cornish Ordinalia.*" *Medium Aevum* 54.1 (1984): 20–32.

———. *The Devil's Rights and the Redemption in the Literature of Medieval England.* Cambridge: D. S. Brewer, 1995.

———. "The Gospel of Nicodemus in Old English and Middle English." In *The Medieval Gospel of Nicodemus: Texts, Intertexts, and Contexts in Western Europe,* edited by Zbigniew Izydorczyk, 210–59. Tempe, AZ: MRTS, 1997.

Matthews, David, and Gordon McMullan. "Introduction: Reading the Medieval in Early Modern England." In *Reading the Medieval in Early Modern England,* edited by Gordon McMullan and David Matthews, 1–16. Cambridge: Cambridge University Press, 2007.

Maus, Katherine. *Inwardness and Theater in the English Renaissance.* Chicago: University of Chicago Press, 1995.

———. Introduction to *Four Revenge Tragedies,* edited by Katherine Maus, ix–xxxi. Oxford: Oxford University Press, 1995.

Mazzio, Carla. "Staging the Vernacular: Language and Nation in Thomas Kyd's *The Spanish Tragedy.*" *SEL: Studies in English Literature, 1500–1700* 38.2 (1998): 207–32.

———. "The Three-Dimensional Self: Geometry, Melancholy, Drama." In *The Arts of Calculation: Numerical Thought in Early Modern Europe,* edited by David Glimp and Michelle R. Warren, 39–66. New York: Palgrave Macmillan, 2004.

Mazzola, Elizabeth. *The Pathology of the Renaissance: Sacred Remains and Holy Ghosts.* Boston: Brill, 1998.

McAlindon, T. "*Doctor Faustus*: The Predestination Theory." *English Studies* 76.3 (1995): 215–20.

McGowan, Todd. *The End of Dissatisfaction: Jacques Lacan and the Emerging Society of Enjoyment.* Albany: State University of New York Press, 2004.

McGrath, Alister. *Luther's Theology of the Cross: Martin Luther's Theological Breakthrough.* Oxford: Basil Blackwell, 1985.

———. *Intellectual Origins of the European Reformation.* Oxford: Basil Blackwell, 1987.

———. *The Genesis of Doctrine: A Study in the Foundations of Doctrinal Criticism.* Oxford: Basil Blackwell, 1990.

McMillin, Scott. "The Book of Seneca in *The Spanish Tragedy.*" *SEL: Studies in English Literature, 1500–1700* 14.2 (1974): 201–8.

McMullan, Gordon. *The Politics of Unease in the Plays of John Fletcher.* Amherst: University of Massachusetts Press, 1994.

McNeill, John T. *History of the Cure of Souls*. New York: HarperCollins, 1977.

McPherson, James. *Shakespeare, Jonson, and the Myth of Venice*. Newark: University of Delaware Press, 1990.

Mercer, Peter. *Hamlet and the Acting of Revenge*. London: Macmillan, 1987.

Metzger, Mary Janell. "'Now by My Hood, a Gentle and No Jew': Jessica, *The Merchant of Venice*, and the Discourse of Early Modern English Identity." *PMLA* 113.1 (1998): 52–63.

Michaud-Quantin, Pierre. *Sommes de Casuistique et Manuels de Confession au Moyen Âge*. Louvain: Editions Nauwelaerts, 1962.

Miller, William Ian. *Eye for an Eye*. Cambridge: Cambridge University Press, 2006.

Milton, Anthony. *Catholic and Reformed: The Roman and Protestant Churches in English Protestant Thought*. Cambridge: Cambridge University Press, 1995.

Minois, Georges. *Histoire des Enfers*. Paris: Fayard, 1991.

Moisan, Thomas. "'Which is the merchant here? And which the Jew?': Subversion and Recuperation in *The Merchant of Venice*." In *Shakespeare Reproduced: The Text in History and Ideology*, edited by Jean E. Howard and Marion F. O'Connor, 188–206. New York: Methuen, 1987.

Montrose, Louis. *The Purpose of Playing: Shakespeare and the Cultural Politics of the Elizabethan Theater*. Chicago: University of Chicago Press, 1996.

Moody, A. M. "The Letter of the Law." In *The Merchant of Venice: Critical Essays*, edited by Thomas Wheeler, 79–101. New York: Garland, 1991.

Moore, A. W. *Infinity*. Brookfield, VT: Aldershot, 1993.

Muir, Edward. *Civic Ritual in Renaissance Venice*. Princeton, NJ: Princeton University Press, 1981.

———. *Mad Blood Stirring: Vendetta & Factions in Friuli during the Renaissance*. Baltimore, MD: Johns Hopkins University Press, 1993.

Muldrew, Craig. *The Economy of Obligation: The Culture of Credit and Social Relations in Early Modern England*. New York: St. Martin's Press, 1998.

Mullaney, Steven. *The Place of the Stage: License, Play, and Power in Renaissance England*. Chicago: University of Chicago Press, 1988.

———. "Mourning and Misogyny: *Hamlet, The Revenger's Tragedy*, and the Final Progress of Elizabeth I, 1600–1607." *Shakespeare Quarterly* 45.2 (1994): 139–62.

Mulryne, J. R. "History and Myth in *The Merchant of Venice*." In *Shakespeare's Italy: Functions of Italian Locations in Renaissance Drama*, edited by Michele Marrapodi et al., 87–99. Manchester, UK: Manchester University Press, 1993.

Murakami, Ineke. "Wager's Drama of Conscience, Convention, and State Constitution." *SEL: Studies in English Literature, 1500–1700* 47.2 (2007): 305–29.

———. *Moral Play and Counterpublic: Transformations in Moral Drama, 1465–1599*. New York: Routledge, 2011.

Myers, David. *Poor Sinning Folk: Confession and Conscience in Counter-Reformation Germany*. Ithaca, NY: Cornell University Press, 1996.

Neill, Michael. *Issues of Death: Mortality and Identity in English Renaissance Tragedy*. Oxford: Clarendon Press, 1997.

———. "Death and *The Revenger's Tragedy*." In *Early Modern English Drama: A Critical Companion*, edited by Garrett A. Sullivan, Patrick Cheney, and Andrew Hadfield, 164–76. Oxford: Oxford University Press, 2006.

————. *Putting History to the Question: Power, Politics, and Society in English Renaissance Drama*. New York: Columbia University Press, 2007.

Nelson, Benjamin. *The Idea of Usury: From Tribal Brotherhood to Universal Otherhood*, 2nd ed. Chicago: University of Chicago Press, 1963.

Neuss, Paula. "The Sixteenth-Century English 'Proverb' Play." *Comparative Drama* 18.1 (1984): 1–18.

Newman, Karen. "Portia's Ring: Unruly Women and Structures of Exchange in *The Merchant of Venice*." *Shakespeare Quarterly* 38.1 (1987): 19–33.

Nocentelli, Carmen. "Spice Race: *The Island Princess* and the Politics of Transnational Appropriation." *PMLA* 125.3 (2010): 572–88.

Noonan, John T. *The Scholastic Analysis of Usury*. Cambridge, MA: Harvard University Press, 1957.

Null, Ashley. *Thomas Cranmer's Doctrine of Repentance: Renewing the Power to Love*. Oxford: Oxford University Press, 2000.

Obermann, Heiko. *The Harvest of Medieval Theology: Gabriel Biel and Late Medieval Nominalism*. Cambridge, MA: Harvard University Press, 1963.

O'Connell, Michael. *The Idolatrous Eye: Iconoclasm and Theater in Early Modern England*. New York: Oxford University Press, 2000.

O'Hara, Diana. *Courtship and Constraint: Rethinking the Making of Marriage in Tudor England*. Manchester: Manchester University Press, 2000.

Orlin, Lena Cowen. *Private Matters and Public Culture in Post-Reformation England*. Ithaca, NY: Cornell University Press, 1994.

Overell, M. Anne. *Italian Reform and English Reformations*. Aldershot, UK: Ashgate, 2008.

Oz, Avraham. "Dobbin on the Rialto: Venice and the Division of Identity." In *Shakespeare's Italy: Functions of Italian Locations in Renaissance Drama*, edited by Michele Marrapodi et al., 185–209. Manchester, UK: Manchester University Press, 1993.

Palmer, Barbara. "The Inhabitants of Hell: Devils." In *The Iconography of Hell*, edited by Clifford Davidson and Thomas H. Seiler, 20–40. Kalamazoo, MI: Medieval Institute Publications, 1992.

Parker, John. *The Aesthetics of Anti-Christ: From Christian Drama to Christopher Marlowe*. Ithaca, NY: Cornell University Press, 2007.

Parker, Patricia. *Shakespeare from the Margins: Language, Culture, Context*. Chicago: University of Chicago Press, 1996.

Partridge, Eric. *Shakespeare's Bawdy*. London: Routledge Classics, 2001.

Paster, Gail Kern. *Humoring the Body: Emotions and the Shakespearean Stage*. Chicago: University of Chicago Press, 2004.

Paster, Gail Kern, Katherine Rowe, and Mary Floyd-Wilson. "Introduction: Reading the Early Modern Passions." In *Reading the Early Modern Passions: Essays in the Cultural History of Emotion*, edited by Gail Kern Paster, Katherine Rowe, and Mary Floyd-Wilson, 1–20. Philadelphia: University of Pennsylvania Press, 2004.

Patterson, Lee. "Chaucerian Confession: Penitential Literature and the Pardoner." In *Medievalia et Humanistica* 7:153–73. Cambridge: Cambridge University Press, 1976.

Pearse, Nancy Cotton. *John Fletcher's Chastity Plays: Mirrors of Modesty*. Lewisburg, PA: Bucknell University Press, 1973.

Pelikan, Jaroslav. *Reformation of Church and Dogma*. Vol. 4 of *The Christian Tradition: A History of the Development of Doctrine*. Chicago: University of Chicago Press, 1984.

Peters, Christine. *Patterns of Piety: Women, Gender and Religion in Late Medieval and Reformation England*. Cambridge: Cambridge University Press, 2003.

Pettegree, Andrew. "Introduction: The Changing Face of Reformation History." In *The Reformation World*, edited by Andrew Pettegree, 1–8. New York: Routledge, 2000.

Pettigrew, Todd H. J. "'Faustus . . . for Ever': Marlowe, Bruno, and Infinity." *Comparative Critical Studies* 2.2 (2005): 257–69.

Po-Hsia, R. *The Myth of Ritual Murder: Jews and Magic in Reformation Germany*. New Haven, CT: Yale University Press, 1988.

Pollard, Tanya. *Drugs and Theater in Early Modern England*. Oxford: Oxford University Press, 2005.

Postles, David. "Penance and the Marketplace: A Reformation Dialogue with the Medieval Church (c. 1250–1600)." *Journal of Ecclesiastical History* 54 (2003): 441–69.

Potter, Robert. *The English Morality Play: Origins, History, and Influence of a Dramatic Tradition*. London: Routledge & Kegan Paul, 1975.

Prescott, Anne Lake. "Intertextual Topology: English Writers and Pantagruel's Hell." *English Literary Renaissance* 23.2 (1993): 244–66.

Prosser, Eleanor. *Hamlet and Revenge*. Stanford, CA: Stanford University Press, 1971.

Randall, Dale B. J. *The Golden Tapestry; A Critical Survey of Non-Chivalric Spanish Fiction in English Translation: 1543–1657*. Durham, NC: Duke University Press, 1963.

Rashdall, Hastings. *The Idea of Atonement in Christian Theology*. London: Macmillan, 1920.

Reynolds, James A. *Repentance and Retribution in Early English Drama*. Salzburg, Austria: Salzburg Studies in English Literature, 1982.

Ricks, Christopher. "Faustus and Hell on Earth." *Essays in Criticism* 35 (1985): 101–20.

Rist, Thomas. *Revenge Tragedy and the Drama of Commemoration in Reforming England*. Burlington, VT: Ashgate, 2008.

Rittgers, Ronald. *The Reformation of the Keys: Confession, Conscience, and Authority in Sixteenth-Century Germany*. Cambridge, MA: Harvard University Press, 2004.

———. "Embracing the 'true relic' of Christ: Suffering, Penance, and Private Confession in the Thought of Martin Luther." In *A New History of Penance*, edited by Abigail Firey, 377–94. Leiden, Netherlands: Brill, 2008.

Rose, Mark. "Othello's Occupation: Shakespeare and the Romance of Chivalry." *English Literary Renaissance* 15 (1985): 293–311.

Rose, Mary Beth. *The Expense of Spirit: Love and Sexuality in Renaissance Drama*. Ithaca, NY: Cornell University Press, 1988.

Rose, Jacqueline. "*Hamlet*: The Mona Lisa of Literature." *Critical Quarterly* 28 (1986): 35–49.

Rozett, Martha Tuck. *The Doctrine of Election and the Emergence of Elizabethan Tragedy*. Princeton, NJ: Princeton University Press, 1984.

Rubin, Miri. *Gentile Tales: The Narrative Assault on Late Medieval Jews*. New Haven, CT: Yale University Press, 1999.

Ryrie, Alec. *Being Protestant in Early Modern England*. Oxford: Oxford University Press, 2013.

Scarisbrick, J. J. *The Reformation and the English People.* Oxford: Basil Blackwell, 1984.

Scodel, Joshua. *Excess and the Mean in Early Modern English Literature.* Princeton, NJ: Princeton University Press, 2002.

Shagan, Ethan. *The Rule of Moderation: Violence, Religion and the Politics of Restraint in Early Modern England.* Cambridge: Cambridge University Press, 2011.

Shapiro, James. *Shakespeare and the Jews.* New York: Columbia University Press, 1996.

Sharpe, J. A. "Last Dying Speeches: Religion, Ideology, and Public Execution in Seventeenth-Century England." *Past and Present* 107 (1985): 144–67.

Sharpe, Kevin. *Remapping Early Modern England: The Culture of Seventeenth-Century Politics.* Cambridge: Cambridge University Press, 2000.

Sheets, John R., S.J., ed. *The Theory of the Atonement: Readings in Soteriology.* Englewood Cliffs, NJ: Prentice-Hall, Inc., 1967.

Sheingorn, Pamela. "'Who can open the doors of his face?' The Iconograhy of Hell Mouth." In *The Iconography of Hell,* edited by Clifford Davidson and Thomas H. Seiler, 1–19. Kalamazoo, MI: Medieval Institute Publications, 1992.

Shell, Alison. *Catholicism, Controversy and the English Literary Imagination.* Cambridge: Cambridge University Press, 1999.

Shell, Marc. *Money, Language and Thought: Literary and Philosophical Economies from the Medieval to the Modern Era.* Berkeley: University of California Press, 1982.

Shuger, Debora. *Habits of Thought in the English Renaissance: Religion, Politics, and the Dominant Culture.* Berkeley: University of California Press, 1990.

——. *The Renaissance Bible: Scholarship, Sacrifice, and Subjectivity.* Berkeley: University of California Press, 1994.

——. "The Reformation of Penance." *Huntington Library Quarterly* 71.4 (2008): 557–71.

Simpson, James. *The Oxford English Literary History: Reform and Cultural Revolution.* Oxford: Oxford University Press, 2004.

——. *Burning to Read: English Fundamentalism and Its Reformation Opponents.* Cambridge, MA: Belknap Press, 2007.

Skidelsky, Robert, and Edward Skidelsky. *How Much Is Enough: Money and the Good Life.* New York: Other Press, 2012.

Smith, Molly. *Breaking Boundaries: Politics and Play in the Drama of Shakespeare and His Contemporaries.* Aldershot, UK: Ashgate, 1998.

——. "The Theatre and the Scaffold: Death as Spectacle in *The Spanish Tragedy.*" In *Revenge Tragedy: Contemporary Critical Essays,* edited by Stevie Simkin, 71–87. New York: Palgrave, 2001.

Snow, Edward. "Marlowe's *Doctor Faustus* and the Ends of Desire." In *Two Renaissance Mythmakers, Christopher Marlowe and Ben Jonson,* edited by Alvin B. Kernan, 70–110. Baltimore, MD: Johns Hopkins University Press, 1977.

——. "Sexual Anxiety and the Male Order of Things in *Othello,*" *English Literary Renaissance* 10 (1980): 384–412.

Sommerville, C. John. *The Secularization of Early Modern England.* New York: Oxford University Press, 1992.

Sommerville, Margaret. *Sex and Subjection: Attitudes to Women in Early-Modern Society.* New York: St. Martin's Press, 1995.

Soni, Vivisvan. *Mourning Happiness: Narrative and the Politics of Modernity*. Ithaca, NY: Cornell University Press, 2010.

Southern, R. W. *Elizabethan Recusant Prose*. London: Sands, 1950.

Spencer, Eric. "Taking Excess, Exceeding Account: Aristotle Meets *The Merchant of Venice*." In *Money and the Age of Shakespeare: Essays in New Economic Criticism*, edited by Linda Woodbridge, 143–58. New York: Palgrave Macmillan, 2003.

Spinosa, Charles. "Shylock and Debt and Contract in the *Merchant of Venice*." *Cardozo Studies in Law and Literature*, 5 (1993): 65–85.

Spykman, Gordon J. *Attrition and Contrition at the Council of Trent*. Kampen, Netherlands: J. H. Kok, 1955.

Stachniewski, John. *The Persecutory Imagination: English Puritanism and the Literature of Religious Despair*. Oxford: Clarendon Press, 1991.

Stallybrass, Peter. "Reading the Body and the Jacobean Theater of Consumption." *Renaissance Drama* 18 (1987): 121–48.

———. "The Value of Culture and the Disavowal of Things." In *The Culture of Capital: Property, Cities, and Knowledge in Early Modern England*, edited by Henry S. Turner, 275–92. New York: Routledge, 2002.

Streete, Adrian. "Calvinist Conceptions of Hell in Marlowe's *Doctor Faustus*." *Notes & Queries* 47.4 (2000): 430–2.

———. " 'Consummatum Est': Calvinist Exegesis, Mimesis, and *Doctor Faustus*." *Literature & Theology* 15.2 (2001): 140–58.

———. *Protestantism and Drama in Early Modern England*. Cambridge: Cambridge University Press, 2008.

Strier, Richard. "Herbert and Tears." *ELH* 46.2 (1979): 221–47.

———. *The Unrepentant Renaissance: From Petrarch to Shakespeare to Milton*. Chicago: University of Chicago Press, 2011.

Strype, John. *Annals of the Reformation*. 2 vols. London, 1735.

Tamburr, Karl. *The Harrowing of Hell in Medieval England*. Cambridge: D. S. Brewer, 2007.

Targoff, Ramie. "The Performance of Prayer: Sincerity and Theatricality in Early Modern England," *Representations* 60 (1997): 49–69.

———. *Common Prayer: The Language of Public Devotion in Early Modern England*. Chicago: University of Chicago Press, 2001.

Tawney, R. H. Introduction to *A Discourse upon Usury*, edited by R. H. Tawney, 1–172. New York: Augustus M. Kelley, repr. 1965.

Tentler, Thomas. *Sin and Confession on the Eve of the Reformation*. Princeton, NJ: Princeton University Press, 1977.

———. "Postscript." In *Penitence in the Age of Reformations*, edited by Katharine Jackson Lualdi and Anne T. Thayer, 240–59. Aldershot, UK: Ashgate, 2000.

Thayer, Anne. *Penitence, Preaching and the Coming of the Reformation*. Aldershot, UK: Ashgate, 2002.

Thomas, Keith. "The Double Standard." *Journal of the History of Ideas* 20 (1959): 195–216.

———. *The Ends of Life: Roads to Fulfillment in Early Modern England*. Oxford: Oxford University Press, 2009.

Tilley, M. P. *Dictionary of the Proverbs in England in the Sixteenth and Seventeenth Centuries*. Ann Arbor: University of Michigan Press, 1950.

Todd, Margo. *Christian Humanism and the Puritan Social Order*. Cambridge: Cambridge University Press, 1987.

Turner, Henry S. "The Problem of the More-than-One: Friendship, Calculation, and Political Association in *The Merchant of Venice*." *Shakespeare Quarterly* 57.4 (2006): 413–42.

Turner, James Grantham. *One Flesh: Paradisal Marriage and Sexual Relations in the Age of Milton*. Oxford: Clarendon Press, 1987.

Turner, Robert Kean. "Collaborators at Work: *The Queen of Corinth* and *The Knight of Malta*." In *Shakespeare: Text, Language, Criticism: Essays in Honour of Marvin Spevack*, edited by Bernhard Fabian and Kurt Tetzeli von Rosador, 315–33. Hildesheim, Germany: Olms, 1987.

Tyacke, Nicholas. *Anti-Calvinists: The Rise of English Arminianism, c. 1590–1640*. Oxford: Clarendon Press, 1987.

Van Beek, Marinus. *An Enquiry into Puritan Vocabulary*. Groningen, Netherlands: Wolters-Noordhoff, 1969.

Vaughan, Virginia Mason. *Othello: A Contextual History*. Cambridge: Cambridge University Press, 1994.

Vitkus, Daniel. "Turning Turk in *Othello*: Conversion and Damnation of the Moor." *Shakespeare Quarterly* 48.2 (1997): 347–62.

———. "Turks and Jews in *The Jew of Malta*." In *Early Modern English Drama: A Critical Companion*, edited by Patrick Cheney, Andrew Hadfield, and Garrett Sullivan, 61–72. New York: Oxford University Press, 2006.

Wagner, Karen. "Cum Aliquis Venerit ad Sacerdotem: Penitential Experience in the Central Middle Ages." In *A New History of Penance*, edited by Abigail Firey, 201–18. Leiden, Netherlands: Brill, 2008.

Walker, Greg. *The Politics of Performance in Early Renaissance Drama*. Cambridge: Cambridge University Press, 1998.

Wallace, Dewey. "Puritan and Anglican: The Interpretation of Christ's Descent into Hell in Elizabethan Theology." *Archiv für Reformationgeschichte* 69 (1978): 248–87.

———. *Puritans and Predestination: Grace in English Protestant Theology, 1525–1695*. Chapel Hill: University of North Carolina Press, 1982.

Walsham, Alexandra. *Providence in Early Modern England*. Oxford: Oxford University Press, 1999.

Waswo, Richard. "Damnation, Protestant Style: *Macbeth*, *Faustus*, and Christian Tragedy." *Journal of Medieval and Renaissance Studies* 4 (1974): 63–99.

Watkins, John. "The Allegorical Theatre: Moralities, Interludes and Protestant Drama." *The Cambridge History of Medieval English Literature*, edited by David Wallace, 767–92. Cambridge: Cambridge University Press, 1999.

Watson, Robert N. "Tragedies of Revenge and Ambition." In *The Cambridge Companion to Shakespearean Tragedy*, edited by Claire McEachern, 160–81. Cambridge: Cambridge University Press, 2002.

Wayne, Valerie. Introduction to Edmund Tilney, *The Flower of Friendship: A Renaissance Dialogue Contesting Marriage*, edited by Valerie Wayne, 1–93. Ithaca, NY: Cornell University Press, 1992.

Weber, Max. *The Protestant Ethic and the Spirit of Capitalism*. Edited by Richard Swedberg. New York: Norton, 2009.

Weimann, Robert. *Shakespeare and the Popular Tradition in the Theater: Studies in the Social Dimension of the Dramatic Form and Function*. Baltimore, MD: Johns Hopkins University Press, 1978.

White, Helen C. *Social Criticism in Popular Religious Literature of the Sixteenth Century*. New York: Macmillan Co., 1944.

White, Paul Whitfield. *Theatre and Reformation: Protestantism, Patronage, and Playing in Tudor England*. New York: Cambridge University Press, 1993.

———. "Interludes, Economics, and the Elizabethan Stage." In *The Oxford Handbook of Tudor Literature, 1485–1603*, edited by Mike Pincombe and Cathy Shrank, 555–70. Oxford: Oxford University Press, 2009.

Whitehead, Lydia. "*A Poena et Culpa*: Penitence, Confidence, and the *Miserere* in Foxe's *Actes and Monuments*." *Renaissance Studies* 4.3 (1990): 287–99.

Wiggins, Martin. Introduction to *Four Jacobean Sex Tragedies*, edited by Martin Wiggins, vii–xxi. Oxford: Oxford University Press, 1998.

Williams, Raymond. *Keywords: A Vocabulary of Culture and Society*, 2nd ed. New York: Oxford University Press, 1985.

Wilson, J. Dover. *What Happens in* Hamlet, 3rd ed. Cambridge: Cambridge University Press, 1951.

Winston, Jessica. "Seneca in Early Elizabethan England," *Renaissance Quarterly* 59.1 (2006): 29–58.

Witte, John Jr. *From Sacrament to Contract: Marriage, Religion, and Law in the Western Tradition*, 2nd ed. Louisville, KY: Westminster John Knox Press, 2012.

Woodbridge, Linda. *English Revenge Drama: Money, Resistance, Equality*. Cambridge: Cambridge University Press, 2010.

Woolf, Rosemary. *The English Mystery Plays*. Berkeley: University of California Press, 1972.

Wrightson, Keith. *Earthly Necessities: Economic Lives in Early Modern Britain*. New Haven, CT: Yale University Press, 2000.

Zimmerman, Reinhard. *The Law of Obligations: Roman Foundations of the Civilian Tradition*. Cape Town, South Africa: Juta and Co., 1990.

Zimmerman, Susan. *The Early Modern Corpse and Shakespeare's Theatre*. Edinburgh: Edinburgh University Press, 2005.

Zupančič, Alenka. "When Surplus Enjoyment meets Surplus Value." In *Jacques Lacan and the Other Side of Psychoanalysis*, edited by Justin Clemens and Russell Grigg, 155–78. Durham, NC: Duke University Press, 2006.

INDEX